First Lady
My Thirty Days Upstairs
in the White House

by **Martha Dinwiddie Butterfield**

as told to

PATRICK DENNIS *pseud.*

Edward Everett Tanner

with photographs by CRIS ALEXANDER

1964

☆ [*William Morrow and Company*] ☆

NEW YORK

WHITE HOUSE

The authoress today—Bosky Dell.

Introduction

entle reader: Having reached the age of more than four score years and ten, the writer's former employer and lifelong friend, Martha Dinwiddie Butterfield, now feels that her secret political and social memoirs as First Lady of the Land can be released to an eager public who still speak of her as the Lady Jane Grey of American First Ladies.

Now "ninety-four years young," Martha Dinwiddie Butterfield is enjoying life's "Injun summer" as a guest at Bosky Dell Home for Senile and Disturbed, where the major bulk of these memoirs was penned with the aid of the writer, whose honor and privilege it was to function as Mrs. Butterfield's Press Secretary during her turbulent month as chatelaine and mistress of our glorious nation's gracious family manse, the White House, and also with the aid of Mr. C. Alexander, who functioned not only as Official Photographer but also as boyhood friend and admirer of our late-lamented President, George W. Butterfield.

Far from being lured by the profit motive for making public the intimate story of her life, Mrs. Butterfield, Mr. Alexander, and the writer have all delved into the Butterfield Papers as a Labor of Love to make clear and clean, once and for all, the political record of "America's Most Maligned Statesman," George W. Butterfield, before, during, and after his thirty-day term as President of these United States.

In this intimate autobiography, actual pages from Martha Dinwiddie Butterfield's diaries will be reproduced. Here also will appear family portraits, photographs, and "snapshots," heretofore unavailable to the casual reader and "armchair historian." Actual menus and recipes will also be included, as well as newspaper cuttings, cartoons, photographs, and engravings that are and have been a matter of public record.

Upon infrequent occasions during the compilation of this volume, Mrs. Butterfield has suffered certain small lapses and caprices of memory. It is then and only then that the writer has taken pen in hand in order to facilitate, simplify, and to weave together certain loose threads of Mrs. Butterfield's literary fabric. Howsomever, the writer would like to have it clearly understood that, save for certain clearly marked passages, the ensuing pages contain exclusively and solely the syntax and opinions of Martha Dinwiddie Butterfield, free and unmarred by the tamperings of any professional author or "ghost writer."

On behalf of Mrs. Butterfield, Mr. Alexander, and himself, the writer humbly begs to acknowledge the invaluable assistance of Miss Mary Margaret McGillicuddy, R.N.; of the entire Occupational Therapy Department of Bosky Dell Home for Senile and Disturbed (with special thanks

to the printing and photographic divisions thereof); of the staff of the Whippoorwill Van & Storage Warehouse; of the Rhoda Fleming Memorial Library; of the Pellagra *News & Sentinel;* and of the Library of Congress. Without them, Mrs. Butterfield's autobiography might never have been written.

But enough of the prologue and on with the show! Pray, gentle reader, permit the writer to step aside and allow Martha Dinwiddie Butterfield, First Lady *Emerita,* to tell in her own words her own story.

PATRICK DENNIS
Press Secretary,
March 4, 1909-April 4, 1909

FIRST LADY

I

To the Manner Born
1870–80

Our ancestral family seat. . . . Clan Dinwiddie, the flower of
Southern aristocracy, reduced to penury by the Carpetbaggers. . . .
Mumsie-love, a fair belle of the Confederacy. . . . Pappa-daddy,
a rising traction executive. . . . Hijinks with my beloved sister
Clytie and that jackanapes Bubber. . . . Lovable old Mammy—a
second mother to us all. . . . Blue blood will tell!

ome! How can I describe my childhood home? Shall I tell you that
it was a lovely old Greek revival mansion set on the banks of the
majestic Pellagra River? Shall I describe first to you the six Ionic
columns of its façade? Or should I commence with its cool, lofty rooms;
its twinkling chandeliers, the graceful sweep of its curving stairway? Or
perhaps ask you to visualize fine carriages filled with ladies and gentlemen charging up the oak-bordered driveway that led from the Pellagra
Post Road to the very verandah of Dinwiddiewood? Should I ask you to
try to hear the chaff and laughter of my family's distinguished guests, or
to listen for the singing of our lovable darkies happily picking cotton in
our cultivated fields? Ah, yes, that was Dinwiddiewood, home of my ancestors, but not the home *I* remember, for I was born just a bit too late to
see it, to enjoy it, to call it home.

Alas, the vicious War Between the States, where often brother fought
brother, came along to reduce Dinwiddiewood to rubble and ashes, to tear
from Pappa-daddy and Mumsie-love their devoted "children" of the Afri-

can race, who were treated just like members of the family,[1] and to reduce to penury the once proud and noble clan Dinwiddie.

By the time I came into the world—a dear, chubby baby girl—the grandeur that was Dinwiddiewood was long gone and grown over with weeds and scrub oak. So completely devastated was Dinwiddiewood that no painting or photograph of it existed by the time of my birth, in 1870.[2] But Mumsie-love could paint more beautiful pictures with words than any artist, could capture more realism with a phrase than with a motion-picture camera. How well I recollect that as a tiny toddler I would wait until the afternoon shadows lengthened and Mumsie-love would sit down in the rocker with her daily tonic, for she was a delicate Southern flower, never hardy or robust. Then I would place my little head in Mumsie-love's commodious lap and lisp, "Tell me about it, Mumthie-love."

"Tell about what, sugar?" Mumsie-love would say. (It was always the same.)

"You know!" I would cry. "About our big plantation."

"Oh, that," she would say teasingly. "Somehow I just can't remember. But maybe if you'd run out to the cool chest and fetch me another glass of tonic . . ."

Eagerly, I would trot out to the kitchen as fast as my plump little legs could carry me, and refill her delicate crystal goblet from the mysterious bottle that she kept sequestered behind the fatback. Then, with brimming

---

[1] In view of the fact that one lady of color—namely, Mammy—remained in the family employ for more than forty years without receiving a salary, there would seem to be some truth in Martha Dinwiddie Butterfield's extravagant statement. P.D.

[2] It is perhaps interesting to note that reasonable doubt exists as to whether or not a property known as Dinwiddiewood itself ever was. After repeated inquiries to the Pellagra County Bureau of Records, no trace of such a holding could be located. P.D.

Mumsie-love

glass, I would rush back to the parlor, where Mumsie-love, as she sipped, would spin out beautiful pictures of the noble family seat granted us by the kings of England. She would tell of gala entertainments given for all the grand plantation owners and their ladies, of the beautiful gowns, the glossy horses, of old Uncle Turney, our faithful major-domo, forever at one's elbow with a tray filled with glasses of Mumsie-love's favorite tonic.

At times, Mumsie-love's memory would seem to go blank. "Pleathe, pleathe, Mumthie-love," I would beg. "Don't thtop now."

"My memory's all of a sudden gone, sugar," she would say. "But maybe if Mumsie-love's little sugar cake could find me a drop more of tonic . . ." Again and again, I would race out to the cool chest to refill my mother's glass.

As the sun sank in the west, and as the tonic diminished in Mumsie-love's glass, she would tell me of her débutante days as the fairest flower of all Pellagra County. She would tell me of her magnificent wedding and of coming first to Dinwiddiewood as Pappa-daddy's blushing bride. But just before Mumsie-love dozed off—she was delicate, as I said, and a great believer in an afternoon nap—she would whisper to me, "Now, don't go telling it to Pappa-daddy. It makes him sad. Dinwiddiewood will just be our secret—you and me, and nobody else. Now, run out to the kitchen and rench out my tonic glass good and proper." With that, Mumsie-love would be eastward of Eden and in the land of Nod.

For some reason, I never did mention Dinwiddiewood to Pappa-daddy, my devoted father, or to my little sister, Clytie, or to my baby brother, Bubber. Once, I asked our favorite servitor and governess, Mammy, about Dinwiddiewood and where I might be able to find it. "Hyuh-hyuh-hyuh!" Mammy chuckled, in her deep, rich voice. "You'll find that place in the bottom of your mother's tonic bottle." But look as I would, I could never see the vast plantation that was my rightful heritage.

Instead of a beautiful white mansion with a pillared portico and stately rooms, we lived in one wing of a humble frame house, which had been partly destroyed by the damnyankees during the War of the Secession. Where the gardens at Dinwiddiewood had rivalled those of Versailles, we had now only a few hollyhocks and sunflowers that, like Topsy, just "grow'd" out beside the house. The rest of our land was closely planted with the mysterious plants and herbs cultivated by Mumsie-love and Mammy.

Yet even as a tiny little girl, I dreamed of living in a great white Greek revival house, with rooms and rooms of beautiful furniture and acres and acres of exquisite gardens. Little did I wot that before too long I would be living in *the* White House, as its mistress and First Lady of the land!

But I digress!

We were poor but we were proud. Our humble home was always spotlessly clean. Pappa-daddy, my beloved father, a rising young executive in the Pellagra County Interurban Traction Company, insisted that the finest

Pappa-daddy, a rising traction executive

of wines and spirits be always abundantly on hand, and adorable Mumsie-love did not gainsay him, but was anxious to comply with her lord and master's wishes.

Dear old Mammy, our faithful servitor, oversaw the care of the house, the kitchen, the herb garden, and our clothing, always making sure that we were simply but impeccably clad and that Pappa-daddy's uniforms were always in flawless order.

Other than my little afternoon talks with Mumsie-love over the tonic, my childhood was in no way unusual. As companions, I had my darling sister, Clytie (the *vivacious* Dinwiddie daughter), who was my junior by

John Sappington Marmaduke Dinwiddie
("Bubber")

The authoress

but one year. Clytie was a born actress, mimic, comedienne, conversationalist, and hostess. Who knows to what further heights she might have risen were it not for her tragic passing, in 1912? And in addition to Clytie and me there was our cosseted baby brother, Bubber, two years younger than Clytie, but so poised, so precocious, so wise in the ways of the world that at times he seemed even older than I. Who would have dreamed, seeing us three Dinwiddie children marching off to school, gambolling on the lawn, performing Clytie's spur-of-the-moment charades and dramas, that he was observing three of Our Lord's children who were marked for fame, for fortune, for greatness, for sorrow, for despair, for tragedy? Certainly not I!

And so passed the first carefree decade of my life as a dreamy little girl in a sleepy little Southern town who, without knowing it, stood on the brink of an unparalleled adventure!

II

Mumsie-Love, A Modern Marie Curie

1880–82

What Mumsie-love learned at Mammy's knee. . . . Mumsie-love and her magic herbs. . . . Mumsie-love's experimental laboratory. . . . A sylvan masque interrupted by a tragic event. . . . A loved one dies, a great product is born—Lohocla! . . . Lydia Pinkham, move over!

I could not continue in the manufacture of my memoirs without pausing here to say a few very special words about our beloved nursery governess, Mammy, who stood with all of us—and especially with me—through poverty and riches, obscurity and fame, adulation and disgrace, sunshine and shadow. Where or when dear Mammy was born, what her real name was, no one will ever know. For a time, I believed that Mammy had been born at Dinwiddiewood, the family estate, and had loyally stayed with Mumsie-love and Pappa-daddy even after the emancipation. But I was wrong. Instead of being one of our old family retainers, Mammy had appeared in our household in 1870, on the very day I was born, just in time to function as midwife. Pappa-daddy, while out anticipating the arrival of his first-born child, had *won* Mammy in a friendly game of cards at the Pellagra saloon!

Up until the time that my adorable Pappa-daddy—always trying to help those less fortunate than himself—turned over the fourth ace that made Mammy his property, poor Mammy had been in the employ of the lowest

Gathering herbs

possible sort of charlatan—the uncouth proprietor of a medicine show! This man had been wont to travel from small community to small community throughout the sunny South, peddling a vile sort of concoction said to be the placebo for all sorts of ailments. It was named Pocahontas Elixir, and was nothing more than a few ill-tasting herbs and straight wood alcohol! Poor Mammy, who may or may not have had some portion of American Indian in her mysterious heritage, was forced by her cruel owner not only to mix up countless bottles of this evil potion but also to appear, in a state of semi-nudity, as none other than Princess Pocahontas herself! (One can somehow understand the appeal of Communism for those of the lower orders so viciously exploited!) Howsomever, during the years of her disgraceful servitude to a "doctor" no better than an animal, darling Mammy had garnered an unbelievable store of knowledge of herbs, their classifications and their uses. Although sweet Mammy could neither read nor write, I feel sure that she would rank as one of our leading herbalists today, were she but here.

While Mumsie-love adored beauty, she was too frail to create it, and more and more the fragrant blooms I feel sure she would have favored were replaced by row upon row of the pungent mysterious plants that Mammy gathered in the swamp out behind our humble home. What an amazing collection! In addition to such common garden-variety herbs as basil, rosemary, sage and thyme, such little-known plants and plant cultures as ergot, nux vomica, mescal, and marijuana flourished beneath Mammy's "green thumb."

Nor was Mammy simply expert at maintaining a thriving herb garden. In addition, she was a treasure-trove of mysterious formulae and recipes. At one time, when Bubber, my cherished baby brother, suffered an agonizing attack of quinsy, the local physician gave him up for dead, poor little tyke. Not so valiant Mammy! Bubber was her favorite and her "baby." Even though all others had forsaken him, Mammy went stalwartly out to the herbarium she kept in an abandoned tool shed, mixed up a magical potion of heaven knows what mysterious herbs, and simmered it for hours on the back of the wood stove. Into this solution she dipped a red stocking —the color, as I recall, was an important part of the remedy—and then tied the stocking around poor Bubber's anguished little throat. Then, as a sort of "absent treatment," Mammy went out to the garden, swung a dead cat counterclockwise around her head three times, mumbled a strange benediction in an unknown language, and buried the cat, along with a chicken's head, under the cottonwood tree. The next morning, Bubber's fever was gone, as was the agonizing swelling of his poor inflamed throat. It was a miracle, and only Mammy had been able to save Bubber.

In addition to such magical feats as the one described above, Mammy could cure almost any commonplace complaint with her various herbal teas. She had a splendid cure for insomnia, which Mumsie-love, always a troubled sleeper, leaned upon more and more heavily in addition to her afternoon tonics. Mammy also manufactured a special kind of cigarette to soothe Mumsie-love's omnipresent asthmatic condition. So interested did Mumsie-love become in Mammy's pharmacopoeia that she, too, began dabbling with herbs, plants, and fermentations. It was a beautiful and touching sight to see Mumsie-love and Mammy set off for the bayou to gather strange and exotic plants and—although I shudder even to think of it—the venom of the dangerous and deadly water moccasin![1] Off they would go, mistress and handmaiden, white and black, bearing with them a dainty picnic hamper and a bottle of Mumsie-love's tonic for use in case of emergencies.

Such an apt student was Mumsie-love, so overpowering her thirst for knowledge, that she even set up a simple form of still in an unused bed-

---

[1] For what purposes, Mrs. Butterfield is now unable to recall. P.D.

An American Madame Curie

room. She always spoke of this as "my laboratory," and Clytie, Bubber, and I were forbidden even to enter this sanctum sanctorum. "Too dangerous, sugar cake," Mumsie-love would say just before locking the door. Only Mammy, Mumsie-love's dusky confidante, was permitted entrance to the laboratory.

Mumsie-love's pathetic demise occurred on my own tenth birthday. It was a balmy May afternoon, filled with the songs of birds. Pappa-daddy, always an ardent lover of music, was away from home, practicing with the Pellagra County Silver Band (his trombone rendition of "Bonny Blue Flag" and other old favorites would bring tears to one's eyes), in preparation for a gala parade. Mammy was in the kitchen icing the cake that she had made for my birthday. Mumsie-love was, as usual, in her laboratory puttering about. As for us children, we were playing "dress-up" so as to perform a sweet sylvan masque that clever Clytie had just that morning penned. (And only eight years old, at that!) I remember the plot to this very day, just as I recall everything else that took place on that fateful spring afternoon.

Having decked ourselves out in "hand-me-down" costumes, we presented for an audience of only ourselves precious Clytie's little playlet. In it, she took the role of a lovely Grecian princess who sets out on a walk through the forest accompanied by her old lady in waiting (the part that was assigned to me) only to be accosted by a handsome Greek god (Bubber), who carries her off to a sylvan dell and there, by some means that was never made quite clear to me, begets a lovely wood nymph (also played by Clytie). We, the Dinwiddie family, were by then the proud owners of a large camera, which had been left on Pappa-daddy's horsecar by an itinerant photographer and never reclaimed.

"Oh, Clytie!" I cried. "You look so lovely do let's show Mumsie-love." Clytie, always at her happiest when all dressed up, agreed and twisted Bubber's little arm until he, too, consented. In all our Grecian finery, we entered the house and bolted up the stairway. "Mumsie-love!" we all shouted. "Come out and look at us!" Mumsie-love's answer was very muffled and indistinct, and I sensed that she was having another asthmatic attack. In any case, I understood our sweet mother to say "Later." Then we rushed down to the kitchen to confront Mammy and to beg her to take our photographs in full costume. Placing her pipe firmly between her gums, she consented, albeit reluctantly, and, camera and tripod in hand, followed us out past the grape arbor to the huge clump of shrubbery that

A Grecian masque

served to screen some of Mumsie-love's and Mammy's more unusual plants from curious eyes.

No sooner had Mammy rounded up Bubber and got us all to stand still and to smile than the earth was rocked by an explosion that shattered windows all over Pellagra Township. The concussion knocked all of us to the ground, and when I opened my eyes—dazed and shocked, naturally, but quite unhurt—the first thing I saw was my adorable mother lying dead on the lawn beside me! So great had been the force of the explosion that it had knocked out an entire wall of the attic bedroom that served as Mumsie-love's laboratory and catapulted her poor, lifeless body clear across the lawn!!! It was a ghastly sight.

Next I was aware of Clytie's whimpering and of Bubber's hysterical laughter (obviously induced by shock) and finally of poor, faithful Mammy wailing, "Fer Gawd, fer Gawd, ole miss done blew up the still! We'll have the sheriff on us yet!" (You can see how the violence of the explosion had temporarily deranged her poor, simple mind.)

☆ [25] ☆

Within seconds, our garden was overflowing with curiosity seekers. The local doctor pronounced Mumsie-love dead and dispatched a boy to fetch Pappa-daddy from the saloon where the Silver Band met for practice. Poor Pappa-daddy! So overcome was he by the shock that he could hardly walk, let alone talk to the reporter from the Pellagra *News & Sentinel*. He simply stood there in his scarlet band uniform dazed and swaying.

Just as a wagon was summoned to take poor, dead Mumsie-love to the local undertaking parlors, beady-eyed little Bubber espied a crumpled slip of paper in Mumsie-love's cold, clenched hand. Controlling his emotions as much as possible, that brave little lad snatched the paper and tucked it into his costume. Later that evening, after a tearful birthday supper in the kitchen, I read—through my sobs—the bit of paper.

"Fer Gawd!" Mammy wailed. "Ole miss done stumble across the Pocahontas Elixir—only she add sarsaparilla and gunpowder!" With Pappa-daddy hard on her heels, Mammy flew up the stairs to that chamber of tragedy, with its gaping open wall. Standing there, quite unharmed because they had been in the very eye of the explosion, were half a dozen bottles of what looked like Mumsie-love's tonic. Mammy sniffed at one of them and then took a cautious sip. "That's it, and I can taste the sarsaparilla," she said, smacking her lips. Then she passed the bottle to Pappa-daddy, who also sampled its contents.

We children were sent immediately to bed, so as to be rested and refreshed for Mumsie-love's funeral. But Pappa-daddy and Mammy remained in the ruined laboratory, sampling poor, dead Mumsie-love's final creation.

No sooner was sweet Mumsie-love laid away in her final resting place than the Dinwiddie household became a veritable beehive of activity. The

laboratory was moved out of the house and established in the empty barn out on the edge of the swamp. "To keep a lot of nosy people from minding *our* business," Pappa-daddy said. Pappa-daddy was able to locate a small hoard of Union dollars that Mumsie-love had painstakingly saved and hidden away in her sewing box, along with her cache of pathetic memorabilia—her marriage certificate, birth certificates for us children, a few faded daguerreotypes, some letters, and personal papers. These Pappa-daddy instructed me to throw into the kitchen stove. Always an obedient child, I was about to carry out his command when I heard a tiny voice within me say, "For what reason should these personal effects of Mumsie-love's be destroyed? It wouldn't be truly stealing if I were to keep them for myself, as long as they are to be disposed of anyway, would it?" I so loved my darling mother that I wanted some sort of keepsake, some reminder—no matter how tiny or valueless—of her gentle presence. And so, saying nothing, I took them to the room that I shared with Clytie and hid them away in the bottom of the mother-of-pearl souvenir box where I sequestered such girlish treasures as a locket, a dead butterfly, a lock of my baby hair, and so on. After that, I forgot entirely about the whole thing.

With the money that Mumsie-love had left behind her, Pappa-daddy invested heavily in bottles, printed labels, a new still, a second-hand wagon, and a pathetic old horse. Very soon afterward, Pappa-daddy resigned his position with the Pellagra County Interurban Traction Company, removed his uniform, and from then on spent all of his days and most of his nights in the new laboratory out near the swamp, with Mammy faithfully working at his side. After a few weeks of feverish activity, consultations with Judge Dimsdale, our local attorney, and a long correspondence with Washington, D. C., Pappa-daddy's plans began to take shape.

How well I recall returning from the nearby schoolhouse one warm September afternoon and seeing Pappa-daddy's wagon standing out in the yard, being decorated by an itinerant sign painter. I gasped in amazement at what he had painted on the sides of the wagon. It read:

Good for what ails you

L O H O C L A

Authentic Indian Spirit Water

For Men, Women & Children

$1 per bottle

H. Gayelord Dinwiddie, President

The first Lohocla plant

In addition, there was also a painting of Mammy, her hair plaited into braids and brandishing a tomahawk. Below this picture, the text read, "Princess Lohocla."

From that moment onward, the days, weeks, and months literally flew past. Pappa-daddy was hardly ever at home. Instead, he scoured the countryside with his wagon and his bottles of Lohocla. On the rare occasions when he was at home, almost every minute was spent in the old barn manufacturing more Lohocla. Mumsie-love's final bequest to her little brood was more valuable than any gold mine. The magic and tragic brew that had brought about Mumsie-love's untimely death brought to her widower and her children the beginnings of a fortune that would soon rival the financial holdings of Vanderbilt, Rockefeller, Morgan, Harriman, Hill, or Fiske!

By the end of only one year, the Lohocla fleet had swollen to twelve wagons, manned by twelve salesmen! Busy in his executive capacity, Pappa-daddy now stayed at home in Pellagra, where, with the aid of a buxom secretary, he managed the entire business. At the end of two years, Lohocla was a household word throughout the whole of Dixie. Pappa-daddy and his secretary, Miss Prouty, had outgrown the old barn at the edge of the swamp and transferred their business activities to a suite of rooms in the Mansion House Hotel, while awaiting the completion of the new Lohocla factory, which was being constructed down by the N.C. & St.L. railroad tracks. Our house, our barn, even Mammy's herbarium were all filled with packing cases and empty bottles, waiting to be filled by the two Negro assistants whom Pappa-daddy had been compelled to employ. By working more diligently than seemed humanly possible, they were able to fill and label one thousand pint bottles of Lohocla per day—only a *quarter* of the daily orders by the time of Lohocla's second birthday, in 1882!

How differently the townspeople felt about Pappa-daddy now! Instead of being despised as an aristocratic dilettante, Pappy-daddy was now a man of parts and a force in the community. He had brought new people, new industry, new money, and new vitality to sleepy little Pellagra Township. Lohocla was on its way, and so were we!

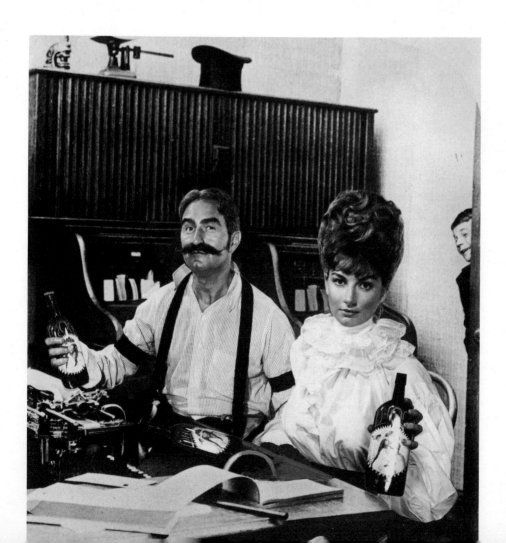

III

A Southern Belle

1883–88

Father struck it rich. . . . Clytie's clever ways with Pappa-daddy.
. . . The new Dinwiddiewood. . . . I dwelt in marble halls. . . .
A bird in a gilded cage? . . . A word in defense of Lohocla. . . .
Pappa-daddy's emerging social conscience. . . . A patent-medicine
heiress. . . . A new popularity. . . . The belle of the ball! . . .
Clytie's quest for culture.

he years between Pappa-daddy's first bottle of Lohocla and my début at Mr. Louis Sherry's, in New York City, fairly flew past. Every day brought more and more wealth to our little motherless family.

While I would never dream of accusing my beloved father of not being generous to a fault, I must admit that he kept careful track of every penny and, naturally not wishing to appear *nouveau riche* or ostentatious, did not squander money on fripperies and vulgar display.

However, my sister Clytie, that mischievous minx, was the apple of Pappa-daddy's eye, and by one way or another she was always able to make him grant her tiniest wish. Our new house—a mansion, really, in every sense of the word—was a case in point. As I may or may not have stated[1] in the foregoing material, our humble frame house, the edifice into which all of us Dinwiddie children had been born, was unattractive, uncapacious, and uncomfortable. But now, with every room, every closet, every nook and cranny overflowing with bottles of Lohocla, it had become simply unlivable. What few pieces of furniture we had had were moved

---

[1] Mrs. Butterfield has. P.D.

out onto the lawn—there to endure the elements—to make room for more and more cases of Lohocla. It was at supper one evening, while being served one of Mammy's famous delicacies—creamed hogs' lungs—that Clytie, aged but twelve, took up the matter of our residence with Pappa-daddy.

"I'm mighty sick and tired of sitting on a Lohocla case every time we come to the table," Clytie said.

"Quiet!" Pappa-daddy said, helping himself from a gravy boat of deep fat—another of Mammy's tempting *spécialités*.

"In fact, Pappa-daddy, it ain't even a table," Clytie continued. "That was thrown out yesterday to make room for twenty more cases of Lohocla."

"Shut up," Pappa-daddy said kindly.

"And another thing," Clytie persisted. "I'm mighty sick of living here in Niggertown, too. I'd like to move into a nice new house over on Jefferson Davis Avenue, with all the swells."

"You're plumb out of your mind, girl," Pappa-daddy said, reaching affectionately across the table for Clytie's pert little face. With that, he filled his tumbler with Lohocla and drained it down in a single gulp. (So great was my father's faith in his own product that he drank several bottles of it daily, both with and between meals.)

"If you weren't such a mean old skinflint—" Clytie began brazenly. I was shocked! Little Bubber tried to suppress a nervous giggle into his table napkin.

"Doggone you, child," Pappa-daddy expostulated. "I've had about enough! Now, young miss, you just march out to the woodshed, and I'll settle your hash once and for all." With that, he swept poor Clytie off her feet and carried her, kicking and struggling, from the house.

Being a born coward about tears and scenes, I was fearfully upset. "Oh, Bubber!" I cried. "Whatever will Pappa-daddy do to poor Clytie?"

"He won't do nothing, mark my words," was Bubber's pert rejoinder.

"Oh, Bubber, dear, how can you be so sure? You know what a terrible temper Pappa-daddy has."

"Maybe so, but ole Clytie happens to know where all the bodies is buried. I'll betcha he don't even touch her."

In agony, I sat for nearly an hour, almost fearing to breathe, and then —just as Bubber had predicted—Clytie marched into the house, calm and serene, with a sweet smile on her elfin face. Pappa-daddy followed—a broken man. He picked up a bottle of Lohocla and retired with it to his room, slamming the door. Calm as you please, Miss Clytie minced upstairs to the room she shared with me and began browsing through illustrated periodicals filled with pictures of the elegant new houses being constructed up North in New York City and Newport, Rhode Island.

"Clytie," I whispered, carefully shutting the door, "what did Pappa-daddy do?"

"He didn't do nothing, sugar," Clytie said. "In fact, he had to agree that we're all living like poor white trash in this tumble-down old hovel. How d'ya like this shingle château built by Stanford White? Kinda plain, if you ask me."

"Didn't he even spank you?"

"He never laid a finger on me. He wouldn't dare. Here's a house by Richard Morris Hunt. Ya like it, sugar?" With that, she took a cigarette out of her dresser drawer and lighted it!

"Clytie!" I gasped. "If Pappa-daddy catches you, he'll—"

"He'll do nothin'," Clytie said, blowing a smoke ring. I was horrified. "He'll do nothin' except maybe offer to light my cheroots for me—like a gentleman should."

"But, Clytie, what did you say to him?"

"I just said a little something that some little old bird cheeped inta my ear. *That* made the old peckerwood sit up and take notice! What color would you like your new bedroom, sugar? I'm gonna have mine in mauve, with gold furniture and a swan bed."

"But, Clytie, Pappa-daddy said—"

"He said I could have a bedroom and a sitting room in the tower. Of course, our *new* house is going to have at least *one* tower. They're all the rage up North."

"But wasn't Pappa-daddy mad?"

"Sore as a crab. But we're moving. We're also going to have a horse and carriage—several—and you and me's going to start going to *private* school. Miss Beaufort's Seminary for Young Confederate Ladies."

"But, Clytie, how ever did you—"

"That's for me to know an' you to find out. But maybe I'll give you a tiny hint, on account of you're so smart. You know that fine creole typewriter that's working for Pappa-daddy—down in the Mansion House?"

"Miss Prouty?"

"That's the one, except she's a *Mrs.* Prouty, and there's a Mr. Prouty, who's just about big enough and mean enough to break old Pappa-daddy in two. He happened to come around here today when you was off to choir practice. Big, fine-looking man. Give me fifty cents to report anything I could to him concerning Pappa-daddy and his—uh—secretary. But I think now I'll just forget what I saw. It's worth quite a lot to old Pappa-daddy.

"Clytie," I said, "I don't understand one word of what you're saying."

"I'm surely sure you don't, sugar. Now, let's plan the downstairs first."

At last, I thought, too excited over the prospects of a proud new Dinwiddie house to ponder further Clytie's mysterious message—at last a beautiful plantation house like the Executive Mansion in Milledgeville, with stately columns, a wide center hall, and a sweeping staircase. But not so sly Miss Clytie! It was she who convinced Pappa-daddy that we would need a new house, and it was also she who chose the architect and the style of house she wanted. Nothing like it had ever been seen in Pellagra County before. The architect described it as "eclectic," and that it most certainly was. Clytie chose every bit of it herself, from the enormous lot, at the intersection of Jefferson Davis Avenue and Stonewall Jackson Street, down to the very lace curtains at the windows. And, mind you, Clytie was but a child of twelve at the time! When I asked her how on earth she managed to plan it, her saucy reply was, "Easy, sugar. I just go down to the library and look through the picture books. Every time I see some part of some old castle I like—well, I tear out the page and give it to the architect. See, sugar? My room, in this here corner tower, is going to have a roof just like that big Taj Mahal place, in Indiana. And these windows here in the dining room are a copy of the ones in some old church in Paris, France. And these stairs on the inside are almost exactly like some in an old Eye-talian castle. And the whole blamed place to be surrounded with a big verandah! Won't that make their eyes pop!"

It certainly did. By the time Clytie's dream house was completed, it contained more than forty rooms and, as the architect said admiringly, more than forty distinct styles of architecture. It was built mostly of wood, shingle, multicolored stone, and wrought iron. There was a porte-cochère and twenty-five stained-glass windows. The interior was just as remarkable. The entrance hall was baronial; the three interconnecting parlors were Spanish, Tudor, and Turkish. The dining room was Chinese, with windows duplicating some of those in Notre Dame. The stairway was gothic with baroque touches.

Clytie's own bedroom—a three-room suite, actually—was, for the most part, rococo and Japanese. The room assigned to Bubber was modelled after a Bavarian *Bierstube,* plus some very masculine suits of armor, battle flags, swords, and shields. Most effective! Pappa-daddy's quarters were inspired by the papal bedchamber at Tivoli. I would have preferred a simple room, with a four-poster bed and a gay floral wallpaper; however, Clytie convinced me that such a room would not be nearly grand enough for a patent-medicine heiress. Therefore I capitulated and settled for a free adaptation of Mme. Pompadour's bedchamber at Versailles. Pappa-daddy was most annoyed to find that the final bills amounted to three times as much as the architect's initial estimate. But Clytie took him aside for a little talk and, as always, was able to wrap him around her little finger with just a word or two. It was ever thus.

And dear Clytie was twice-blessed in having an adoring father who was also wealthy as her extravagant demands grew and grew and grew. Obviously, Mammy could not care for a house so large singlehanded, and so, after a brief conference with Pappa-daddy, a veritable army of Negro retainers appeared, dressed in plum velvet liveries, ordered specially all the way from New Orleans, and powdered wigs for formal occasions, from a special hairdresser in Richmond! According to Clytie's wildest dreams of grandeur, there were two grooms for every carriage (of which there were several—a victoria, a phaeton, a brougham, a landau, and an adorable little governess cart drawn by a sweet shetland pony, for brother Bubber); a footman behind each chair at every meal; six men just to tend the gardens, which boasted an orangery, a grotto, a waterfall, two fountains, a reflecting pool, several classical statues, and numerous iron deer; and also personal maids for each of us girls.

Pappa-daddy would become almost apoplectic with anger whenever the immense bills for Clytie's frivolous expenditures arrived, but pretty, personable Clytie could always step into Pappa-daddy's library and win him over to her way of thinking in a trice. And no wonder Pappa-daddy preferred my sister Clytie to me. She was a gay sunbeam of a lass, overflowing with high spirits and charm, while I was shy, serious, and retiring, given to overweight and introspection. In many cases, I felt that Pappa-daddy was right in trying to curb Clytie's extravagance and her wild spending sprees. No matter how rich we were, it seemed morally wrong that a girl still in her early teens could have at her casual disposal so much money—money to burn. But when I, as an older sister, would attempt to take Clytie to task for her profligate ways and encourage her to mend them, Clytie would simply laugh merrily and say, "If I didn't spend it, the old soak would only put it where we could none of us get our hands on it. Can't you see that I'm spreading prosperity all over the town of Pellagra?"

What Clytie said was somewhat true. Wealth begets wealth, and very soon after Pappa-daddy established Lohocla as *the* patent medicine of the South, numerous opportunities to invest in other business ventures came his way. Businessmen of Pellagra were skeptical of Pappa-daddy at first, but their sneers were soon changed to cheers as year by year, month by month, week by week, day by day Pappa-daddy became more prosperous and influential. I had to laugh when, at the end of Pappa-daddy's first year, Mr. Peavey, president of the Pellagra County Trust Company, came to our humble home[2] with his hat in his hand to offer Pappa-daddy one million dollars in cash (as well as generous royalties) for the Lohocla formula. Pappa-daddy literally threw him out of the house!

Word of Lohocla spread like wildfire, and very soon distinguished gentlemen from all parts of the country—and even one from as far away as Toronto, Ontario, Canada—travelled all the way to sleepy little Pellagra, trying to coax Pappa-daddy into leasing distribution franchises for his miraculous product.

So much that is unpleasant, unkind, and untrue has been written about Lohocla, until its recent emergence as a product vital to national defense, that I feel called upon to say a few words in Lohocla's behalf.

It is all very well to accuse the Dinwiddie family of charlatanism and humbuggery because certain unschooled users of Lohocla put too much faith in the product. But I have before me a label from the *original* bottle of Lohocla, as well as advertisements appearing in such respected and respectable magazines as *Woman's Home Companion, Modern Priscilla, Delineator, Munsey's,* and *Liberty.* In no place do we claim that daily dosages of Lohocla can or will *cure* such widely diversified ills as arthritis, beriberi, constipation, dropsy, epilepsy, female complaints, gout, hives, impetigo, jaundice, kidney stones, leprosy, mononucleosis, neuralgia, otitis, pregnancy, quinsy, rabies, social diseases, tularemia, urethritis, varicose veins, warts, xenophibia, yaws, Zulu fever, all of which are listed on the label. Pappa-daddy, being a gentleman of probity, simply stated that Lohocla would *"relieve the discomfort of"* [3] such ailments.

If those who scoffed at Pappa-daddy could but read the sincere, unso-

---

[2] By "humble home," Mrs. Butterfield refers to the house in Negrotown where she was born and *not* to the mansion described in the foregoing.   P.D.

[3] Italics Mrs. Butterfield's.   P.D.

licited endorsements of Lohocla that poured into the Lohocla laboratories daily (always accompanied by orders for still more of this liquid) they would see for themselves what my father truly was—a dedicated man of science who, by dint of hard labor and philanthropic zeal, miraculously brought euphoria within the reach of millions of sufferers for a mere dollar a pint.

Although rival patent-medicine manufacturers hired people to claim that they had gone deaf or blind from dosages of Lohocla, although the Communist-inspired Pure Food and Drug Act, spawned by the inquitous regime of President Theodore Roosevelt (who was actually jealous of my dear husband's political power, and tried to wound him through me and my devoted family), struck many a foul blow at Lohocla, it was not until the gangster-engineered passage of the terrible Volstead Act that the mighty banner of Lohocla was lowered to half mast. All I can and will say about Lohocla Authentic Indian Spirit Water is that if it was *not* good, *not* beneficial, and did *not* offer nirvana to multitudes of people suffering from disease or depression, *why* then did so many millions of satisfied customers keep ordering bottle after bottle after bottle? My case rests!

However, I digress.

Before the end of the first year, Pappa-daddy and Lohocla became the largest depositors in the Pellagra County Trust Company, and the following year, dissatisfied with the rates of interest paid by the Pellagra County Trust, Pappa-daddy opened the Lohocla National Bank right next door, paying double interest. It was not long before the Pellagra County Trust was forced to close its doors, while the Lohocla National flourished until Franklin D. Roosevelt (another Roosevelt enemy of Clan Dinwiddie) and his so-called "New Deal" declared its Socialistic bank moratorium of 1933, thus wiping away a grand old family tradition as well as devouring the life savings of widows, orphans, and humble folk all over the glorious South.

Nor was it long before other tempting business arrangements made themselves known to Pappa-daddy. By attending auction sales, he was able to pick up many a fertile bit of farm land in the immediate vicinity. Once but a hireling of the Pellagra County Interurban Traction Company, Pappa-daddy eventually purchased that tottering firm outright. He did so at a propitious moment—just in time to provide transportation for several hundred Lohocla employees and their families, who had been brought to Pellagra Township and settled in the Gayelord Dinwiddie

Mansions, which Pappa-daddy built on the opposite side of town and, out of the goodness of his heart, rented for a mere pittance to his delighted workers. In fact, when Pappa-daddy heard that some Pellagra landlords were charging exorbitant rentals for substandard housing, he made it obligatory for members of the Lohocla Family to rent from him and only from him. That soon put a stop to profiteering! Equally indignant to discover that Lohocla employees were going deeper and deeper into debt by purchasing food, clothing, and furniture from the merchants of Pellagra County, Pappa-daddy opened company stores of his own, where members of his staff and their families could charge their purchases for an unlimited length of time, the only proviso being, naturally, that they must settle their debts to the company stores before terminating their employ with Lohocla.

It was not long before Pappa-daddy became *the* leading citizen of the county. He was its largest manufacturer, its largest landlord, its chief merchant, its transportation firm, and its newspaper publisher.[4] Can you wonder that these simple Southern folk so loved Pappa-daddy?

After Lohocla had been in business for only four years, the little township of Pellagra had more than doubled its population! It was estimated that more than fifty per cent of the townspeople were employed, in one way or another, by my father.

At sweet sixteen, I suddenly realized that I was the most eligible girl in the county, the chatelaine of the most elaborate and costly house in the state, and a patent-medicine heiress.

Being unaggressive and painfully shy, I was timid about entertaining anyone except the girls I had grown up with. They had always been my friends when we were poor, and so why would they not be our friends when we were rich? Happily, levelheaded Clytie made me see the folly and snobbishness of my ways.

"You are being nothing but an old stick-in-the-mud," Clytie would storm when I felt leery of inviting girls from Miss Beaufort's Seminary to our splendid new house. "I think it's just plain stuck-up and snobby not to ask Margaret Peavey and the other girls from old Miss Beaufort's. Instead, you just want to run around with a lot of trash from Niggertown, like we had to when we were poor."

"But, Clytie," I would say, "they were our friends when Maggie Peavey and the others wouldn't even speak to us."

---

[4] Following a series of defamatory articles in the Pellagra *News & Sentinel,* Mr. Dinwiddie purchased that periodical and became its publisher and editor-in-chief. P.D.

"And now that they want to be our friends, you are just so all-fired mean and exclusive you stick your nose up at them."

"I don't," I said. "But people like the Spratling girls and the Sockdolagers have always been our friends."

"That's right," Clytie said. "And now you just want to make them feel miserable and no-account by dragging 'em here to show off how rich Pappa-daddy is. Do you think *that's* nice?"

How right Clytie was! Tortured by my own shyness, I had been making my old friends feel insignificant and uncomfortable in the presence of so much grandeur while snubbing new acquaintances who were anxious to be our friends, too.

"Very well, Clytie," I said, feeling shocked and much abashed. "*You* handle the invitations for my sixteenth birthday party. And I'll just be surprised."

"You bet you will," Clytie said.

Chums—with Margaret Peavy at Miss Beaufort's

On my sixteenth birthday, just sixteen girls were present—only the members of our two classes at Miss Beaufort's Seminary. And Clytie was correct, as always. I was surprised—surprised that they had accepted our hospitality and surprised at how much friendlier they had all become in just a few years. I was astounded to notice that suddenly I had lost my shyness and had become one of the most popular girls in the town. At first, I could scarcely believe that plain, pudgy young Martha Dinwiddie could cause such a sensation with the social leaders of Pellagra. Naturally, nothing that Clytie ever did could astonish me. My younger sister was so pretty and sweet, so naturally vivacious and gregarious that I would have *expected* her to be the belle of *any* ball. As for young Bubber, he was perhaps the most completely precocious boy I have ever seen or heard of. At thirteen, small, lithe, dashing, wiry Bubber affected long trousers and sideburns. (He was still too young to grow a mustache or even to shave.) He smoked panatela cigars quite openly, although I pleaded with him not to, telling him that they would stunt his growth, in which matter I was entirely correct.[5] Not only did he dress the role of the dandy, but he scented himself liberally with bay rum, patchouli, and lilac vegetal! He had a way with the ladies, from the elderly aristocratic spinsters living along Jefferson Davis Avenue down to the very colored girls who functioned as maids in our home. Irresistible, that was Bubber.

Like his sister Clytie, I would have *expected* Bubber to be the heart and soul of any social group, for they both had the certain *je ne sais quoi* that made all sorts of people from all walks of life sit up and take notice. But as for my own popularity I found it just too difficult to believe at first. Yet it was true! Just like an ugly grub emerging from its drab cocoon to turn into a dazzling butterfly, I was suddenly in the greatest demand with boys as well as girls. The innocent pleasures of youth were suddenly mine. At our first youthful evening parties, my dance program was always filled weeks before the event took place. Before I was even eighteen, I had received marriage proposals from Ned Hitt, Wade Lamprey, and Ted Pottinger—three of the town's most eligible beaux. I was a Southern belle in every sense of the word—as poor, dear, dead Mumsie-love must have been before the War of the Secession.

My situation was a sort of Judgment of Paris in reverse. On the night of my eighteenth birthday (in spite of Pappa-daddy's loud objections, the

---

[5] A moot point. John Sappington Marmaduke (Bubber) Dinwiddie's full height at the time of his death was five feet four and a half inches. P.D.

event had been celebrated by a large cotillion in the ballroom of our house, owing to sweet, unselfish Clytie's intercession on my behalf), I crept into Clytie's bed to tell her of my dilemma in choosing the correct cavalier and to ask her advice.

"Don't talk like a fool!" Clytie snapped. "You'll marry none of them."

"But, Clytie, dearest," I said, "I'm eighteen now. I can give my own consent whether Pappa-daddy likes it or not."

"You idiot! Who cares about Pappa-daddy? He'd be only too glad to get rid of every last one of us."

"Clytie! What a dreadful way to talk! When he's been so sweet and generous . . ."

"Have it your own way, stupid," Clytie said. "Marry any of those one-horse-town red necks you like. But first *you're* going to do a favor for *me.*"

"Why, certainly, dearest," I said, quite mystified. "Anything you like."

"Good. You and me's going to New York, and we're going to come out."

"Come out of what?"

"I mean come out in society. The Four Hundred and all like that. Then we're going to take the Grand Tour of Europe—Paris, London, Rome, Vienna—big fashionable places, with dukes and princes and the rest of those high mucky-mucks. Then you can come back to this little jerk-water place and marry some black field hand for all I care."

Darling Clytie! But for her loving concern and sound advice, I might never have met the man of my dreams—that statesman and President of these United States, George W. Butterfield!

IV

Glamour and Romance

1888

We invade New York. . . . Business before pleasure. . . . My début to the Four Hundred. . . . Getting away from it all. . . . The White Star Line. . . . A dashing stowaway—George W. Butterfield. . . . My shipboard romance. . . . Pappa-daddy intervenes.

ew York! Can my gentle readers imagine what the magical city meant to a young country miss of eighteen, who, though the heiress presumptive to a large fortune, had never before been out of Pellagra County?

Yet there it all was—North America's greatest city—just waiting to be conquered! But there was, alas, dissension in the ranks of our little "Confederate army" even before we set out on what would prove to be the greatest adventure of my adventurous life. Pappa-daddy was furious with Clytie when she even so much as suggested going to New York. As for Europe, he turned livid with anger even at the mention of the name! If I live to be a hundred,[1] I will never know what magical words Clytie used on Pappa-daddy in her do-or-die efforts to persuade him. Heretofore, charming Clytie had only to sequester herself in Pappa-daddy's study for a few moments in order to talk him around to her way of thinking. But this time Clytie's little whim involved his taking at least a year off from the daily grind of the Lohocla plant. Hardly had Clytie begun her whee-

---

[1] Which is entirely within the realm of possibility, Mrs. Butterfield having been born in 1870 and enjoying perfect health under circumstances where she is the recipient of the ultimate in excellent physical care. P.D.

dling and "sweet talking" than I heard a roar that carried all the way from the closed door of the study out to the conservatory. I raced to the hall just in time to hear the door of Pappa-daddy's study close with a bang. Dear Clytie, ashen, leaned weakly against a suit of armor, rubbing at an angry red spot on one of her cheeks.

"Clytie, darling!" I cried. "Whatever in the—"

And then—or did my ears deceive me?—Clytie uttered a term I had never before heard used. Shaking loose from my solicitous touch, she raced furiously up the stairs, calling, "Bubber! Bubber!"

Pappa-daddy did not dine with us that evening. In fact, he rarely took any of his meals at home, preferring, I suppose, the hearty companionship of other businessmen at the Pellagra Club or the Planters' Club, to both of which he had recently been elected. It was a strange and rather lonely meal, with Clytie and Bubber looking remote and secretive, exchanging occasional dark glances and speaking only to each other, in what might well have been a code or an extinct foreign language. The term "yellow girl" kept popping up, as well as other strange words. My poor attempts to draw my younger brother and sister into general conversation were rejected. I retired early that evening with a recent copy of *Harper's Weekly*.

The next morning, I was up with the birds and, before the day grew too warm, off to visit a family of poor whites on the far side of the town. I breakfasted lightly on mush, grits, greens, fatback, bread, drippings, and sorghum, alone but for faithful old Mammy, who circled the table chuckling softly to herself.

Before the others were up, I was away in the governess cart with my parcels of food, castoff clothing, and the Bible from which I read aloud to the impoverished family whom I had "adopted." It was late afternoon before I returned to Dinwiddiewood. The driveway was filled with a great cortège of carriages—*our* carriages. Leading off the procession was the victoria, which contained Clytie, a vision in lavender, looking cool and collected (and, if the truth were told, a trifle smug) beneath her twirling parasol. Behind her, in the phaeton, sat Bubber, calmly smoking a cheroot and whiling away the time with the pretty quadroon upstairs maid. Beneath the porte-cochère, in the landau (which must have been stifling, as the folding top was closed), sat Pappa-daddy, looking hot, impatient, and angry.

"Hey, you-all," I cried, waving gaily. "Is this a circus parade?"

The door of the landau sprang open, and Pappa-daddy, looking apoplectic with anger, began shouting at me.

"You better be careful, Pappa-daddy," Clytie called mischievously. "We're not out of Pellagra County *yet*."

"That's right, Pappa-daddy," Bubber chortled, his beautiful boy-soprano voice now, alas, settled once and for all into a manly tenor. "Them Ku-Kluxers can get mighty ornery in this hot weather." Both he and Clytie laughed delightedly.

Almost frothing at the lips with rage, Pappa-daddy shook his fist at me and babbled incoherently. Then, seeing a horse and buggy racing along Jefferson Davis Avenue, he bolted back into the landau and slammed the door.

"What Pappa-daddy is *trying* to say, Martha," Clytie called calmly, "is that you'd better get a move on. We almost left without you."

"Left?" I said. "Left for where?"

"Why for New York City, where else, silliness?" Clytie said, twirling her parasol flirtatiously. "New York City and our début, and then our Grand Tour."

There was an absolute roar from Pappa-daddy, in the landau.

"Better hurry, sugar!" Clytie called.

"But I haven't packed. I'm just wearing this old calico hack-about dress and mended gloves and—"

"Don't you fret about that, sugar," Clytie laughed. "You won't be wanting to wear any of these tacky old small-town duds any longer. We'll be buying our *toilettes* in big fancy dry-goods stores, like Stewart's and Lord & Taylor and Benjamin Altman's and Arnold Constable's—and, of course, at Worth's in London, England, and Paris, France. Ain't that right, Pappa-daddy? Ain't that what you just said?"

The landau positively shook, but there was no sound.

"Better get a move on, Big Sister," Bubber called.

"B-but . . ."

"Just climb in here with me," Clytie said. "Wouldn't pay to look too conspicuous—use up too many carriages. Pappa-daddy's travelling in mufti. Ain't that right, Pappa-daddy?"

There was no reply from the landau. It simply shuddered upon its springs once more. A groom assisted me out of the tiny governess cart and helped me hastily up into the victoria.

Our convoy was off! First the victoria, then the phaeton, and, last of all, Pappa-daddy, in the tightly closed landau. Even the blinds were drawn. I looked back and gazed upon our happy home for the last time in many a moon.

We boarded the train not at the new Pellagra depot, as I had expected, but well out of town, at the Lohocla plant's private siding. In spite of my tardiness, our timing was perfect. I could hear the romantic whistle of the four-fifty-seven just as we drew up to the tracks. The train was flagged to a halt, and we were helped aboard the very last car—a private one, hastily reserved at who can fathom what expense. It was nicely fitted out in rosewood and green plush, with a large sleeping compartment for Clytie and me, individual compartments for Bubber and Pappa-daddy, and a comfy lounge where our little family could sit and also where our meals were served. Darling Pappa-daddy, always the salt of the earth, had even hired a private boxcar for our two darky porters.

"But why the suddenness? Why the mystery? Why board the cars way out here in the wilderness instead of going to the depot?" I kept asking. "What did you ever say to Pappa-daddy to make him decide to take this long and costly trip on the spur of the moment?"

"Curiosity killed the cat," was all Clytie would say. "Now, why don't you sit here by the window, sugar, and watch the scenery?"

Poor Pappa-daddy! He was so undone by the speed of our departure that he went straight to his own compartment, pulled down all the shades, and refused to come out even for meals. Happily, his valet had had the foresight to include a case of Lohocla among our scanty personal possessions, so as I watched a dusky servitor hustling in and out of Pappa-daddy's compartment, each time replacing an empty bottle with a new full pint, I had the satisfaction of knowing that my dear parent was drawing the strength and sustenance needed for so sudden and arduous a journey, while we young folk picnicked on cold Georgia Banner ham, cold fried chicken, grits, corn bread, pickled sowbelly, molasses, fruit, and scuppernong wine. So excited was I by my first glimpse of every new hamlet and village, every barn and cow that I sat rapt at the window, watching this thrilling new world unfold itself before me. And sooner than I could possibly believe, we were pulling into the station at New York.

At the time of our arrival in Gotham, Manhattan was a far different place from the overcrowded "tight little island" that it is today. In 1888, Madison Square, with its magnificent trees, its smart hacks and carriages with their dapper jarveys (coachmen) gliding smoothly along the Belgian-block pavement, its Parisian-style hotels—the Hoffman House, the Albemarle, and the Fifth Avenue—was the center of smart social life. Fifth Avenue below Twenty-third Street was known as Ladies' Mile, with its double white row of tempting specialty shops. Above Twenty-third Street, this mighty thoroughfare was still largely residential, with its fashionable clubs, its stately mansions, St. Patrick's Cathedral, the Vanderbilt houses, "Marble Row," and "Millionaires' Row." The elegant old Waldorf-Astoria (so recently pulled down to make way for the new Empire State Building) was but a dream on the architect's drawing board at the time of our arrival, its site then occupied by the town houses of the John Jacob Astors and the William Waldorf Astors. Even more imposing was the marble mansion of the late A. T. Stewart, leased to the Manhattan Club at the time of our first visit.

Although Pappa-daddy suggested—and with a certain amount of prudence, I felt, for he was a godly man whose strict religious scruples made him abhor anything that smacked of worldliness—that my sister Clytie and I put up at a hostel for Baptist girls, while he and Bubber sought lodging with a lady in the Tenderloin district, Clytie would have none of it. She insisted upon taking two enormous suites at the new Windsor Hotel, overlooking the Jay Gould residence, at Fifth Avenue and Forty-seventh Street.

I will grant that our accommodations were opulent in the extreme. Clytie and Bubber, however, seemed to take the Hotel Windsor in their stride. It had quite superseded the older Fifth Avenue Hotel as the uptown center of high finance. Our near neighbor Jay Gould and swarms of financiers peopled the public rooms every evening, and Pappa-daddy, who had been so staunchly against this trip to New York, soon became heart and soul of this cluster of tycoons. Even Mr. Gould had to admit that my father had taught him "umpteen new ways of skinning a cat." In addition, its register contained the names of notables and aristocrats from every corner of the globe. I was sick with shyness in the presence of such illustrious personages, but Clytie and Bubber seemed right at home with the greatest of them. Such was the magnetism of my dear sister that she had but to walk through the lobby of the hotel and the door of our suite was simply besieged by captains of industry and leaders of the social whirl from all over the world. Their wives, mothers, and sisters, however, were more reticent about calling upon us.

No sooner had Clytie established us in the Windsor, and had our many rooms abloom with fragrant blossoms from Siebricht & Wadley's Rosehill Nurseries (a firm that, even then, proudly boasted "Flowers by Telegraph to Any Part of the World!"), than she hired carriages and grooms for each of us and started on a whirlwind shopping tour of New York. Shoes from

Cammeyer and J. & J. Slater; jewels from Black, Starr & Frost, Tiffany, Udall & Ballou, and Dreicer & Company; gowns from Lord & Taylor's on Broadway, Arnold Constable, and Margaret A. Howard; furs from Jaeckel and Revillon Frères. Meanwhile, brother Bubber gave vent to his masculine vanity with stylish new suitings from Brooks Brothers' store, at Broadway and Twenty-second Street, and smart haberdashery from such awe-inspiring firms as Kaskel & Kaskel and Budd, both established at that crossroads of the *haut monde,* Fifth Avenue and Twenty-third Street, whence originated the expression "Twenty-three skiddoo!"

As for me, my tastes were more modest. I loved browsing through the books at Brentano's Literary Emporium, in Union Square, and gazing fondly at the tiny tots agog in the fairyland of wonderful toys at F. A. O. Schwartz, on East Fourteenth Street. Clytie often chided me for my lack of interest in the world of fashion, but I sensed that I was a homebody at heart, while my sister and brother were better adapted to the hustle and bustle of high society.

Even then, Clytie was a born social leader, urging my father to join such venerable clubs as the Union, the Union League, and the Knickerbocker. For some reason, although Pappa-daddy eventually indicated a willingness to mix with these yankee gentlemen, his election to membership never came up. So busy, however, was Pappa-daddy talking business to his new associates—such men as Russell Sage; James R. Keene; H. M. Flagler; Washington Conner; F. Work; Samuel C. T. Dodd, the brilliant attorney for John D. Rockefeller; Edward Harriman; James Hill; and even that famous lady mogul, Mrs. Hetty Green!—that he had but little time for things social. Instead of taking a year's holiday, Pappa-daddy was able to amass a still larger fortune in the way of stocks and shares simply for confiding to these great tycoons a few of his simple business methods. Even Mr. Rockefeller and his associate, Mr. John Archbold, were speechless with admiration for some of Pappa-daddy's sweeping reforms, and he was known the length and breadth of Fifth Avenue as "one of the slickest operators this side of Ossining," a great tribute to a man of Pappa-daddy's retiring modesty.

As long as his considerable holdings were growing every day in New York, he became more lenient—in fact, totally indifferent—in the matter of Clytie's profligate spending, and it was then that my sister, weary of the mercantile pleasures of the Ladies' Mile, began to think seriously of our début before New York's Four Hundred. At first, Clytie tried to get none other than Mrs. Astor's court chamberlain, Ward McAllister, to serve as our social mentor in New York, on the grounds that the McAllisters and the Dinwiddies were *both* leading aristocratic families of the more gracious old South. Although Clytie wrote to Mr. McAllister time and time again, and even went personally to call on him, she had the bad luck to find him never at home. Then, armed with Mr. Louis Keller's interesting new book, the Social Register, Clytie and I set out in our carriage, leaving cards on all of the families listed therein. Once having established the fact that we were in town and "at home" at the Windsor, it seemed certain that they would return our calls—a matter of course among neighbors in Pellagra—and would surely be delighted to attend our débutante ball.

Since I was too shy and diffident myself to do very much more than stand for hours in the atelier of Mme. Margaret A. Howard—then *the* couturière to society—being fitted for my ball gown, Clytie took over all the arrangements for our début, with the assistance of a Mrs. Ada Civet, an acquaintance of Bubber's, who promised that for a certain fee she would oversee such details as invitations, notices to the press, and plainclothesmen to keep the uninvited from "crashing" the gate on the gala night. "It will be," Mrs. Civet guaranteed as she folded the large check drawn by Pappa-daddy on the Lohocla National Bank, "the most exclusive party in the history of New York society."

Clytie found it difficult to choose between Delmonico's splendid new establishment, which stretched for an entire block on Fifth Avenue at Twenty-sixth Street, and Sherry's. The matter was finally settled by a toss of a coin, and all of Sherry's was reserved for the evening of our début, although Mrs. Civet had been most forceful about suggesting that the party be held in the town house of one of her many highly placed relatives (which was, on very special occasions, rented out at a high figure), saying that the *haut monde* of New York was too conservative to attend a private party held in a public restaurant. Perhaps she was correct.

Clytie did, however, yield to Mrs. Civet's wishes concerning the floral decorations. Mrs. Civet was very firm about having the flowers sent in from the greenhouses of her palatial estate in New Jersey, saying that these privately owned flowers "removed the tinge of commercialism" from the ball.

I will never forget the evening of my début. I was dressed in white with a simple strand of pearls, which was, according to Clytie, the "uniform" of the débutante. Clytie, although my junior, chose rose tulle and diamonds. Our little family arrived at Sherry's shortly after nine, happy to

Mrs. Civet (l.), "Bubber" (r.)

find ourselves the first of the merrymakers. Mrs. Civet had not yet appeared nor had any of the guests, although the entire Social Register had been summoned. The restaurant had been transformed into a veritable fairyland, but even as early as nine o'clock the garlands of Mrs. Civet's flowers, looped from the chandeliers, entwining the balustrades, and forming arches and bowers, were a great deal the worse for wear. Having something of a "green thumb" myself, it seemed to me that Mrs. Civet's estimate, which had been accepted and paid some weeks in advance, was rather high for flowers of such short-lived bloom. An orchestra—rather smaller than the one we had been led to expect—played popular tunes of the day in the empty ballroom. Several hundred round tables festooned the supper rooms, each attended by a retinue of handsome flunkies in knee breeches, gold-laced liveries, and powdered wigs. Champagne flowed like water, but Pappa-daddy had brought his own private stock of Lohocla. (Although a teetotaller, save for certain light table wines, Pappa-daddy had no objection to other ladies and gentlemen imbibing delicately of fine vintages or even, upon occasion, spirits.)

With our bouquets in our hands (and my heart in my mouth), Clytie and I stood in a bower of roses, jasmine, freesia, and smilax, to await the first guests, with Bubber and Pappa-daddy loyally at our side. Ten o'clock arrived but no guests—not even Mrs. Civet, one of whose duties it was to keep out the uninvited.

"I think it's mighty inconsiderate of them to be so tardy," I remarked. "The orchestra has been playing for more than an hour, and the waiters have been on their feet since—"

"*Their* feet?" Bubber sneered, gazing down at his narrow patent-leather pumps.

"That's what it's like in New York society," said Clytie, who was *au courant* with such things. "I asked 'em all, from Astor to Vanderbilt, and they're probably just now getting up from their dinner parties before the ball."

Pappa-daddy called for a chair, a small table, and a large bottle of Lohocla.

"Perhaps you're right, dear," I said.

Another hour passed and still no guests had appeared. Nor had Mrs. Civet seen fit to take over her duties at the door! By this time, my feet, wedged into high-heeled satin slippers, were torturing me. "Do you suppose there could have been some mistake?" I asked.

"Martha, sugar, you just don't understand big town high life," Clytie said reassuringly. "Everything starts late here." Bubber, too, called for a chair, and for another bottle of champagne. Still we girls stood and still I smiled.

At midnight, the major-domo called out the names of the first arrivals. A very elderly lady and gentleman made their way slowly up the grand staircase from which the once festive floral garlands now drooped brown, shrivelled, and dead. The Lohocla bottle was quickly withdrawn, as was young Bubber's magnum of champagne. Pappa-daddy, quite weary by now, was helped to his feet and we formed a small receiving line.

"Good evening," I said, curtsying. "I am Martha Dinwiddie."

"How?" said the old gentleman, obviously quite hard of hearing.

I was about to repeat my name when he said to his wife, "Oh, pshaw! We must have come the wrong night. Mrs. Fish said it was going to be a real circus."

"Won't you-all join us?" I said.

"Hush up," Clytie whispered angrily. "They're just a couple of old nobodies trying to get a free drink." Very tactfully, she steered them back down the stairs, while the old gentleman kept muttering about how much he enjoyed a circus. The next morning, their visiting card was presented to me. I have it still—Cyrus West Field, paper merchant, financier, and guiding light behind the great Atlantic cable, had attended our début! It is my only souvenir.

At one o'clock in the morning, Mr. Sherry himself appeared at Clytie's side and announced that the elaborate collation—oysters, terrapin, squab, canvasback duck, medallions of beef, lobster, crab, galantine of chicken,

Coming out

crayfish, suckling pig, and Mammy's own delicacy sent from down home, creamed hogs' lungs—would be spoiled if it were not eaten. Although none of the guests had yet arrived, we repaired to the supper room, Bubber and two waiters supporting Pappa-daddy, who was by then dropping with fatigue. It was a lonely feast, attended by none but the hired photographer, although Clytie—always democratic—struck up a lively conversation with one of the bewigged young men engaged to wait upon table. At half past four, when the rosy-fingered dawn was lighting the skies above Long Island, Pappa-daddy, now dead to the world, was carried to a brougham. Bubber excused himself to visit a Turkish bathing establishment located nearby in the Tenderloin district, and Clytie and I were driven wearily back to the Windsor. On the following day, no newspaper carried a single word concerning our début. From Mrs. Civet, all we received was a postal card bearing a Canadian postmark and showing a picture of Niagara Falls. On it, in a rather unsteady hand, she had written, "Didn't I tell you that your party would be exclusive?" Upon looking the word "exclusive" up in a dictionary, I found that it was defined as "excluding or inclined to leave out others." When I showed the postal card to Clytie, she was furious. In her anger, obviously brought on by fatigue from the onerous evening before, Clytie used language that I have never heard a lady use, vowed vengeance, and announced that we were leaving for Europe. "And I'm not coming back," she cried, "until I've got all these highfalutin New York snobs licking my shoes!"

Useless of me to try to explain to Clytie that the absence of guests on the previous evening had surely been caused by some enormous mistake (probably made by Mrs. Civet, who had never struck me as an efficient person, although she was ladylike and kind in the extreme). My sister was adamant. Pappa-daddy, however, proved to be a stumbling block once again to Clytie's plans for an immediate sailing. Having seen New York at first hand, albeit against his will, Pappa-daddy was now quite content with staying there and exchanging secrets of success with well-to-do yankee gentlemen. He had even gone so far as to rent office space in a building on lower Broadway in an attempt to establish a Northern office of Lohocla. However, Clytie had met in the lobby of the Windsor Hotel a Miss Ida Minerva Tarbell, a young woman not many years older than I, who had established quite a reputation as a newspaper reporter, of all things! (In those days, it was known very occasionally for a woman of good family but limited means to accept a position with the press, writing social goings on and such, but Miss Tarbell dealt mostly with business and spoke of herself as a "muckraker." It was most unusual.) Clytie had only to invite Miss Tarbell to tea one afternoon when Pappa-daddy awoke from his nap. With pad and pencil in hand and asking only a few simple questions about Lohocla, its origin, its contents, and the structure of the Dinwiddie business holdings, Miss Tarbell had an almost magical effect upon my father. From having been dead set against a European trip, Pappa-daddy, still in stocking feet and galluses, raced down all six flights of stairs to have the hall porter book passage to England on the very next ship. In the meantime, quite mystified by the eccentric-seeming behavior of my parent, I tried, to the best of my poor ability, to answer some of Miss Tarbell's questions. But she seemed quite dissatisfied at having only me to interview and kept speaking of the "inside story."

The next morning, we all boarded the White Star ship *S.S. Euremic*—then the fastest ship on the North Atlantic run. Although the weather was still mild—warm, even—Pappa-daddy insisted that Clytie and I be bundled in furs from ankles to eyes and that we be heavily veiled. He himself was carried aboard on a stretcher and taken immediately to his stateroom. (A larger, adjoining stateroom was completely filled with cases of Lohocla—"Enough," Pappa-daddy said, "to get me to Europe and back home to Pellagra where a white man can run his own affairs without some snooping hen from *Munsey's Magazine* sticking her nose into his business.") So anxious was Pappa-daddy to sample the joys of European culture that he did not even leave his darkened cabin to see the bright new Statue of Liberty, standing guard over New York Harbor! At high noon, with a great blasting of whistles, the *Euremic* set sail, and I was off—off to the greatest adventure of my life!

Perpetually shy as a violet, perpetually nervous as an aspen, and ever—although my popularity with both sexes back home in Pellagra had proven me wrong time and time again—the perpetual wallflower, I was awe-struck by the enormous oceangoing hotel, with its grand saloons, its many decks, its unusual terminology, its ranks of cabin stewards, mess stewards, deck stewards, bar stewards, and bath stewards. But not so, need I add, our Clytie. My sister acquired her "sea legs" immediately, and was soon darting thither and yon about the great ship, seeking out the dashing young junior officers and being taken on many a private tour to parts of the ship no passenger had ever visited before.

We would have been seated at the captain's table, as was our due, but, for reasons best known to himself, Pappa-daddy had boarded under an assumed name, took all his meals in his stateroom, eschewing wine for bottles of Lohocla, and chose not to make his true presence known. We junior Dinwiddies were seated at the second mate's table for the first luncheon at sea, and before the tempting and nourishing brown Windsor soup was served, Clytie had made this dashing young mariner stop brooding about the wife and kiddies awaiting his return to Liverpool. With such a social gift of always making others—especially lonely men—feel at home and at ease in her presence, who knows to what heights in the diplomatic world my precious sister Clytie might not have soared had she been allowed but a few more years of radiant, passionate life? Bubber, too, sparkled like some rare gem, and it was not too many hours before I found him in the bar, downing brandy Alexanders and playing an innocent game of cards with the first divorced woman I had ever met!

As for me, I have always been a poor sailor as well as a retiring person, so I betook myself to my berth to lie supine with a cold compress on my forehead, while the stewardess chafed my wrists with eau de cologne. Having lunched lightly upon Portuguese oysters, brown Windsor soup, delice of Dover sole, saddle of mutton à la dauphine, boiled potatoes, Brussels sprouts, vegetable marrow Prince Edouard, Roman punch, trifle, and savory, I soon felt my eyelids growing heavy and lapsed into a dreamless slumber. But who knows if I would have slept had I but realized that the man among men, the one great love of my life, my beau, lover, husband, and the father of my child was but a scant foot away from my very pillow?

Just as a steward was passing outside in the corridor, striking the gong that announced afternoon tea, I opened my eyes to see a strange young man in our stateroom, wolfing down most of the five-pound box of bonbons sent to us as a memento from Mr. Louis Sherry. I lay there terrified as I watched him consume first the fondants, then the marzipans, then the nougats, and lastly the dragées. As he removed a candied violet from the top layer, I sat bolt upright and cried, "Young man, I believe you are in the wrong stateroom!" I was about to ring for the steward when I felt myself caught up in a hot, fierce, firm embrace. I opened my lips to scream, but before I could utter a sound, a horny, virile hand was clapped over my mouth, and I felt myself choking on a liqueur chocolate (filled with crème Yvette). But even though I should have feared for my very life, I distinctly remember feeling no sense of panic in the arms of this forceful stranger. Struggle as I would, I could not free myself from his overpowering grasp. After a few moments, I gave up the fight and relaxed in his arms. Just then, the cabin door burst open and there stood Clytie, having returned to change her costume for tea. "Oh, excuse me, Martha, sugar," she said. "I had no idea you were entertaining." The bold stranger let loose his hold and sprang from my berth. He looked like some desperate wild animal cornered by unfriendly hunters in his lair.

"Really, Martha," Clytie said, "if you had to go and pick yourself a gentleman friend, I don't know why you couldn't have chosen one of those *good*-looking young English officers instead of this—"

"Clytie!" I cried. "I haven't any idea who this gentleman is. I awoke from my nap to find him eating all of our candy, and—"

"Ladies, I can explain," the stranger said, in a deep, thrilling voice—a voice that set my very soul on fire. My romantic intruder then introduced himself. His name, he said, was George Washington Butterfield (and right then and there I knew that it was a name destined to become immortal), and he came from a small village named Albumen, Indiana, the eldest of eleven sons of a widowed matriarch. It had long been his desire to see the world, but, lacking funds to purchase a ticket, he had seen fit to stow away aboard the *Euremic,* stealing onto the ship in the guise of a visitor seeing friends off, and, finding our stateroom unoccupied, had lain hidden under my berth until the ship was safely out to sea. Then, famished, young Mr. Butterfield said that he had ventured out from his hiding place to see a "beautiful princess sound asleep"—I still thrill when I think of those words!—and, after "drawing strength from her eternal beauty" (how my heart leapt and sang!), had proceeded to still the pangs of hunger at our box of bonbons.

"Clytie!" I gasped, clutching both my hands to my heart. "Isn't that the most romantic thing you ever did hear?"

"If true," Clytie said. (One of the great sorrows of my life was that my darling Clytie and my worshipped George never got on as brother- and sister-in-law should. From the very outset, suspicion, mistrust, and animosity hovered between these two otherwise saintly people, ruining what should have been a perfect relationship.)[2] "I'm going to ring for the steward and have this common damnyankee sneak thief tossed into the hoosegow where he belongs."

But for once in my life I took the initiative and overruled my impetuous younger sister. "No!" I said, more firmly than I had intended. "This

---

[2] Far from being blind prejudice on the part of Mrs. Butterfield, there is evidence that during his term as President of the United States Butterfield attempted to deny entry into this country to his sister-in-law. The plan was scotched by the Secretary of State. P.D.

young man is *my* discovery, and *I* shall be the one to make any and all decisions." Strong language from one as reticent as I!

"Have it your own way," Clytie said, wiping her nose with a chamois dipped into *poudre de riz*. "That cunning second mate has invited me to have tea in his cabin. Just be sure you get this yankee trash out of here before it's time to dress for dinner." With that, my sister turned smartly, gave her train a slight kick, and marched out, slamming the door. Left alone with my "marauder," shyness once again overtook me. Coloring deeply, I said, "Would you like another candy? I believe there are some coconut kisses in the second layer." At the very word "kiss," I blushed crimson.

"Yes, ma'am. Thank you, ma'am," Mr. Butterfield said. "I believe I will." Silently he offered the box to me, and just as mutely I selected a bit of crystallized ginger and nibbled on it delicately, avoiding his gaze. When Mr. Butterfield had devoured the entire box of candy, I poured out a glass of Lohocla for him, feeling that his ordeal might have weakened him, and took a glass of it myself. Its tranquillizing powers were instantaneous. Even I began to unbend. "Why don't I order tea?" I said.

"Swell!" he said. I was quite shocked at the word, but deliciously so. Hiding him in the wardrobe, I summoned the steward and ordered an enormous tea for just one wee slip of a girl—sandwiches, crumpets, scones, honey, jam, two kinds of cake, and a large tart. Then I gazed spellbound as my uninvited guest sat down and greedily consumed it all! I have always loved to watch men eat. Show me a man with a large appetite and I will show you a man with a large heart! When the empty teacart had been removed by a somewhat surprised steward, I said, "And now, Mr. Butterfield, what do you propose to do for the *next* nine days of our journey?"

An idealistic dreamer, he seemed to have no ready answer to that question. Therefore, I took it upon myself to march to the purser's office and purchase—with my own letter of credit—a first-class passage for young Mr. Butterfield, explaining haltingly (it was the first time in my life I had ever told a lie, even a little white one) that he had come to see us off, had been taken ill, and had not been able to get ashore. As luck would have it, Mr. Butterfield was put into Bubber's cabin, adjacent to ours. I am ashamed to say that, for once in his life, my younger brother did not display the hospitality that has made the Southland famous; however, I forgave him on the grounds of his age, the unaccustomed motion of the ship, and the fact that he had drunk quite enough Alexander cocktails to make a grown man (not to mention a boy of fifteen summers!) tipsy.[3]

As Mr. Butterfield had not packed any garments suitable for an ocean voyage, we were able to dress him quite adequately in some things of Pappa-daddy's.

"When the cat is away," it is said, "the mice will play," and I am afraid that without Pappa-daddy's constant paternal vigilance I was a wee bit swept off my feet by my stowaway. For me, it was love at first sight, and the feeling must have been mutual for Mr. Butterfield never left my side (during my waking moments). At first, I was pleased, flattered, and surprised that he had not chosen gay Clytie, as all other men seemed to do. But no, this young man had eyes only for me! Clytie said, causing my face to flush the color of fire, that Mr. Butterfield followed me "like a bloodhound," while Bubber (again under the iniquitous influence of that divorcee and too many cocktails) said, "And he's just about as pleasant to share a cabin with." I took him sternly to task.

But I digress! Mine was a true shipboard romance in every sense of the word. Here I was, a débutante in my first season, "out" with my first love on my first sailing. Shy and diffident, I was speechless with fear that Mr. Butterfield's eye might be caught by some of the truly lovely American and English girls aboard and that he would soon abandon plain old me for one of those more experienced charmers. But, to give the other girls aboard full credit for good sportsmanship, every last one of them went out of her way to avoid Mr. Butterfield. You can always tell who is—and who is *not*—a lady! In my own poor halting way, I tried to draw Mr. Butterfield out, knowing from an article I had read that men like to talk about themselves. It worked! From then on, I had no trouble at all. Mr. Butterfield would begin discussing his views, his plans, his hopes, and his dreams over the breakfast table and would not stop until I, heavy-eyed and all but dropping with fatigue, would excuse myself long after midnight for some well-earned rest. I was in seventh heaven.

I recall that then Mr. Butterfield's goals had not been political, for he was far too modest a man to think then—even to dream—that he might ascend to the highest office of our native land. A poor boy with little education save what he had been able to pick up for himself, his aim was business (*big business*), a wife, and children. At this I brightened, for who was in a better position to supply all three than I?

---

[3] A habit Dinwiddie *fils* was to continue throughout his life's span.   P.D.

On the night of the captain's gala, Mr. Butterfield "popped the question." My heart was in my mouth as I whispered, "Yes, Mr. Butterfield, yes. But you must ask my father."

Leading him down the companionway to Pappa-daddy's stateroom, I evoked a silent prayer that my father would give his consent, for I could never have dreamed of marrying without it. Indicating Pappa-daddy's door to Mr. Butterfield, I daringly blew him a kiss from the entrance of my own cabin and then went inside hopefully to wait. The pause seemed endless, and then suddenly I heard a wild animal roar and the sound of crashing glass. Dashing to the passage, I got there just in time to see Mr. Butterfield, hair awry, bounding up the companionway while Pappa-daddy, dressed only in his nightshirt and roaring incoherently, pitched empty Lohocla bottles at my lover's retreating figure. What could the exchange between these two men whom I loved have been? I shall never know. My poor father was in such a state of hysteria, seeing things—animals and other fanciful creatures—that did not even exist, that the ship's doctor had to give him heavy sedation and put him immediately back to bed.

I, too, retired, but I did not close my eyes, and my pillow was drenched with tears when the British Isles hove into sight. Love, which had seemed so close that I could reach out and touch it, had suddenly vanished into thin air.

Grand Tour

1888–90

London—we visit the Queen. . . . Gay Paree. . . . Italian Suite. . . . Alt Wien. . . . Count Przyzplätcki—a romantic encounter. . . . Wooing in Bosnia-Herzegovina. . . . Bubber's distressing behavior. . . . Clytie wins the coronet. . . . I choose democracy and George W. Butterfield.

ondon—what can I tell you of that city of fog? So heavyhearted was I that I do not even recollect the name of the hotel where we were quartered. Suffice it to say that with Clytie in command, it was opulent. So, too, I imagine, were the carriages and body servants that Clytie hired for the visit. I had eyes for nothing but the dream-visioned face of George Washington Butterfield. Even an experience so thrilling as to see *two* exiled empresses—Eugénie of France and Carlota of Mexico—driving in the same park on the same afternoon did nothing to raise my drooping spirits. Clytie, of course, was thrilled by the many fine shops, and Bubber nearly went mad with delight rushing from tailor to shirtmaker to hatter in that world capital of gentlemen's finery. Even Pappadaddy, a bit steadier on his feet after a few days on dry land, rode occasionally to the City to see if there was a future British market for Lohocla. And, indeed, there was! But all of this was wasted on me. I walked, talked, ate, and slept like some sort of automaton, thinking only of Mr. Butterfield—my lost love.

But Clytie was determined to live life to the hilt during our brief stay in the English capital. Whilst examining jewels at Spink's, my beloved sister made the acquaintance of a most attractive gentleman, who

claimed to be a natural son of the Dowager Queen-Empress Victoria. Extremely interested in the diamonds that Clytie was purchasing, he struck up a conversation and opined that Clytie might be interested in being presented to his mother. The Queen, he explained, was in a pepetual state of mourning and did not receive. However, owing to his close relationship with the sovereign, he could arrange a private audience. All that would be necessary was a contribution of a thousand pounds, which would be paid over to one of the Queen's favorite charities. Clytie was thrilled, and even I rose temporarily from my torpor, so excited was I at the prospect of meeting this amazing woman.

Clytie paid the gentleman in hundred-pound notes, and arranged to have him meet us at the photographer's (where we were to be immortalized in our splendid presentation costumes) and then take us immediately to the family entrance at Windsor Castle. Once our pictures had been taken, we waited to be called for. An hour passed, and then another. Teatime came and went, and still no sign of Clytie's gentleman friend. Finally, the studio closed for the evening and we were forced to return to our hotel in a common hack.

Poor Clytie suffered a complete *crise de nerfs,* and kept moaning incoherently about receiving a "royal screwing from that big bastard," which I realized was not intended as profanity, but described her friend's position in the palace household. Clytie packed immediately for France, swearing vengeance, but I understood that even though English and Americans speak the same language, many little misunderstandings can arise.

Never a good sailor, I was dreadfully ill crossing the English Channel to France, while poor Pappa-daddy had to be carried onto the train for Paris. Gay Paree, the City of Light, was neither light nor gay to me, for my poor heart was broken. Mr. Butterfield had simply disappeared from sight after his tragic interview with Pappa-daddy. As for my parent, once, when I gathered up the courage to inquire as to what had transpired during that tragic tête-à-tête, he denied having any memory of the meeting whatsoever! I was at my wits' end.

Clytie and Bubber naturally adored Paris. Clytie loved the dressmakers, milliners, booters, furriers, and jewelers. As for Bubber, dressed like a dandy, he could scarcely wait until sundown to pursue the riotous round of pleasures that Paris offers the single man. Pappa-daddy seemed more or less content to remain in his bedroom, picking at the truly Lucullan dishes of the hotel. At times, I feared that the dear man might fade completely away—a second anguish to add to my already overflowing heart—but happily Lohocla was at hand to keep up his strength. One night, I grew so concerned for poor Pappa-daddy that I begged the maître d'hôtel to allow me the use of the kitchens to prepare for Pappa-daddy one of Mammy's succulent dishes from dear, sleepy little Pellagra, and with trembling hands I lovingly concocted a sow jowl à la créole. But when I offered it hopefully to my father, he flung the whole platter into the bidet and called for a Bourbon at any price. The concierge sent a chasseur out and in this way Clytie and I were presented to the ranking Pretender to the throne of France. Pappy-daddy became only worse.

As for me, I spent every evening alone in my room, writing letters of love to George W. Butterfield—letters that never would (never could) be mailed, as I knew not where to reach my love. I was as sad as Clytie and Bubber were gay, and that *tristesse* is my only memory of the first time I saw Paris.

Because of some silly misunderstanding between Bubber and the unduly jealous husband of a much older Parisienne, ending in my baby brother's being challenged to a duel in the Bois, our visit to France was cut short and we escaped to Italy. Because of the heaviness of my poor

Art Treasures—Firenze

Clytie's Papal audience

heart, I do not recall very much of our journey. My recollections are of a series of suites in various Grand Hotels—in Naples, Florence, Rome, and Venice—of smoldering volcanoes, endless art galleries, ruins, and opera houses. Through it all, I moved like a somnambulist, neither knowing nor caring where I was, what I was seeing, what I was eating, so full was my heart for my lost love.

Venice was very damp, and Pappa-daddy was far from well. It seemed that he had developed some sort of strange Italian malady, and he was so weakened that he could barely stand. Darkly distrustful of all foreign physicians, Pappa-daddy became his own doctor and forwent all food, existing exclusively on Lohocla and, occasionally, a little Valpolicella table wine. Miraculously, it pulled him through. It was with vast relief that I helped Pappa-daddy into the corner of a railway compartment and we left beautiful Italy for the more bracing air of Vienna and the North.

Once established in the Imperial Suite of the Hotel Sacher, overlooking the glorious Vienna Opera, and getting poor Pappa-daddy bedded down, I felt that a great weight had been taken off my shoulders *and* my heart. True, I still pined for Mr. Butterfield, but I was rewarded and relieved by seeing my beloved father able to sit up and take notice of what was going on about him. Although I pleaded with him to go to Bad Gastein and at least *try* taking the cure with those astonishing radioactive waters, he refused. Still and all, I was greatly encouraged to see him supplementing his diet of Lohocla with a daily bottle or two of Liebfraumilch and some harmless dark beer between meals. Once more or less free of that particular burden, I tried to forget my cares and my aching heart and take some measure of pleasure in this great city, which was, at that time, *the* capital of *the* greatest empire of all Europe. With Clytie, I strolled the Ring each day, shopped at the modistes lining the Karntnerstrasse, bought lovely gloves at shops along the Graben, and went twice a day, without fail, to Demel's for coffee (*mit Schlagober*) and the delicious pastries concocted there. In fact, I made so free with Nicholas Demel's rich cakes, tortes, and strudels that all my lovely new gowns had to be let out after I burst the seams of three ravishing Worth creations!

But although I may have been a trifle too plump for the extravagantly silhouetted models put out by the House of Worth, my figure was pleasing to at least *one* romantic stranger!

One pleasant afternoon, while Clytie, who had remained as *shlank* (as one says in German) as ever through rigorous dieting, purges, and tight lacing, was visiting a world-famous corsetière in the hope of becoming even more wasp-waisted than a kindly Dame Nature had made her, I ventured out in a public hack and up into the lovely hills of Grinzing, quite alone save for the driver and, of course, the horse.

While admiring the view and humming ageless Strauss waltzes to myself, my reverie was interrupted by a sight that would make any red-blooded American woman fighting mad. There, before my very eyes, I saw a distinguished-looking gentleman, in clothes neat but shabby and of exquisite cut, being thrown out of a humble shop and set upon by not one, not two, not three but *four* hulking Austrian waiters.

"Halt!" I said, in my uncertain German. *"Was ist der matter?"*

One of the surly brutes who had been belaboring the poor gentleman

Finding a suitable memorial for Mumsie-love

spoke a bit of English and told me that his victim had ordered half a litre of wine and then had found himself without funds to pay for it.

"And how much is his bill?" I asked. It was a trifling amount—only a matter of a few pennies. "Here," I said, flinging some coins in the ruffian's face. "Now, unhand this man!"

I had meant for the encounter to begin and end there, remembering with a pang how I had suffered—and how I still suffered—from my last encounter with a penniless male stranger, but this gentleman was not to be put off. Dusting himself with great *élan,* he produced a slightly stained visiting card and presented it to me with a click of his heels. Beneath an elaborate crest I read his name:

COUNT STANISLAUS PRZYZPLÄTCKI

Schloss Przyzplätcki   *Przyzplät, Bosnia-Herzegovina*

"My name," the stranger said, in his thick, colorful accent, "is pronounced simply 'Splatsky.'" I was ever so relieved to know. With that, he took back his card, explaining haltingly that it was the last one he had, the engravers in Bosnia-Herzegovina being unaccountably dilatory. Then, without so much as a by-your-leave, the nimble Count Stanislaus leaped into the fiacre beside me and said, "You are perhaps returning to Vienna, no?"

Before I could reply, he instructed the driver, in fluent German, to return to my hotel. Although annoyed, I could not but admire his suavity and forcefulness. All the way back down to the city, he chatted amiably, telling me that he was a lone bachelor, temporarily embarrassed for lack of funds; describing his stately ancestral castle in Przyzplät (pronounced "Splat"); and asking lively and intelligent questions about me, my family, and my life in America. At the end of the ride, he said, "It would give me such pleasure to offer you tea, but you of course understand that I have not a sou." Before I could refuse, I found myself propelled into the lounge of our hotel and heard my "host" ordering a lavish spread in his rapid German. Protest as I would that I was on a rigorous diet, great trays of cakes, tortes, and pastries appeared, which the Count, with miraculous ease, was able to consume with frightening speed.

While devouring an entire terrine of *pâté de foie gras,* for which the hotel was justly famous, Count Stanislaus made further inquiries as to my family, our travelling plans, the hotels we had visited, what we had done.

When I began to describe Clytie's and my ill-fated presentation to Queen Victoria, he interrupted to explain to me how he and the Queen were sixty-fourth cousins thrice removed. He was also kin to the Bourbon Pretender to the throne of France, whom we had met so briefly in Paris. Simply to make conversation, I mentioned to him having seen the former Empress Eugénie and the tragic Empress Carlota. It developed that he was related to both of them. I tried many times to make it clear that I was not acquainted with any of these august personages, but Count Stanislaus was too busy talking and eating to take in my words. As I have said, if there is anything I love it is to see a man with a hearty appetite, and the Count ran a close second to even my adored and lost George Washington Butterfield. I was spellbound with admiration at the efficient way in which he could pile small mountains of fried mushrooms and tartar sauce onto thin slices of hot toast and consume them without spilling a morsel or missing a word.

"Be still, my heart," I heard a distant voice say within me. "This man is a total stranger. Attractive though you find him, can you be certain that it is not simply an infatuation on the rebound?"

He was just finishing off the strudel and explaining to me that it was the custom of his family and his country to offer himself in marriage to the one who had saved his life—*to me!*—when suddenly he stopped, mid-strudel, and stared openmouthed. Following his gaze, I saw that his attention had been caught by none other than Clytie, returning from the corsetière's, superb in almond green from the House of Worth, her supple figure a perfect hourglass. As she made her way through the lobby, the hall porter, the reception clerks, the page boys all bowed respectfully, murmuring, *"Gnädige Fräulein," "Bitte,"* and *"Küss die hand."* There was even something that sounded incredibly like a long, low whistle, but, of course, that must have been a noise from the street.

Clytie caught a glimpse of me at the tea table and hurried over. "Martha Dinwiddie!" she said, "I knew it! Here you sit stuffing yourself like a Christmas goose when you're already so portly you can't hardly squeeze into your stays. I wouldn't fill up on that truck if . . ." The words died on her lips. "Oh. 'Scuse me. I didn't know you were entertaining a gentleman caller."

I happily introduced Count Przyzplätcki to my sister. *"Hélas!"* Clytie said, with a flutter of her parasol. "But I'm simply famished—so much shopping—fittings, gloves, jewels. I know you-all won't mind if I join you for just the tiniest little second—a cup of tea or maybe chocolate and just one or two of those little old *petits fours*. I feel absolutely faint from fatigue." She swayed dangerously.

"Clytie, dearest!" I cried.

Count Stanislaus leapt to his feet and assisted poor Clytie to one of the Maria Theresa chairs. "Oh, thank you, Count," Clytie said, from beneath fluttering eyelids. "Martha, sugar, would you be a pearl and run up to the Imperial Suite for my swoon bottle? I'd send one of the help, but the Imperial Suite is so large that I'm afraid the boy would never find it. It's in the fourth drawer of my jewel box, right between the diamond tiara and the emeralds. Now, Count, what were you saying?"

I had considerable trouble locating Clytie's smelling salts, which turned out to be in her medicine chest. When I returned to the table, I was relieved to see that my delicate little sister had recovered to such an extent that she had allowed Count Stanislaus to order another complete afternoon tea, and was forcing herself to take a bit of nourishment. The roses seemed to have returned to her wan cheeks, and she was chatting vivaciously with our guest, who was still paying us the greatest of all compliments by leaving every platter clean.

"Martha, sugar," Clytie said, "can you imagine, Count Stan, here, knows Vickie and Jennie and Lottie, and ever so many of our best chums. Like I was saying, it's such a small world." I was not quite certain as to the identity of the acquaintances to whom Clytie referred, but then she was ever more gregarious than I and knew far more people.

"Clytie," I said, squeezing her wasp waist, "I want you to be the first to know. Count Przyzplätcki has just asked for my hand in marriage."

Clytie's rosebud mouth fell open, her lovely brown eyes widened. "Why, Martha, sugar. If that isn't the dandiest news ever! May I kiss my new brother-in-law?" With that, warmhearted Clytie threw both arms around the Count's neck and kissed him with such ardor that the whole populace of the hotel was shocked into silence. Even I confess to having felt a bit uncomfortable. The reader must, however, bear in mind that the year was 1888, when any public display of emotion was considered *infra dig*.

Pappa-daddy, whose mysterious illness had left him with rapidly shifting moods from the heights of elation to wild, unreasonable rages to—in his worst moments—fancying that strange animals were in the room, and down to the very depths of tearful despair, seemed to regard Stanislaus with somewhat more favor than he had poor, sweet, simple, honest George. It is true that, owing to their vastly divergent accents when speaking the English language, neither was able to understand very much of what the other was saying. And then Stanislaus had a natural way with sick people. He confided to Clytie that his own dear father, the late Count Szigiszmund Przyzplätcki, had suffered from (and, alas, been claimed by) a very similar disease, contracted while on a wine-tasting tour of the Cognac region of France. In addition to his gentle—and, I am sorry to confess, somewhat devious—way with the infirm, he was blessed with the knowledge of certain old Balkan remedies, handed down from generation to generation of his noble forebears, so, rather like Mammy, he could cure, by mysterious means, ailments that even the most eminent physicians of Vienna—then the medical mecca of the world— had given up as hopeless. By sending to the maître d'hôtel for a few innocent-looking wine bottles, he could always enter Pappa-daddy's sick-room, where at times the poor dear might be raving with the torments of his illness, and leave him but minutes later sleeping like a baby.

Stanislaus also had an endearing way of fitting himself into almost any situation. Sensing that he might be needed at a moment's notice to see our dear father through a moment of crisis, he quietly moved his few pos-sessions into Bubber's capacious bedchamber, transferring Bubber to a cot in the adjoining dressing room. For once, Bubber, who, I must confess, was becoming abominably willful and spoiled on his Grand Tour of Europe, did not complain. Rather, he seemed to dote on Stanislaus and to look up to him like an older brother. And it was Stanislaus who took him out on tours of the city night by night—"to a Vienna no tourist knows," as Bubber explained—introducing him to the common people and per-fecting the boy's German. Clytie, as I have heretofore indicated, adored her prospective brother-in-law, and Pappa-daddy was as gentle as a lamb in the capable hands of this charming foreigner.

Being ultra-proper and slavish in his devotion to Old World customs (and let me say right here that Stanislaus was one of the most reverent of fiancés, never once having even kissed me, so observant was he of the code of a gentleman), the Count insisted on asking Pappa-daddy for my hand in marriage. Thinking of the last painful encounter between a suitor and my parent, I trembled at the prospect. And yet I confess to having been of two minds about the whole thing. Although I was fond of Stanislaus, *did* I truly love him? Pappa-daddy was restive at the time of the rendezvous, but Stanislaus, impeccably dressed in one of Bubber's Savile Row frock coats, marched fearlessly into the parental bedchamber, taking with him three mysterious bottles. I sat in the drawing room, ill with apprehension, but try as I would, I could hear nothing through the closed door. An hour later, Stanislaus reappeared, perfectly poised, to announce that his proposal had been accepted and that Pappa-daddy was dozing comfortably. With that, he kissed me for the first time, very gently on the cheek, and said that my beloved father had drowsed off before the question of my dowry could be brought up. For some days after that, Count Przyzplätcki tried to settle this matter, but, alas, poor Pappa-daddy seemed to have reached a stage in his illness where it was utterly impossible for him to remain awake during any business discussions.

It was then that Stanislaus said that the air of Vienna was undoubtedly causing my father's terrifying lethargy, and he invited us all to be his guests at Schloss Przyzplätcki, high in the hills of Bosnia-Herzegovina. There, my fiancé explained, Pappa-daddy would have not only the benefits of the high, clear air, but he would also be at the very source of some of Stanislaus' most miraculous cures. In addition, I would be able to become acquainted with the castle of which I was soon to become chatelaine, so that I could plan, well in advance, any changes, repairs, or renovations I desired before the date of my occupancy.

It was a long and arduous trip before we finally detrained at Sarajevo, that tinderbox which, but a quarter of a century later, was to ignite the entire world. Here we were to transfer to the Przyzplät Czyümsyàvnöia Dbrvyüshka,[4] a so-called "crack" train. However, the Bosnia-Herzegovina railway system being what it was, there was a delay of several hours, during which we had time to kill in Sarajevo. Establishing Pappa-daddy in a Moorish suite of the Hotel Visegrad-Vranje, safely equipped with two bottles of Lohocla in case of emergencies, the four of us set out on foot to sample the mysteries of this ancient city. It was like stepping into "A Thousand and One Nights." For here was a purportedly modern city, later—after the tragic assassination of the Archduke and his lovely consort—to become the capital of Bosnia-Herzegovina, still living in the past of its Turkish rule. Side by side with the new Catholic cathedral, even then awaiting consecration, were the minarets of a hundred mosques shrill with the muezzins' call to prayer.

"Why, it's just like our third parlor back home," Clytie cried, gazing with rapture at the Oriental architecture, the grilled windows, the veiled women, for even as late as 1888 nearly half of the population was Moslem.

---

[4] The Przyzplät Cannon Ball. P.D.

Although I found the place picturesque and fascinating, I wondered how I—a simple girl from Dixie—could fit into this exotic milieu. We strolled through the market place, cacophonous with the haggling of merchants and their patrons, and finally into the bazaar, redolent of pungent spices, where carpets, copper pots, brassware, ivory, and gems were being hawked. As I stopped to admire an intricately worked golden bracelet, I felt a tugging at my sleeve.

"You—English lady—you want guide? English. I speak." I turned and saw an incredibly filthy vagabond in a ragged burnoose.

"Shoo!" I said indignantly. Yet there was something about that voice, that touch—a feeling of familiarity I could not describe.

Then suddenly this uncouth street Arab exclaimed, "Martha!"

"George!" I cried, and fainted dead away. I came to just in time to find a noisy crowd gathered around me and to hear Count Stanislaus and two native policemen berating my poor lover. "Come on, sugar, let's get out of here," Clytie kept saying.

"George!" I cried. "George Butterfield!"

"She's gone off her head, Bubber," Clytie exclaimed. "Come on, help me with her."

I was hurried away from the close, ill-smelling bazaar just as my darling George was being hustled out by two burly-looking officers. In the confusion, I was just able to slip away from Clytie and Bubber and whisper into George's ear, "Schloss Przyzplätcki, Przyzplät. I'll wait for you forever." With that, we were torn apart—George to heaven knows what sort of unspeakable dungeon and I to a refreshing cup of minted tea at the Café de la Gare whilst awaiting the train.

Just twenty-eight hours later, we descended, weary, creased, and travel-worn, from the train at the village of Przyzplät, high up on a mountain near the Montenegrin border. The village's one street was paved with muck and mud. Swine wallowed lazily in the deep ruts. There were a few small buildings—a wineshop, an inn, another shop or two—all very quaint and picturesque in their way, but falling to ruins. I was relieved to see that a church (*not* a mosque), in a shocking state of repair, was the focal point of the village square, for I had not, until my arrival in Bosnia-Herzegovina, even once stopped to consider what my future husband's religion could be.[5] At least, Stanislaus was a Christian!

_____

[5] The religio-political history of the Przyzplätcki family of Przyzplät is not without color and interest. Originally of Polish origin, the Przyzplätcki founder settled in Bosnia-Herzegovina in 1146, after becoming hopelessly lost en route to the Holy Land at the time of the

After a wait of something more than an hour at the station, we were greeted by several of Stanislaus' old family retainers driving two dilapidated *oxcarts!* We piled aboard the first of the oxcarts while our luggage was loaded onto the second. Up, up, up we travelled, at almost a ninety-degree angle, along a rutted, rocky, twisting donkey path overhanging a sheer drop of thousands of feet. Fearing to look down, I could only look

---

Second Crusade. Here he set himself up as sole ruler, took a concubine, sired children, and established a dynasty. For nearly seven centuries, the Przyzplätcki tyrants reigned as absolute monarchs of their self-styled "kingdom" of Przyzplät—48 sq. mi. (mostly perpendicular), est. pop. 351—a wild, arid, mountainous area in southwest Bosnia-Herzegovina, bordering upon the independent state of Montenegro (today *all* a part of Yugoslavia). As the land was infertile, inaccessible, and totally undesirable, the Przyzplätcki claim to a monarchy was never challenged by the Serbian Kingdom or the Ottoman Empire. Nor was the territory ever invaded during the Middle Ages by marauding Turks, Venetians, Hungarians, by Mongolian tribes or the House of Hapsburg. The tiny kingdom first came to political attention in 1804 (the time of Napoleon's founding of the South Slavic State), when Bonaparte said: *"Rien est Przyzplät!"* The King of Przyzplät, Ignace the Vile, declared war upon the French Emperor as a result of this mortal insult. As the armies of Napoleon did not deign to attack Przyzplät, and as the army of King Ignace could not raise the necessary funds to invade France, the war raged for more than a decade without a life being lost, a prisoner being taken, or a shot being fired. At the Congress of Vienna, after loudly but unsuccessfully importuning the victors to be included at the conference table, King Ignace gracefully renounced the kingdom and permitted Przyzplät to become annexed by Bosnia-Herzegovina in exchange for the title of Count, a listing in the *Almanach de Gotha,* and a small annual allowance.

Religiously, the professed faith of the Przyzplätckis was that of the Hrnjödivniján Rite of the Serbian-Orthodox Church, a little-known branch of Serbian Orthodoxy of which one of Count Stanislaus' forebears, Kaszimir the Uncouth, was the founder in 1380. Originally Roman Catholics, the Przyzplätcki rulers broke with the Vatican at Rome at the time of the Great Schism, when Clement VII was crowned Anti-Pope at Avignon, France. Presumably feeling that he was better qualified to reign as Pope from Przyzplät, King Kaszimir (later Saint Kaszimir the Uncouth) proclaimed himself as Pontiff at Schloss Przyzplätcki in 1380, notifying Pope Urban VI of Rome that his services were no longer required. This decree, the original of which reposes in the Musée Przyzplätcki at Przyzplät, was incorrectly addressed and travelled from place to place for several years before reaching its intended destination at Rome, where it was dismissed as the work of an unknown practical joker and returned for insufficient postage. By the time it arrived back in Przyzplät, Pope Kaszimir (who had, during his own lifetime, canonized himself as Saint Kaszimir the Uncouth) had been poisoned by his mistress, Sophie-Asafoetida, who was later beatified and (in 1389) canonized as Saint Sophie the Deliverer. Kaszimir's son, Thaddeusz, having inherited little of his father's deep religiosity, had no interest in continuing the struggle with Rome. It was he who liberalized the Hrnjödivniján Rite, which was later merged with the Serbian-Orthodox Church as an autonomous sect. Count Stanislaus Przyzplätcki and Miss Dinwiddie were subsequently married by the Patriarch of Przyzplät, at the Cathedral of St. Kaszimir the Uncouth, and although various complications later arose, their marriage was considered a valid Christian sacrament. P.D.

"Stan"

up, and when we approached Schloss Przyzplätcki—much of it dating from the Crusades—my heart sank as, drawing nearer, I saw that it was in even worse repair than the village below. Once beneath the rusted portcullis (an iniquitous remnant of the Dark Ages, which had fallen twice before, I learned later, claiming the lives of three peasants and a cow), the courtyard of the castle was a sight to behold. Festering piles of refuse and offal attracted swarms of insects. Half a dozen broken-down carts stood in various stages of neglect and disrepair. Of livestock, dogs, cats, chickens, pigs, sheep, and cattle wandered about on far from the best of terms with one another. I was speechless with dismay, but dear Clytie—always eager to put people at their ease—cried out at the Old World charm and quaintness of the place.

The interior of Schloss Przyzplätcki was primitive in the extreme, cold, draughty, and damp beyond description. After seeing that Pappa-daddy was placed—as comfortably as possible, under the circumstances—in a bedroom high in the keep, I was shown to a vast, echoing, vaulted stone room, which Stanislaus told me, to my horror, was the chatelaine's bed-room, bridal chamber, and confinement room. Heartsick and weary, I asked if I might have a bath. A large wooden wine barrel was rolled into the room and placed before a porcelain stove (of the Seventeenth or Eighteenth Century), which gave but little heat. While waiting for the servants to fill it—a project that took more than an hour—I pulled a richly brocaded Venetian chair (but one stained, worn, and torn, out of which the stuffing fell by great handfuls) to a crude deal table and tried

to seek some consolation by writing in my diary. As I still have the book—indeed, it has been an invaluable reference and refresher of my memory after these more than seventy years—I will reproduce the page here to show you my exact emotions at the time.

Dear, dear Diary,

We are at last at dear Stanislaus' home, Schloss Przyzplätcki, and it is <u>not</u> what I expected <u>at all</u>!!!! Old, dirty, and falling apart like some ~~nigger~~ Negro hovel Down Home. Was I wrong in accepting the Count's proposal? Do I love him? And if I do will I be able to stand living in this strange wild place?

But, dear Diary, yesterday in the bazaar at Sarajevo—a terrible Turkish town—who should come up to me disguised as a dragoman but my o.a.o, GEORGE!!!!!! My heart stood still and I literally fainted. I knew then and there that as sweet and thoughtful as Stanislaus is, as much as he worships me for myself alone, I could never find happiness with him whilst tortured by the knowledge that the man of my dreams still walks this very earth.

I tried to tell Georgie where I would be, but in this barbarous place, with these strange foreign names, did he hear me? Did he understand me? Will he come??? I can only hope and pray.

Haven't seen Clytie's rm. as yet. It is right next to Stan's. Pappa-daddy is in the tower far fro~~m~~

At this point, a *rat* ran over my foot! I screamed and dropped the pen, leaving a terrible splattering of ink on the page. That is all I was able to write.

☆ [74] ☆

After a large but wholly indigestible luncheon of mutton, onions, and the dark red wine of Dalmatia, Stanislaus took Clytie and me on a tour of the castle, armed with a great sheaf of rolled-up paper. It seems that he was not unaware of the deplorable condition of Schloss Przyzplätcki, and had called in an architect from Ragusa to draw up extensive plans for restoring and modernizing the castle. Although I knew nothing of architecture, I could see that the project was an exhaustive one, with gas lighting, William Morris wallpapers, a hydraulic lift in the main tower, several bathrooms, a Byzantine stable block, and an entire new wing in the style of Baron Georges Eugène Haussmann (the rebuilder of Paris). I gasped at the complexity of the work, and wondered where all the money necessary for such a lavish renovation could be coming from. Count Stanislaus had led me to believe—from casual conversation—that he was well-to-do, but a restoration as elaborate and all-embracing as this one would cost—I knew not what. Dear Clytie, whose taste was so exquisite and who was *au courant* with the latest styles of architecture and décor, "oh-" ed and "ah-" ed over the plans, even going so far as to suggest a few even more costly additions. Weary, disillusioned, troubled, and upset as I was, I was able only to say that almost anything would be an improvement and that the castle would certainly profit from a few added creature comforts.

I was, however, grateful for just one thing. Stanislaus had been able to make Pappa-daddy comfortable at last. By giving him alternate doses of Lohocla and some miraculous Balkan medications called, if memory serves, Blatina, Zilavka, and Slivovitz, he was able almost immediately to give my poor father the relief he so needed. Within an hour, Pappa-

daddy was propped up in his bed of state, eyelids drooping, a sweet, sad smile about his lips. And then, just as Stanislaus was about to reintroduce the subject of my dowry, Pappa-daddy's eyes closed, and his dear, dulcet snoring was indeed music to my ears.

Thus the days dragged on. Without having said a word to darling Clytie, she seemed to sense my quandary and did her best to monopolize Stanislaus' time both day and evening. They were forever together, examining the empty rooms of the castle, strolling through the village, taking sylvan walks (sometimes packing a lunch and remaining out for the entire day), and Bubber, too, managed to amuse himself with the simple, rustic pleasures of the average peasant of Bosnia-Herzegovina. In his friendly, outgoing, one-hundred-per-cent American way, he even brought out bright paste jewels to trade with the native girls while they tended their goats and sheep high up in the grazing lands.

But though my loved ones seemed happy and well enough amused by the quiet life of Przyzplät, I still kept hoping against hope that I might hear in some way from my darling George. And finally, one night in the

second week of our visit, it happened. Wearing a merino manteau (against the mountain chill) and standing on a chair (as protection from the rats), I was giving my hair its customary one hundred strokes with a brush when I heard a tapping at my window. Peering out, I saw in the faint light of my tallow candle none other than the fabulous face of my beloved George! Throwing discretion to the four winds, I struggled to open the ancient casement to admit the man of my dreams. "George!" I cried, and fell into his arms.

"Martha," he mumbled, too broken by manly emotion to speak clearly, "can you let me have a hundred dollars? I'm hungry."

"Well, don't try to eat the food here, my darling," I said, emptying the mystifying array of strange foreign monies from my reticule into his trembling hands. "Where are you staying?"

"Well, I *was* sleeping in a haystack not far from here, but your brother and some dame moved in on me, and—" He was interrupted by a tapping at the door.

"W-who is it?" I cried, terrified that my illicit rendezvous might be discovered. What a position! I, the future bride of the lord of the manor, with a man in my room!

"It's Clytie. Let me in."

"You must go, my love," I whispered to George. "Meet me in the cathedral tomorrow morning at ten."

"Swell," he said, shockingly. "And thanks for the loan. Maybe you can bring some more tomorrow." With that he was gone.

Heart pounding, I opened the door to admit dear Clytie. She was wearing a peignoir trimmed with passementerie and carried the prayer book I had given her for her last birthday. "Why, Clytie," I said, "whatever are you doing up at this hour?"

With lowered eyes, my sister replied, "I've been praying, Martha, begging forgiveness for a terrible, terrible sin."

"You, Clytie? Never!"

"Yes, Martha. I don't know what came over me, but I've gone and done a terrible thing, and now I must pay the price."

"What can you be talking about?"

"Sister, I'm going to have a baby. *Stan's* baby."

"Oh, Clytie!" I cried, a seething turmoil of mixed emotions. What overwhelming stroke of fate had come at just this very moment to solve so many of my problems?

"Yes, Sister," Clytie cried. "I love Stan and Stan loves me, and—"

"And I, dear Clytie, love another. Go to Count Stanislaus and tell him that I release him from his promise. He is to marry you, and true love will out."

"You mean you don't *want* to have a title?" Clytie asked, dumfounded.

"No, Clytie, my heart belongs to a simple yankee man of the soil. Go to your love with my blessing, and I shall go to mine."

In a burst of girlish emotion, Clytie threw her arms around my neck. "Hot damn!" she cried. "Now I'm going to be a countess and show all that trash in New York society who's who!" With that she was gone. My heart was bursting with joy. Not only was I free of my own foolish promise, not only was my gallant suitor awaiting me but a few miles away, but I had been able to give my adorable baby sister the man of her dreams. Dazed with happiness, I got into bed and slept the whole night through for the first time since I had met Count Przyzplätcki.

The following morning, the castle was a beehive of activity, with Clytie planning a trip to the not too far distant town of Mostar, where she could order wedding invitations and announcements, cable to Paris for her bridal gown and her trousseau (the village of Przyzplät boasting neither postal nor telegraphic services), and send word of her betrothal to the *Tatler, Country Life,* the *Spectator,* the *Bystander,* and the *Court Circular* of the *Times* in London; to *Le Figaro* and one or two other Parisian society journals; to the New York Press; and to the Pellagra *News & Sentinel*. I was able to slip quietly away to the Cathedral of St. Kaszimir for a tryst with my cavalier.

The church was empty, save for a goat and George. There I was able to tell him, in an excited whisper, of the wonderful events of the night before that had set me free of my pledge to the Count and made it possible, once again, for me to become Mrs. George Washington Butterfield. George seemed stunned by the news. All he could mutter was, "Well, I guess if your old man's so sick, it won't be long before you inherit the whole Lohocla works." What odd and ofttimes senseless things we frequently say in moments of strong emotion!

Quietly we made our plans: I would wait, presumably free and unattached, until after Clytie's wedding, and then—with or without Pappa-daddy's permission—I would become Mrs. George Washington Butterfield. There was a slight confusion within the gloomy interior of the cathedral as the Pzärdjást[6] and a youthful acolyte tried in vain to remove

---

[6] In the hierarchy of the Hrnjödivniján Rite of the Serbian-Orthodox Church, this would rank roughly with monsignor. P.D.

the goat in preparation for matins. Hastily I drew my veil over my face, pressed my lover's hand, and fled discreetly from the church.

As the wedding date drew nearer and nearer, Stanislaus *and* Clytie grew more and more importunate in pressing Pappa-daddy for the bride's marriage settlement. I was shocked to learn that Clytie and her intended had arrived at a figure of more than *one million dollars* as the bride's *dot!* When poor Pappa-daddy fell asleep during the abortive discussions, Clytie even attempted to shake him awake!!! "I am amazed at you," I said sternly. "How could you for a moment doubt that Pappa-daddy, who is the salt of the earth, would deny his favorite child *anything?* If you will only be patient and wait until this lingering illness has passed, you should know as well as you know your own name that our father will be generosity personified."

Clytie began to reply quite hotly: "Martha, if you had the sense God gave a goose, you'd know what's the matter with that old hound. He ain't any sicker than I am. He's just . . ." I would hear no more. Drawing myself to full height, I strode from the room.

Nor was Bubber's conduct making matters any easier. Being an open, outgoing American youth, he had mistaken the friendly, hospitable attitude of the native girls for something more than it was obviously intended to be. He had also failed to reckon with the stern, patriarchal Old World attitude of their fathers. That Bubber had, in the innocence of youth, perhaps overstepped the boundaries of discreet behavior, was made abundantly clear one afternoon when, while sunning himself in the courtyard of the castle, a long, treacherously sharp dagger was thrown from who knows where, removing just the tiniest bit of poor little Bubber's left ear and embedding itself in the hayrick against which he was leaning! Needless to say, the poor little tyke was *most* unnerved.

At last, the glorious day of days arrived for Clytie to become Countess Przyzplätcki of Przyzplät, in the Cathedral of Saint Kaszimir the Uncouth, with me as her only attendant. The service, conducted by the Patriarch of Przyzplät—a cousin of Stanislaus'—was lengthy and most impressive, if unintelligible, marred only by the appalling ventilation of the cathedral. Pappa-daddy, after many days' preparation, was able to rise to the occasion and to give the bride away, which he said jovially he was only too happy to do. The bridal couple was pelted with flowers and, oddly enough, vegetables (a little-known Balkan custom, the symbolism of which is, I should imagine, a wish for plenty). Then we made our way back to the castle, where just the five of us partook of a large wedding

breakfast of spitted ox, chili peppers, onions, *hrjävádja,* a sweet peculiar to Bosnia-Herzegovina (a cuisine that reminded me of Mammy's and made me homesick), and literally gallons of Przyzplätja, a rather vine-gary white wine that is a specialty of the region. It all proved too much for Pappa-daddy. After the third bottle, he had to be helped up the tower stairs, undressed, and put to bed. I knew that his reason had again escaped him when I heard him mutter, "Thank God, I'm rid of at least one of 'em." But, not wishing to mar the happiness of my sister's day of days, I hurried back down to the merrymakers and assured Clytie that Pappa-daddy was in the best of health, knowing how she would worry were the sorry truth but hinted. Bubber and I waved the honey-moon couple off at the portcullis—standing well back—and then I hustled to my room to commence supervising the packing of our many, many bags and trunks.

No sooner had I removed the tight slippers and tighter stays of my wedding costume than a tremendous racket riveted my entire attention. There in the center of the courtyard stood a great hulking peasant, shout-ing imprecations and gesticulating wildly. He was accompanied by his daughter, a plump young thing, who was weeping torrents of tears. As the bailiff's command of English was sparse to say the least, I could only understand, when he came to tell me about it, that the man wished most urgently to see Bubber. Excusing myself, I hurried to Bubber's bedroom to find the place stripped clean of his possessions. This note was pinned to his pillow:

Dear Sister

I have gotten into some trobble with a girl from the vilage and have to leave pronto.

Sorry but I took your perls and some other stuff on acount of I havent any money I will head for Paris where there is a lady freind that said she woud wait for me. Say "good buy" to the old soak. I hope he crokes.

Bubber

I nearly fainted! Fancy a boy of Bubber's age—merely a child—left to fend for himself in this barbarous land filled with bandits, murderers, and worse! I summoned the bailiff and told him, with all the composure I could muster, to inform Bubber's callers that Master Dinwiddie had been called suddenly out of town. From the courtyard below came a terrible roaring and cursing, accompanied by shrill wails, but I had not the heart to listen. Instead, I went directly to Pappa-daddy's bedchamber, where I found him in a semiconscious condition. As gently and tactfully as I could, I broke the news of Bubber's unceremonious leavetaking. My father sat bolt upright in his bed. "Say that again, Martha!" he shouted. "Say it again!"

Trembling with fear at the effect this tragic message might have, I repeated my carefully chosen words. "You mean he's gone? Gone for *good?*"

"I'm afraid so," I whispered, brandishing his note of farewell.

"Great Jehoshaphat!" Pappa-daddy roared. "Two of them bloodsuckers off my back in one day! Now, if you could only . . ."

Realizing that the happy, the tragic, the exciting events of the day had totally unhinged my father, I resolved not to burden him with the problems of my own nuptials. Instead, I would see that he was sent back to America, where Mammy could minister to him as only she knew how.

"Goodbye, Pappa-daddy," I said. "I shall leave you now."

"Yeah, do that. A mighty good idea. Mighty."

I stepped forward to plant a kiss of farewell on his dear fevered brow, but the madness overtook him again. "Scat!" he shouted, and threw an empty bottle in my direction. Hurrying to the door with as much dignity as I could muster, I turned back for one more glimpse of my beloved father, but then a veritable rain of empty bottles shattered on the stone wall behind me. Without further ceremony, I made my *congé.*

Throwing a few essential garments into my portmanteau, I summoned the bailiff, tipped him generously, and gave him my final instructions regarding the transportation of my father back to his native land.

I hastened on foot down the steep corkscrew donkey path to the inn in the village, where my darling George was drinking Zilavka in the tap-room. "George!" I cried. "My life, my love, my all! Here I am—your bride! Yours and yours alone! Let us fly!"

"Did you bring any money?" he asked.

VI

George Washington Butterfield, an Horatio Alger

1890

The Butterfields of Indiana—a capsule genealogy. . . . Unto them a son is born—George Washington Butterfield, future President! . . . Will the baby live? . . . A mother's despair. . . . Exit Butterfield père. . . . A full house. . . . Early struggles. . . . "Let nature be your teacher."—Wordsworth. . . . The will to succeed. . . . Travel is broadening. . . . Elopement! . . . Our wedding night. . . . George presents an interesting business proposition. . . . A rosy future.

efore continuing with my story, it seems but just and fair that I devote a few words to describing that paragon among men—the glorious prize awarded to me by fate—George Washington Butterfield, my husband.

George was a striking figure: perfectly proportioned; not overly tall, but standing almost a full head above me; of powerful, robust physique (although, later in life, given to excessive avoirdupois); with a fine baritone singing voice and the orator's gift of swaying multitudes with his spellbinding words, delivered in the golden tones of a trained public speaker.

A President's Birthplace

My George had sprung from humble beginnings, like Lincoln. He was born in a log cabin on the outskirts of Albumen, Indiana. This is not to infer, by any stretch of the imagination, that the Butterfields were one whit less aristocratic or descended from less distinguished ancestors than my own family, but they were not blessed with the worldy goods that had made us millionaires.

George's father, Hezekiah de Lafayette Butterfield, and his dear, valiant mother, Poultice Grout Butterfield, had been late settlers in the Hoosier State of Indiana, travelling arduously overland from New Jersey in a covered wagon with California as their goal. The equipage, unfortunately, broke down completely on the outskirts of the tiny village of Albumen, Indiana,[1] and that is where they chose to live and raise their family.

From the very beginning, Dame Fortune seemed firmly allied with the Devil himself against the struggling young couple. Everything that the hopeful Hezekiah turned his hand to seemed doomed from the outset. Visionary schemes for raising cotton, tobacco, oranges, papaya, pineapples, and mangoes were all frustrated by the bitter winters and the icy winds off Lake Michigan, not too many miles distant. A plan to breed

---

[1] The hamlet of Albumen is now entirely defunct and no trace of its remains, save for a very small plaque located on the northeast side of Highway No. 130, equidistant from the towns of Elkhart and Goshen, proclaiming the locale as the birthplace of President Butterfield. P.D.

ostriches to supply the ceaseless demands of the millinery trade came to an end when my father-in-law was kicked severely in the groin by the the first of his expensive birds. An idea—decades in advance of its time—for raising domesticated chinchillas was scotched when the "Adam and Eve," so to speak, of the Butterfield Chinchilla Farm were carried off by predatory hawks. A plan to raise and train performing bears very nearly cost my father-in-law his life. Nothing he touched ever seemed to work out successfully.

Meanwhile my saintly mother-in-law busied herself as best she could, building with her own two hands the small log cabin in which her fine family of sons was to be born; cooking; scrubbing; washing clothes; plowing; coaxing a small vegetable garden from the unyielding soil of their homestead. In addition, she also did laundry for the wealthy Alexander family (manufacturers of quality buggy whips) whose impressive estate[2] abutted the Butterfield homestead. A delicate and finely bred young woman, it is a miracle that she was able to perform such exhaust-

---

[2] Now the site of a Howard Johnson Restaurant. The house, gazebo, and conservatory were razed in 1932, although part of the stable—a structure of only middling historical interest—remains standing. P.D.

My darling mother-in-law

Little George

ing tasks and still bear a son quite without aid or physical amenities. But it was touch and go! Frail and exhausted by her hard lot in life, Mother Butterfield came perilously close to miscarrying the precious burden that lay beneath her heart more times than once. At last, in the fury of a February blizzard (was it a Sign that, like so many in the Hall of Fame, my George was first to see the light of day during the month of February???) and after untold hours of agonizing labor, the eldest of the Butterfield sons arrived—a tiny, wizened, premature baby covered with black hair. "W-we will call him George," the proud, exhausted mother whispered triumphantly. "George Washington."

So overcome was the new father by emotion that he could only say, "We ought to call it Rover."

Weighing but four pounds at birth, the fragile infant was washed, wrapped in worn but clean blankets, and placed in the open oven of the old wood-burning stove (the backwoods equivalent of the incubator in those far-off days), where a hideous tragedy was narrowly averted when his father absent-mindedly shut the oven door and stoked the stove in order to brew a pot of coffee. The tremulous cries of the babe were all that saved his gossamer little life, and my husband's high color in later years was often attributed to this early misfortune.

Nor was my husband's frailty the only cross that his gallant mother had to bear. Once he had achieved sufficient weight to give him a fighting chance at life, it developed that he was a sickly, colicky baby, prone to stomach distress and to crying the night through. (A parallel to President Theodore Roosevelt might be drawn here, but I would prefer not to do

A virile September Morn

so, as *neither* of the Presidents Roosevelt were men whom I admired, for good and sufficient personal reasons that shall be disclosed later in my story.)

As though my poor mother-in-law had not worries enough with a presumably moribund baby to tend, she was struck a further cruel blow by fate when she awoke one cold spring morning to administer her infant son's two-o'clock feeding to find her marriage bed empty. Hezekiah Butterfield, defeated by the rigors of life on their humble homestead, had cracked beneath the strain and had decamped, leaving behind no word of apology or explanation, no money on which to rear his sickly offspring— nothing. My husband and his mother forever after tended—quite under-standably, it is true—to be bitter about Butterfield *père's* seemingly heart-less abandonment. And who could blame them? Yet I was able to under-stand that for many of us too gently born and too highly strung to face the grim realities of life, his "coward's way out," so to speak, was the only possible one. But such knowledge did little to comfort Mrs. Butterfield or to make her lot in life easier. Through the kindly patronage of the Alex-ander family, she continued to work as a laundress, doing her best to feed herself and to look after her sickly little son. A year later, however, the tiny family was enlarged by still another son, Thomas Jefferson Butter-field, and eleven months after that by yet a third, Zachary Taylor Butter-field, and in rapid succession by eight other brothers—Abraham Lincoln Butterfield, Rutherford B. Hayes Butterfield, Ulysses S. Grant Butterfield, Andrew Jackson Butterfield, Millard Fillmore Butterfield, Martin Van

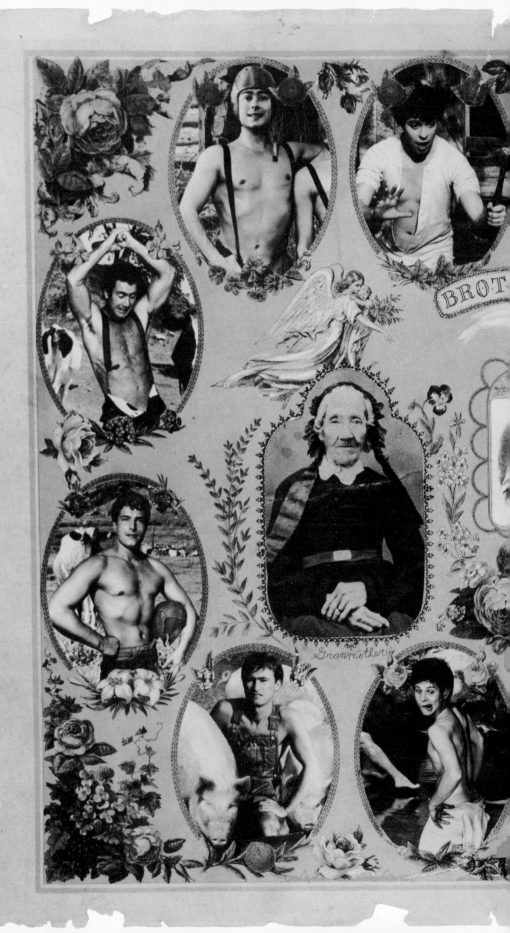

BROT

Granmother

HOOD

WASHINGTON & LINCOLN. (APOTHEOSIS.)

Buren Butterfield, and finally by twin boys, James Knox Polk ("J.P.") Butterfield and John Quincy Adams ("J.Q.") Butterfield. What a brood for a lone mother to raise without the aid of a husband!

Yet this sterling woman of the plains persevered, knowing that she would somehow manage, and manage she did! Rarely has so fine a lot of brothers walked this earth. But the finest of them all was manly little George.

It was he who took it upon himself to be man of the house, to assign tasks and chores to his younger siblings, to maintain order in the midst of chaos, and to do his bit to keep the wolf from the door of the humble home that had served as a President's birthplace.

Like Lincoln, my George had been born in a log cabin, and also like Lincoln, he had an insatiable thirst for learning. After a long day of tilling the soil, attending school whenever it was possible, working at any job he could find (peddling newspapers, sweeping out the local general store, dong piecework at the Alexander Manufacturing Company, helping neighboring farmers during threshing season—anything to turn an honest penny), George spent his nights at the hearthside reading by the flickering light of the dying fire. And, always eager to share his knowledge, it was my George who tutored his younger brothers, ever anxious that they could go forth into the world to a better life than the one they had been born to.

"J.P." and "J.Q."

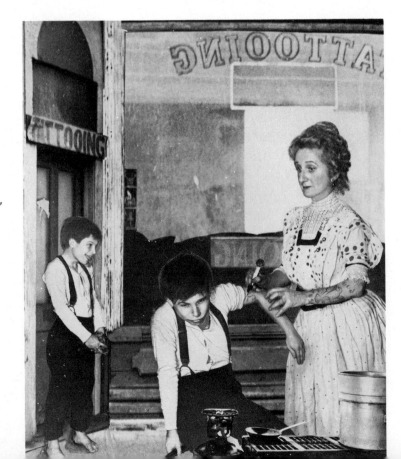

George Washington Butterfield

. . . an Horatio Alger

Hunting

Pigskin

Batter up!

George was a natural athlete, and, who knows, had there been the means to send this born scholar and sportsman to Harvard, Yale, or Princeton, he might also have left his mark as one of the gridiron greats of all time. Instead, he had to content himself with the rowdy rough-and-tumble of his younger brothers, but cope he did.

"Mens sana in corpore sano," that was the Butterfield brothers through and through. And to demonstrate that this is not merely wishful thinking, seen through a roseate mist with the hindsight of many, many decades, I have reproduced in this chapter priceless photographs to prove my point. As the seniors of the wealthy Alexander family—good neighbors, in every sense of the word—were kind enough to supply Mother Butterfield with housework, castoff clothing, and occasional odds and ends from their well-stocked larder, so did the young Cris Alexander keep an ever-watchful eye out for George and his brothers. It is to Mr. Cris Alexander, a gifted young amateur—nay, boy genius—with the camera, that I am indebted for these splendid action photographs of the Butterfield brothers. Whatever the boys were up to—and you may rest assured that it was

The Ole Swimmin' Hole

aplenty!—Mr. Cris was always on hand with his camera to immortalize it. And to show how strange are the manipulations of Dame Chance— many years later when George had long been gone from the place of his birth and had just been nominated for the Vice-Presidency, he was visited by none other than the same Cris Alexander, who came bearing the unheard-of (at that time in history) suggestion that he be appointed Official White House Photographer in case my husband won the election.

George, being both modest and conservative in the extreme, immediately said no, and considered the interview at an end. However, Mr. Alexander had brought with him a portfolio of photographs, taken during those halcyon boyhood years in Albumen, Indiana, to refresh my husband's memory. One glance and George was immediately convinced of the wisdom of Mr. Alexander's suggestion; photographs like those were not easily available. Thus fate rejoined my George, the poor boy from a log cabin who was soon to enter the White House, and Cris, the rich boy from a mansion who was soon to forsake his role as heir apparent to the Alexander buggy-whip fortune to become the first Official Photographer. How often have I said to myself, "Life *is* strange."

But I digress!

Reaching the age of eighteen, young George Butterfield paused to look objectively and honestly around the place of his birth and take stock. What future lay in a tiny village like Albumen for a young man seething with ambition? None!

A disagreement with the owner of the general store over some missing merchandise had made it impossible for young George to continue as general handyman in that humble emporium. Some odd pennies that caused a discrepancy amounting to only a very few dollars had brought to an end George's career as a vendor of newspapers. Things were slack at the Alexander Manufacturing Company, and the Butterfield farm was so small and so well supplied with able hands to bring in its pitiful har-

Master Alexander

vests that there was no need for yet another pair. And so, with a heart saddened at parting from his beloved mother and his adored brothers and yet filled with hope for the future, George, like his father before him, crept away by dark of night (in order to spare his mother the pangs of a more formal leave-taking) and headed east, working his way from town to town, from job to job—no task too mean, none too taxing—until the day of our romantic meeting aboard the *S.S. Euremic*. The rest of my tale is history.

Once safely reunited with my lover, my one thought was to escape the village of Przyzplät, lest Pappa-daddy discover me missing from the castle and send out a search party. Hastily penning a note of farewell to him, I gave it to a peasant boy and asked that it be delivered the following morning. Then George and I rushed to the station for the same miserable train that had brought my family and me up to this mountain aerie to enact our odd true-life drama, which was, indeed, much stranger than fiction.

We were married in Athens at a simple Protestant service and, with our few belongings, checked into a humble room in the Aphrodite Hotel, adjoining the ruins of the stately Acropolis. At last, my wildest dream had come true. I was Martha Dinwiddie Butterfield, *Mrs. George Washington Butterfield!*

Once alone with my new husband in the small but immaculately clean hotel room, a terrible sort of stage fright overcame me. The only male I had ever seen in a state of undress was Bubber, and even that had been many years before, when he was but a babe.

We dined, nervously and silently upon *spanakopetaropeta* and a bottle of heady, resinous Retzina, and then retired once again to our room, where I sat terrified at the window, pretending to watch the Acropolis by dusk. So tense and overcome with embarrassment was I that I was unconscious of any noise in the room until I turned around and saw that George, clad only in his long underwear, was climbing into the bridal bed with a bunch of grapes and a back issue of the *Saturday Evening Post,* which he had borrowed from the American Embassy.

Realizing that I could wait no longer, I began to prepare for bed, but where could I possibly disrobe without being seen? In a panic, I grabbed up my bag and stepped into the large armoire, slamming the door behind me. Struggling there in the dark, confined space, I prayed that all would go well on our wedding night. Somehow or another, I got out of my dress, petticoats, corset cover, and stays and into the white batiste

nightgown I had brought along, but when I tried to open the door of the stuffy armoire, I discovered that it had no handle on the inside! What to do? Tentatively I tapped gently on the thick, tufted wall and whispered, "George?" There was no reply. A bit more firmly, I rapped again and called his name in my normal speaking voice. Still no reply. Now, quite upset, I pounded on the door and shouted, "George! Let me *out!*" This time, I heard an answer: my husband's dulcet snoring from the bedroom beyond.

It was not until nine o'clock the following morning that George, searching for his shaving gear, opened the armoire to release me—more dead than alive. Thus we spent our first night in holy wedlock.

I had very little left on my letter of credit. George, of course, had no money at all, so that returning to the United States was imperative. Finally, we booked second-class passage on a small ship sailing from Piraeus. As we stood at the rail, I grasped George's hand and sighed.

"What?" George said, freeing his hand to scratch himself. (The mosquitoes in Athens had been vicious that year.)

I said sadly, "It will be nice to be back home with Mammy to help me nurse Pappa-daddy back to health."

I felt George's arm wind about me. "And while your old man is so— uh, *sick,* Martha, maybe he'd like me to step in and run the Lohocla works for him. What do you think?"

"Why, I'd never thought about it at all," I answered quite truthfully. So blissful had I been as a bride that such mundane problems as where we were to live or how had never entered my silly head.

"But I bet you could ask him for me, couldn't you, baby?"

How could I refuse? George had such a tender, masterful, subtle way about him that I was putty in his hands. And what, I ask you, could be more natural than for my father, whose health was failing rapidly, to want his business affairs placed safely in the hands of an adoring son-in-law? "Why, of course I could," I said. "And I know that Pappa-daddy will be delighted if we catch him at just the right moment."

"After about how many quarts is that?"

"And we could all live together at Dinwiddiewood. It's big enough, heaven knows, and poor Pappa-daddy will be so lonely with Clytie and Bubber gone. We have a rosy future ahead of us, George, my beloved," I said. "A beautiful, beautiful future for hundreds and hundreds of years."

"And with millions and millions of dollars."

"What did you say, dearest?"

"I said where's the bar?"

A Father's Forgiveness

1891

*Homecoming. . . . Rebuked at the front door. . . . False friends?
. . . Nesting. . . . Sweetheart, bride, wife, and homemaker. . . .
Hard times. . . . Among my souvenirs. . . . George takes an in-
terest in my financial situation. . . . George's interview with
Pappa-daddy. . . . A father's forgiveness. . . . Starting at the bot-
tom—George becomes Treasurer of Lohocla.*

ome! What a beautiful four-letter word that is! To see that grand
old flag, with its thirteen stripes and forty stars, was worth all the
ruins and art museums and architectural wonders in the world!
Checking with the New York office of Lohocla, on lower Broadway, I
discovered that Pappa-daddy, feeling considerably better, had arrived
several days before me and had even felt up to talking business with
some of his influential Northern associates. Then he had been sent back
to Pellagra in a private railway car belonging to one of these titans of industry. My heart leapt for joy to know that my dear father, vastly restored, was now safe and sound at home. What a reunion it would be!

However, when I requested a loan of two hundred dollars to put us up
in a nice hotel for a day or two and to purchase Pullman accommodations
back to Pellagra, my request was rudely refused.

"But there must be some mistake," I said patiently. "I am Mrs. Butterfield, the Miss Martha Dinwiddie as was. Surely you could wire my
father and—"

"No mistake and no loans," was the rough rejoinder. "The boss's
orders."

Still incredulous, I asked to see the manager of the New York office, only to discover that it was the manager by whom I had just been insulted. Although I tried to control my temper, it got the best of me. "Take your happiness while you may," I snapped. "You will not be employed by the Lohocla Company for very much longer!" With that, I wound my feather boa about my shoulders and marched out of the office.

By sitting up all night in the station and by existing on a diet of coffee and rolls during our long wait, I had just enough money to purchase two day-coach seats to Pellagra. It had been so long since I had had to deny myself anything that the experience was something of a lark for me. George, however, felt quite differently.

After an arduous trip on the notorious Southern roadbeds, we finally arrived at Pellagra, heavy-eyed and weary. I had not even enough money left to pay for two fares on the Pellagra County Interurban trolley car— my own family's company! "Come, George," I said. "At least we can arrive in style." We made our way across Confederacy Street to the town livery stable. "May I please have a hack to take my husband and me to the Dinwiddie residence on Jefferson Davis Avenue?" I asked of the "cracker" who was lounging in the office.

"That'll be one dollar," he said, not even bothering to rise to his feet.

"I happen to have left my money behind me," I said. "However, my father, Mr. Dinwiddie, will be delighted to reimburse your driver when we arrive at Dinwiddiewood. I am—"

"Sorry, lady, no buck no buggy." With that he got up, turned his back rudely on me, and strode off to the box stalls. I was stunned. To think that I, a Dinwiddie born and raised in this town that my father virtually owned, could be treated with such disrespect and total lack of consideration!

Rather than worry poor George with these trifling problems, I said, "It's such a lovely day, dear, and there are so many beloved old places I should like to point out to you, why don't we walk? It's just a short way— barely three miles."

My husband showed little enthusiasm for such a trek, but walk we did. On the way, I pointed out places of interest—the Lohocla National Bank, which cheered George considerably, as it was a splendid example of Victorian architecture; the church where I had always worshipped; Miss Beaufort's Seminary, my old school; the Planters' Club, and other sights rich in local color. The town had changed and grown greatly even in my absence. I noticed two new hotels on Main Street—the Lohocla

House and, directly diagonal, the Hotel Dinwiddie, both, I assumed, family property—and a five-story office building called the Dinwiddie Block.

"Does your old man own all of this?" George asked in wonderment.

"Yes, love, I suppose he does. But, of course, his *real* business is patent medicine. These are just sidelines." George gave my waist a firm squeeze right there on the street! He was a man of towering passions.

Just then, whom should I spy coming along the street but my dear old friend Margaret Peavey. "Maggie!" I called, waving frantically. "Maggie!" But apparently she did not see me, as she quickly crossed the street in the middle of the block, narrowly averting what might have been a serious accident with a big red Lohocla wagon, and disappeared rapidly into Nussbaum Frères Department Store. I was at a loss to understand it. Could it have been that Margaret actually did *not* see me at a scant hundred yards' distance? Had I changed so very much in such a short period of time that even my oldest and dearest friends did not recognize me? I was sorely troubled.

George's spirits brightened as we approached Dinwiddiewood from the Stonewall Jackson Street side. "There it is," I said, forcing a gaiety I no longer felt. "Home, sweet home."

Gazing appreciatively at its towers and turrets, its chimneys and stained-glass windows, George said, "Jeest, some lean-to!" in his lovable picturesque fashion. "I'll bet that set him back plenty simoleons!"

"It was rather expensive, I believe, but it was built to last and, of course, it will never go out of style."

Hand in hand, we passed through the wrought-iron gates and strolled up the front walk. As we reached the steps of the verandah, I stopped. "George, dear, aren't you going to carry me over the threshold?"

"What?" George said.

"It's a tradition that the bridegroom always carries his little bride over the threshold of their first home. And even though this isn't *our* home—strictly speaking—it is the place where we will live until we find a dear little cottage of our own."

"You know I've got terrible back trouble," George said, hesitantly. The door opened and there was Pappa-daddy standing before us, armed with a double-barrelled shotgun.

"Pappa-daddy!" I cried. "Put that gun down. It's all right. We're married." I held up my left hand, with its simple gold wedding band.

"Get off my property and *stay* off!" he shouted. Poor man! Once again, I knew that his illness had got the best of him.

"Pappa-daddy!" I cried. "Don't you know me? It's your little girl—Martha. And this is my—"

"I don't care if you're Webber and Fields. Get out and stay out or, by God, I'll shoot." With that, he slammed the front door squarely in our faces. There was nought for us to do but comply with the poor invalid's fever-born wishes.

By withdrawing the small savings account that I had tucked away in Pappa-daddy's bank (feeling quite wisely that no matter how wealthy one was, the thrift habit was a good one), we were able to lease a small flat above a mean shop in a depressed part of the town. As poverty was more or less a novelty to me, I got enormous pleasure out of shopping about for inexpensive bits of furniture, painting chairs and tables, running up my own curtains, cooking and washing and ironing just for two. George, however, was frankly miserable. And who could blame him? He had always been a poor boy, and it must have been a blow to his pride that he could not immediately treat his wife to a lovely home, clothes, servants, a horse and carriage—all the luxuries he had always dreamed of possessing. Day after day, he sat morosely in our prim little parlor, reading the Pellagra *News & Sentinel* over and over and over. As he had nothing to wear but a suit of most unusual European cut, purchased for our wedding

in Athens, it was imperative that he have some decent-looking clothes to put on when out seeking employment. With the last of my precious cash, I sent him to the tailoring department of Nussbaum Frères to buy a new suit, some shirts, a hat, and a pair of good shoes.

Imagine my amazement when he returned home with six suits, two dozen shirts and collars, an overcoat and two topcoats, four pairs of shoes, many, many neckties, underwear, nightshirts, dressing gowns, socks, five hats, waistcoats, spats, garters, braces, gloves, scarves—everything.

"Good heavens, George," I said as I helped him unload his new finery onto our little brass bed. "How did you ever manage to buy so much on the small amount of money I gave you?" To my horror, he replied that he had not. Instead, he had opened an account with Nussbaum Frères! Married only a month and already in debt! However, George—while a man in every sense of the word—was like a child in many respects. It was one of his most lovable characteristics.

I wondered why George, fully outfitted to accept any sort of employment, did not seek some gainful occupation, but he complained that all the positions advertised in the *News & Sentinel* were too menial for the son-in-law of Gayelord Dinwiddie, and that to accept such a humbling position as a shoe clerk, a shipping assistant, a feed-and-grain salesman, or a teamster would so lower him on the scale of the Pellagra business world that he would never be able to rise to a position worthy of his talents. Knowing nothing of business or its hierarchy, I felt certain that he was right, but I also knew that with no money, with another month's rent coming due, and with two mouths to feed, something would have to happen immediately.

Sitting up late one night, long after George had gone to sleep, I wrote a frank, friendly note to Pappa-daddy, "laying my cards on the table." Two days later, it reappeared marked "Return to sender." The handwriting I recognized as Pappa-daddy's own. With heavy heart, I burned the letter in the stove, choosing to say nothing about it to George.

Another fortnight passed and matters had grown desperate. Suddenly, the thought came to me that I had left all my girlhood possessions behind in the big house on Jefferson Davis Avenue—dresses, books, underthings, warm coats, a sealskin dolman, mementos, and souvenirs that could be of no value, sentimental or otherwise, to Pappa-daddy. Many of these things, all of the finest quality obtainable in the state, could be sold at some fraction of their value. I knew that only Mammy, who still functioned as housekeeper for Pappa-daddy, could help me.

Yet how to reach her? She could neither read nor write, so a letter would be useless. The year was 1891, and the town of Pellagra had no telephone system. But see Mammy I must.

I waited until dusk, and then, putting on a dark, hooded mantle, made my way on foot to Jefferson Davis Avenue. Through a window I could see lovable old Mammy, seated in the servants' dining room, telling her fortune with an ancient deck of cards. I rapped on the pane.

"Why, Miss Martha! Shoot my shoes if it ain't you!" Mammy said, with a rich chuckle. Then she added darkly, "You better not let your daddy catch you around here. Not if you know what's good for you."

"Poor Pappa-daddy," I said. "Is he no better?"

"Mean as ever—meaner, even."

When I told Mammy of my request, she shook her head doubtfully, her big gold hoop earrings swinging. "I don't know. He's already given Miss Clytie's duds to his fancy lady. Yours was too big, but you never know what size the next one will be." But when I explained the terrible financial embarrassment in which I found myself, she took pity on me and said that she would send over whatever she could find.

True to her word, the next day the governess cart rolled up to our squalid dwelling place piled high with reminders of my former life although certain lacunae, such as the sealskin dolman and the few simple pieces of jewelry I had worn as a subdébutante, were notable. After several trips, I got them all upstairs, where George was getting out of bed.

"Look, dearest, what darling Mammy has sent me. By selling these things, we may be able to squeak through yet another month until you become established."

George paid but little heed and asked when breakfast would be served. I pointed out that it was nearly time for luncheon, and that luncheon would consist solely of warmed-over lady peas and part of a loaf of stale bread, and for that reason I had sent for my old belongings to see if we could raise enough cash on them for rent and to give the grocer a small payment on account.

Pawing through the pile of forgotten finery, George gave estimates as to the prices they might fetch in the colored second-hand store. The maximum total sum was a depressing one. Suddenly he came up with my old mother-of-pearl souvenir box. "What's this?" George asked.

"Oh, it's nothing—just a lot of mementos I've hung onto since I was a child. Nothing in it is worth anything. You might as well throw it in the

stove. At least we can keep warm." Then I remembered that the little
mother-of-pearl box also contained our birth certificates, baptismal
records, and other documents of some significance. "No, wait," I said
just as George lifted the lid of the stove. "There are some papers in there
that might be important. Just let me look through them, please." Im-
patiently, George banged the lid down on the stove and tossed the box
into my lap, saying something about being hungry. Poor lamb, he hadn't
had a mouthful of food all day.

Going through the box, I found Mumsie-love's marriage certificate, a
few personal papers, an old locket of mine, a curl of my baby hair, and—
of all mysterious things—Mumsie-love's last will and testament!

With hands trembling with emotion, I held up the yellowed sheet of
paper and began to read:

Last Will and Testament

*I, Eulalia Silversides Dinwiddie, being of
sound mind and body do hearby make this
my last will and testement. I havent got
nothing to leave except my recipe for a
dandy poison to use on potato bugs.*

Here Mumsie-love wrote out, word for word, the formula for Lohocla!
That wonderful product, it seems, could do almost anything. Then the
will went on to say: "I devide this between my husband, Gayelord Dinwiddie, and my three children, Martha, Clytie, and . . ."

George," I said. "Come and look at this."

The will had been witnessed by Mammy, who had signed with
an "X" at the place where Mumsie-love had written her name, and also
by the reverend of the Baptist church, who lived but a few streets away.
As Executor, Mumsie-love had named kindly old Judge Dimsdale, who,

although in his eighties, was still hale and hearty and still practicing law in his offices on Main Street.

George could hardly speak. "H-how long have you had this thing?" he asked finally.

"Oh, for years. Ever since I was ten. I'd forgotten all about it."

"Martha, don't you see what this means? It means we're rich. Your crazy old man can't kick you out of no house that's one-quarter yours. It's just as much yours as it is his, and so is the Lohocla plant and the hotels and the Dinwiddie Block and the bank and everything else in this town that he owns. Your ma left this to all four of you—share and share alike. Now, where is this Judge Dimsdale?"

Dressed in our best, we entered Judge Dimsdale's offices. Judge Dimsdale, of course, remembered me from childhood. He courteously offered us chairs, read Mumsie-love's will twice, arched his eyebrows, and excused himself from the office. When he returned, he said that he had every reason to believe that the will was valid and watertight. Then he and George fell into a legal discussion of such complication that it made my poor head swim. Two hours later, when we left the law offices, we had received from Judge Dimsdale not only his assurance that he would handle our case but also an advance of one thousand dollars against our future expectations! I was never so happy. It meant that now I would have legal authority to take care of my poor, deluded father, and to nurse him back to the vigorous, robust, loving, kindly Pappa-daddy he had once been.

We returned to our little nest only long enough to pack up our possessions and remove them to the Bridal Suite of the Mansion House. (We were not welcome at either the Lohocla House or the Hotel Dinwiddie.) I confess to feeling a slight twinge of remorse when we left the three little boxlike rooms that had been my first home with my husband. When would I have another for just us?

For the next few days and nights, I barely saw my George, so busy was he seeing to the terms of Mumsie-love's will. I was of a mind to notify Clytie and Bubber, but, alas, I knew not how to reach them. Bubber was presumably in Paris, but where? As for my sister, the lovely Countess Przyzplätcki, I knew that no mail would be delivered to so remote a spot as her husband's feudal estates.

It was Yuletide, and, for George, on our first Christmas together I bought all sorts of lovely surprises—bedroom slippers with his initials worked in petit point, a meerschaum pipe, a morocco cigar case, and a

stylish carryall for his business papers for such time as he found employment. And for darling Pappa-daddy, who would soon have me on hand to care for him, all the comforts an invalid needs—a *chaise percé,* a hot-water-bottle cover in petit point (I stayed up well beyond my bedtime each night, in a desperate rush to finish it; every stitch a stitch of love), a special sickbed pillow filled with fragrant balsam, and a small bedside Bible, printed on India paper so that it would not be too taxing to hold. I wanted to deliver these gifts early (or, at least have them sent by one of the hotel employees), but George kept saying, "Hold your horses, Martha. Let's wait and give him a *real* surprise." It sounded such fun that I was all too eager to fall in with my husband's plans. But when December 24th finally rolled around and Pappa-daddy's gifts were still piled in the sitting room of our suite, I became impatient. "When, Georgie?" I kept asking. "When?"

"Tonight, baby. Tonight. Can you wait to see the expression on the old—"

"Oh, it's going to be such fun!"

On Christmas Eve, we set off—George, Judge Dimsdale, and the Baptist minister who had witnessed the will, in the first hack; I in the second with my gifts for Pappa-daddy. Almost as though by prearrangement, the side door at the porte-cochère of Dinwiddiewood was opened not by the Negro major-domo but by Mammy herself. I fell into her arms, but George pulled us apart and said, "You just wait out here in the hall, baby. I've got a little Christmas surprise for the old man first. Where is he, auntie?"

"In the library, white man, and I ain't no relation of yours, thank God," Mammy said. Always full of jokes!

I seated myself gingerly on the canework seat of the *chaise percé,* and waited patiently while Mammy ushered George and the other gentlemen into Pappa-daddy's library, then entered that room herself, closing the door firmly. What seemed like an eternity crept slowly by until the ominous silence was shattered by a roar from the library. The door flew open, and I saw Pappa-daddy stagger out, wearing his smoking jacket and cap, his hand clutched to his heart. Darling George, always on hand at any crisis, followed him. "All right, by God," Pappa-daddy cried, "you win this round. Now, git!"

"Go, Pappa-daddy?" George asked incredulously. (Even now, he was calling my father by his pet name.) "We're all going to be living here together."

"In *my* house?"

"In *our* house, I believe. Besides, Martha wants to be where she can keep an eye on you, *and so do I.*" The darling! "Now, you'd better wipe your mustache. There'll be a photographer here from the *News & Sentinel* to take a picture of our happy reunion."

"My newspaper?"

"No, *our* newspaper. And I've already prepared the announcement for you to give to the reporter. You don't have to read it aloud—just hand it to him."

"What does it say?" Pappa-daddy asked, groping for his spectacles.

"It says that you've appointed me Treasurer of the Lohocla empire. I don't mind starting as a minor official of the company. I'm still young and—" George said no more. Pappa-daddy had collapsed.

Lohocla Company Names New Treasurer

Firs

...thru a series ...lations since he experienced no .oms, and has only shot to look for-

been captured at relative and placed ber 14. Roger, who Ir. and Mrs. Robert ried it to East Am- , show the creature smates.

s either not feeling .se it was the wrong or bats to be lively. mates tried to stir e action.

kept blowing on it", "I think they made kd. It climbed to the jar and bit me on the

d, he said, was not deep leed. Nevertheless when n to the school nurse, rchand for treatment, decided that if the comatose, perhaps

George Washington Butterfield, of Albumen, Ind., son-in-law of Beauregard Dinwiddie, president and founder of the Lohocla Corp., has been appointed treasurer of the internationally famed patent medicine firm. With tears of joy in his eyes, Mr. Dinwiddie made the announcement in an exclusive interview with porte

The thru Monday An observ cars were blinding ped acre day.

Ten were recor by Coo Donald

VIII

Motherhood

1892

Peace and Harmony. . . . A suitable standard of living. . . . To-getherness. . . . George takes hold. . . Fête champêtre. . . . A near disaster at Lovers' Leap. . . . First twinges. . . . My beautiful secret. . . . George's pathetic attempts to disguise his pride and pleasure. . . . Waiting. . . . A mother's ordeal. . . . We call the baby Alice. . . . A perfect family unit.

he Christmas of 1891 was one of the happiest I had ever known. There I was with my beloved new husband and my adored old father, all under the sheltering mansard roof of Dinwiddiewood together. The Chinese dining room, with its stained-glass windows and its impressive Louis Comfort Tiffany central gas fixture making the room glow with rich, cathedral-like color; the long fumed-oak table covered with ivory damask; the massive Victorian silver; the plum velvet livery of the footmen; the rose-shaded gas candelabra. George's eyes nearly popped out of his head as course after course of Mammy's delicious Southern cooking appeared, culminating in a large plum pudding drenched in Lohocla and ignited. Although my eyelashes and a bit of my "ratted" pompadour went up in flames, it seemed a small price to pay for such warmth, security, and gladness.

During Christmas week, our belongings were moved in from the Mansion House, and many, many old friends came to call after the news of my whereabouts appeared in print. How foolish and wrong I had been to assume that a dear old chum like Margaret Peavey had cut me intentionally on the street. She explained that she had simply been concentrating very hard on a special shade of blue thread that she had wanted to purchase at Nussbaum Frères on the day of our return to Pellagra and had not seen me. To show how glad she was to welcome back her old friend *and* the husband of the old friend, Margaret gave a lovely dinner party in our honor, with only members of the Lohocla executive Family as guests, so that they could all meet their new Treasurer. It was a gay and heart-warming evening. On New Year's Eve, we attended the dancing party at the Planters' Club, George dashing in his brand-new evening clothes and I causing heads to turn in a beaded Worth ball gown. (My European wardrobe, which was mysteriously missing a few weeks before, when I had asked Mammy for my old clothes, had just as mysteriously been located high in the attics of Dinwiddiewood. Mammy had such a knack for finding things.) Needless to say, I was the belle of the ball, so many friends from the past being anxious to see me once again and catch up on old times.

In the meantime, George was exceptionally busy taking hold at the Lohocla plant. I knew then that I had picked a winner. For a man with little formal education and no exact experience, he showed nothing short of genius at handling the complicated system of bookkeeping that Pappa-daddy had developed. Although the method was unique, George understood it at first glance, and he and Pappa-daddy had many a long, long nighttime session locked in the library, while I, happy and content to be with the two men I loved most, sat in one of the drawing rooms with my needlework.

While Pappa-daddy was still unsteady on his feet, still given—although far less than before—to flying off the handle, still apt to be unclear in his speech, he seemed vastly improved, and no one could ever deny that he was a demon for work. On the nights when he was not closeted with George, explaining certain apparent discrepancies in the books, he was out of the house—I knew not where—with his secretary hard at it. "You must take it easy," I said to him. "You're a sick man and no longer as young as you once were. George can do this nightwork for you."

"In a pig's eye he can. Not while I've got a breath in my body," Pappa-daddy answered jovially.

George was also very firm about my drawing up my own will, which was done properly through the offices of Judge Dimsdale, correctly dated, signed, sealed, and witnessed, with copies on file in the Lohocla National Bank as well as in George's own personal vault. George had only to point out the many sad misunderstandings generated by Mumsie-love's somewhat irregular will to make me see the wisdom of this.

Thus the happy days passed, the busy, cold winter melting early into a warm, balmy Southern spring. One lovely sunny Sunday after George and Pappa-daddy had spent almost every night airing some of the Lohocla firm's knottier problems (and, I am sorry to say, not always agreeing), I decided that it would be nice to have a complete change and, without saying a word, planned a surprise picnic instead of the usual heavy Sunday lunch at home.

Taking Mammy into my confidence, I planned the menu myself: sowbelly in aspic, catfish mousse, collard greens au surprise, and Mammy's heavy but delectable lump cake. The meal was to be washed down with scuppernong wine and, for Pappa-daddy, half a dozen bottles of chilled Lohocla. No servants were to accompany us, as I wanted this to be Just the Family alone together on an outing where George and Pappa-daddy could settle the differences that had arisen between them during the week.

When I sprang my surprise at the breakfast table, the two men were lukewarm about the whole idea, but they got the first scent of spring and decided that an impromptu *fête champêtre* might be more fun than otherwise. We loaded the picnic hampers into the phaeton and, George taking the reins, got an early start for one of my favorite picnic places—Lovers' Leap. Lovers' Leap (its name is derived from an old Indian legend) was generally conceded to be the highest point in the state, and from it on a clear day one could see *five* different counties!

As it was early in the season, the picnic grounds were deserted, and we three were the only merrymakers on hand to take advantage of the lovely view and the tender green buds of *primavera*. The luncheon was a huge success, with Pappa-daddy eating more than I had seen him consume in years. After draining the third bottle of cool Lohocla, that fine old gentleman stretched out for forty winks, and George and I went off on a nature walk. George had just acquired a new camera and had become quite a bug on taking photographs. Suddenly nothing would do but that I pose for a picture at the very edge of the precipice from which the two Indian lovers leapt to their deaths.[1] I was only too happy to oblige.

I posed both with and without my parasol, smiled and said "Cheese" several times, but, still something of a novice with the little black box, George was not quite satisfied that he had me in perfect focus. After tak-

---

[1] Height 2,067 feet above sea level. P.D.

ing several different poses, he said, "I've got just one more plate left, and the sun is perfect. Now, step back a little." I obliged. "Back just a little more," George called from beneath his black cloth. I took another cautious step. "Now, just one step more, baby. Now, lean against the railing." Doing so, I heard the rotten wood give. I suddenly lost my footing and felt myself in midair, falling, falling, falling. And then, with a terrible impact, I found myself in the thorny embrace of a wild plum tree. The pain was excruciating, but, looking both upward and downward, I discovered that I had not fallen more than twenty feet, and the flowering plum tree, for all its agonizingly sharp barbs, had saved me from a hideous and instantaneous death.

"Poor George," was my first thought. "I must get to him to prove that

I am still alive. He will be beside himself with anguish." Extricating myself from the uppermost branches of the stunted tree, I grasped at a bush growing from the side of the cliff, then a stout-looking vine, then a gnarled root, and so on, until finally, my smart striped picnic ensemble torn to shreds, I reached the lip of the precipice.

Poor George, indeed! He was worse than I had ever imagined. He was rolling on the ground clutching his sides, wild, maniacal laughter issuing from his lips. The miserable man was in advanced hysterics, too upset even to have awakened Pappa-daddy. "Georgie!" I cried. "It's Martha. I'm safe!" He looked as though he had seen a ghost. Ashen, the laughter died on his lips, and then he burst into tears. So upset was George that he drank the remaining three bottles of Lohocla singlehanded. With George still shattered from the horrendous experience and Pappa-daddy having suffered a slight touch of the sun, it was I—a pathetic thing of thorns, bruises, rags, and tatters—who had to drive the horses home. Never again did we attempt another picnic.

It was shortly after this eventful outing when, still bearing a few telltale black-and-blue marks from my terrifying fall, I began to feel certain strange twinges—a general malaise. Thinking little or nothing of it, I put my faith in Lohocla—after all, it had done a great many other things for the Dinwiddie family!—and went about my daily round of visiting, shopping, entertaining, and homemaking for my two "boys." But the discomfiture continued, and I discovered that I felt fearfully ill every morning to such an extent that I could not even bear to look at some of Mammy's famous specialties, such as mush in sorghum, grits poached in possum drippings, or fried bread with chinaberry jelly. Could it be . . . ? I wondered! Knowing nothing of the facts of life and too modest to expose myself to a male doctor, I took Mammy into my confidence. She poked and prodded; then she got out her trusty old deck of fortune-telling cards and consulted them. At last, she came chuckling to my room. "Honey," she said, "you sure is." She asked a few mystifying questions of me, and then, again consulting the cards, set the date of my baby's birth for the following October or November. I was so thrilled that I could hardly speak. To think of it! Me! A *mother*! The mystery and the wonder of it were so electrifying that I swore Mammy to silence and planned to have it just my own beautiful secret until such time as I began to "show." Then, and not before, would I tell my George!

A more than adequate sempstress and gifted with knitting needle, tatting shuttle, and crochet hook, I began to spend my afternoons running up tiny garments of gossamer delicacy, to be bound later with pastel ribbons. (Would they be pink? Would they be blue?) At the same time, I listened to fine classical recordings, made by such distinguished divas as Dame Nellie Melba and Dame Clara Butt, so that my sweet lambkin would grow and grow within me under the auspicious influences of the finer things. Likewise, I studied heavy volumes illustrated with masterpieces of painting, sculpture (properly clad), and architecture and in the evenings, without telling him why, urged George to read aloud from books of poetry by Alfred, Lord Tennyson, Ella Wheeler Wilcox, and—should the baby be a boy—the rugged verse of Rudyard Kipling. This George flatly refused to do, although I am certain that had he but known my—*our*—beautiful secret, he would have read himself hoarse for the cultural betterment of our unborn child.

Although I had ever been delicate, I bore up nobly beneath the strain of expectant motherhood. Mammy, the only one who shared my knowledge before it became obvious to anyone who observed my silhouette, was adamant about the wisdom of "eating for two" so that *my* baby would have the best possible start in life. Instead of three meals a day, I was given six—a midmorning snack, a heavy afternoon tea, and a fair-sized supper at bedtime to supplement the already Lucullan diet of Dinwiddiewood. In addition, she was forever surprising me with rich eggnogs; a delicious mixture of Lohocla, goat's milk, cream, Bourbon, and beaten egg-whites; sherry flips; hot toddies (even though the summertime temperatures in Pellagra hovered at 100° Fahrenheit!); and with omnipresent silver dishes filled with pralines, fudge, molasses taffy, and tipsy cakes.

Oddly enough, I began to "show" far sooner than most expectant mothers. I knew that the "jig was up" one evening when we were dressing for a formal dinner party to be given in George's and my honor by the Lohocla purchasing agent and his sweet wife. It was a very warm evening, and try as she would, Mammy could not get me laced in tightly enough for any of my beautiful evening dresses to fit. I childishly flung myself onto my bed and burst into tears.

"What's the matter *now?*" George asked, fitting the diamond studs into his evening shirt.

"It's—it's j-just that I haven't a stitch I can get into," I sobbed, still guarding my treasured secret.

"Well, if you'd stop eating like a sow and get a little exercise . . ."

With that, my sobs redoubled, and then, ashamed of myself for my petulant tears when I should have been carolling with pride and joy, I wiped my eyes and blew my nose and said, "George, darling, we're going to have a little stranger come to visit us."

"Who now?" he asked. "Not Clytie and that hunky husband?"

"No, Georgie, no. We—you and I—are going to have a b-a-b-y."

"Huh?" he said.

"A baby! Our own little bundle of joy."

With that, George bolted out of the room, and I could hear his pumps pounding down the grand staircase. A few moments later, he returned to the room with two bottles of Lohocla.

"A toast for our own little babykins?" I asked, beaming.

"Hell, no," George said. He quickly downed both bottles and then said, "Now, say it again—slowly, this time—and don't go spelling any fancy words."

Men! Just great big overgrown boys, as I have so often said. Anyone with half an eye could see that my George was as pleased and as proud as Punch, but, naturally, he didn't want to show it. On the other hand, Pappa-daddy displayed a loud and unexpected reverence when I told him the happy news. "Oh, my God," was all he could say.

Although Mammy kept me in as robust health as was possible for one of my fragile constitution, I grew too large to be seen abroad on the streets. (Please bear in mind that this was 1892—a time when mothers-to-be did not flaunt their joyous secrets to the public, especially in the South, where pregnancy was considered indelicate in the extreme for *white* ladies.) Owing to Mammy's excellent care, I had gained eighty pounds! Surely my baby would be one of the strongest, healthiest little creatures ever born of woman. However, Mammy's calculations did not agree with Mother Nature's. October—Mammy's first prediction—came and went. November arrived, and with it my constant expectation of being delivered.

December came, bringing the usual hurly-burly of the Yuletide season. Still there was no sign of my baby's arrival.

And then it happened!

On Christmas Eve, just as our faithful servants had begun their round of carols—"Massa Dinwid-*dee* looked out on Pellagra Ci-ty," [2] and so on—I felt the first sharp pain. "George!" I cried. "I think it's coming."

"Shut up and listen to the nigrahs," he said. "That's what we're paying them for." How like George to be gruff in his usual lovable way, trying to

[2] An annual tradition instituted by Countess Przyzplätcki, née Miss Clytie Dinwiddie.   P.D.

Waiting

Baby Alice

Mammy—my midwife

A dainty nursery

still my fears and jolly me along. But no, this time it was no mistake. This was the real thing, and on Christmas Eve, too!

Immediately, Mammy went out into the garden and buried a dead frog, which she had been saving in the cold chest since Michaelmas. She made up the delivery bed with sheets especially dyed in cochineal for the occasion, sprinkled them with dried ergot, and repeated a magic chant three times in a language totally unintelligible to me. Then the pains began in earnest. No words of mine will ever describe the tortures I suffered giving life to my priceless child. One hour, two hours, three hours, four—the time crept slowly forward and my agony was unendurable. Six hours, seven hours, eight hours. Nine hours, ten hours, eleven. And then finally, after having lost consciousness for some time, I heard a lusty cry, opened my eyes, and saw a beautiful, sunny Christmas, dawning through the lace curtains at the bay window. 'It's a girl!' Mammy announced, holding up a tiny, red-faced cherub. "Fifteen pounds—more, even. Weighs more than the Christmas turkey and has a full set of teeth."

"May I hold her?" I whispered.

I cradled the rosy little darling in my arms and then lost consciousness again. Christmas had passed by the time I awakened, and it was more than a month before I could rise from my bed.

Finally, on a fair, clear day in early spring, the baby—who by then tipped the scale at twenty-one pounds—was declared strong enough to endure the ordeal of being accepted into the church. Dressed in my finest,

George's garnets

but still unable to manage lacing and stays, I accompanied George, Pappa-daddy, the officers of Lohocla and their wives to our dear little white house of worship, where our gift from Him was christened Alice, from the Greek meaning "truth." This was the only little one Our Lord was ever to give me.

At last, our joy was complete. Now we were a family. Together we could conquer the world. And together we did!

Dinwiddie-Butterfield, Clan and Empire

1893-1901

George takes hold of Lohocla. . . . Manipulations. . . . Coal, Oil, Railroads, Lumber, Shipping, and Steel join the fold. . . . Tycoons of the times. . . . The Butterfield brothers take an active interest. . . . Baby Alice. . . . The return of the prodigal—Bubber comes home. . . . Clytie and Stanislaus—an indefinite visit. . . . Sharing the wealth. . . . One big, happy family. . . . The end of an era—President McKinley is shot.

fter the birth of Baby Alice, the happy years fairly flew by. So busy was I with my little girl, with the management of stately Dinwiddiewood, with my manifold activities—church groups, charities, clubs, and committees—with my position as social leader of Pellagra (a role that I did not play especially well and neither wanted nor deserved; it was simply thrust upon me, as the eldest daughter of the town's richest and most influential citizen and the wife of its leading businessman; my old school chum Mrs. E. Gottbutt Hitt, née Margaret Peavey, would have filled the niche so much better, with her inborn charm and presence) that I barely had time to notice the many changes going on about me. Pellagra, thanks largely to the ever-increasing expansion of Lohocla and its related enterprises, had ceased to be a sleepy little Southern town and had grown into a small city, even boasting a suburb or two ("outskirts" we called them then), a country club, and a population (counting colored) of nearly 25,000!

SARGENT: *Mrs. Butterfield and Daughter, 1901. Oil, 90 x 64½".*
Collection Mrs. Jane Seeman-Lambert, Lexington, Ken.

So if I did not notice the steady burgeoning of the town through which I moved constantly day after day—new business, new faces, new districts —because of the gradualness of its growth, how could a simple homebody like me be expected to observe or understand the hydra-headed organization that Lohocla had become?

Lohocla was to me a family enterprise, and so it was only natural that my husband should take a hand in the affairs, thus lightening the burdens of my dear father. I was proud, too, of the way George had taken hold, of his complete understanding of Pappa-daddy and of Pappa-daddy's business methods. Little did I realize in my provinciality that in Wall Street, in the City in London, and on the Paris Bourse the word "Lohocla" meant not only a phenomenally popular cure-all but oil, coal, railroads, lumber, shipping, patents on parts for the new "horseless carriages," and all manner of things in the world of high finance, and that the names Dinwiddie and Butterfield were as well known to big business as Montgomery Ward and Sears, Roebuck were to the simple farmwife who had never left her home county.

Yet perhaps in my case ignorance *was* bliss, for I should have been speechless with stage fright and timidity when giving dinner to tycoons such as Henry Clay Frick, George Jay Gould (of course, I remembered his father from my débutante year in New York), Edward Harriman, H. M. Flagler, and others. Sometimes I was so busy greeting them and putting them at their ease that I did not even catch their august names, and even when I did, so sheltered was I in the proper Southern tradition that they meant little or nothing. To me, John Pierpont Morgan was just a shy man with a big red nose (a drinker, I wondered, in a temperance household like ours?) and a very small appetite, for he said almost nothing and scarcely touched Mammy's succulent *pièce de résistance,* roast possum with yams. John D. Rockefeller—of course, even *I* had heard of *that* name—was but a pitifully thin, quiet, older man, who, as Mammy put it in her colorful, colloquial way, needed "a good cleanin' out an' a good fattenin' up!" And so it went.

George, a born businessman and leader, was able to size up any business situation and to get the best of any bargain, quite like dear Pappa-daddy had been in New York before his mysterious European malaise had overtaken him. And as for Pappa-daddy, he did not relinquish the reins too easily or too happily. A rugged warrior, he still held control of mighty Lohocla and although my two "boys" worshipped one another and were lost in mutual admiration, many was the night I all but cowered in my

Dinwiddie-Butterfield Enterprises—the Board of Directors

boudoir at hearing their voices raised in heated argument from the library below. But the course of true love never does run smooth, does it? And I was also pleased when George's younger brothers arrived, one by one (save for the twins, "J.P." and "J.Q.," who could never be separated,[1] and appeared on our doorstep together), for it meant that family bonds were being strengthened. For each of his brothers, loyal George was able to find an executive position in the Lohocla empire. Pappa-daddy was of two minds about this, but by the time he could call a meeting of the directors, so many of George's brothers had become directors that my father, for once in his life, was overruled.

As a baby, Alice was as bright as she was beautiful, precociously learning to talk at an extremely early age (three and a half!), and so avid for learning that Miss Beaufort's Seminary (Clytie's and my old alma mater) enrolled her in the first grade at the unusually early age of six! As musically gifted as the young Mozart, little Alice had the throat of an angel and I thrilled to hear her sweet, piping voice raised in such beloved operatic arias as "Habañera," "Una Voce Poco Fa," and the lovely "Bell Song" from "Lakmé," singing the French and Italian lyrics with her cunning little Southern accent. It was enough to bring tears to one's eyes. In fact George was so moved each time Baby Alice sang that he had to excuse himself from the music room.

Alice was in all ways Terpsichore's favored child, for in addition to her singing, she played the piano with a feather touch—such classical favorites as "The Confederate Drummer Boy" and "Where the Fairies Meet" ringing majestically throughout Dinwiddiewood—and danced so beautifully that had she not been born at a time when no "nice" girl went on the stage, I feel certain that she would have become a *ballerina assoluta,* in a league with Pavlova, Markova, Danilova, and Hayden. The very sight of Alice poised on her points in her little pink tutu was to see poetry in motion. At painting and sculpture, she was also talented to a marked degree, even having done a most expressive mural with orange Crayola in her nursery at the age of three! It was perhaps because my Alice was so extraordinarily gifted in things artistic that she was not able to give her full attention and brilliance to matters academic at school. "Alice does not apply herself," was Miss Beaufort's perpetual comment on the child's monthly reports. But, of course, I realized that poor Miss Beaufort was becoming quite

---

[1] By this possibly misleading statement, Mrs. Butterfield does not mean to imply that the twin brothers John Quincy Adams Butterfield and James Knox Polk Butterfield were what is popularly known as "Siamese twins," but that they were constant companions. P.D.

elderly, and was at a loss to cope with so exceptional a little girl as mine.

And so the years went past—years of happiness, wealth, success, and sunshine. Soon our happy family was to be enlarged by still another person, a very handsome, very dashing, very Europeanized young man —none other than that jackanapes Mr. John Sappington Marmaduke Dinwiddie, *our Bubber!*

Almost ten years to the day from the time he had taken his hurried leave of Bosnia-Herzegovina, he reappeared on the threshold of Dinwiddiewood, very much the grown-up man of the world, complete with mustache, monocle, cigarettes (considered fast, effeminate, or foreign—or all three—for a man at that time), and engraved visiting cards, proclaiming him to be no longer just plain "Bubber" but "Mr. J. S. Marmaduke Dinwiddie," if you please! Still, he would always be darling Bubber to me.

Not a day had passed since his disappearance from Schloss Przyzplätcki that I had not worried and prayed for my beloved baby brother. I saw now that either I need not have worried or that my prayers had been answered, for that rascal was in the pink of condition—manicured, massaged, brilliantined, scented, and kept in bandbox condition by an English valet. How he had managed to exist on but a few of my jewels for all these years was a mystery to me, and so it shall always remain. "That is for me to know and you to find out, Sister, old thing," he said, in his clipped English accent. But manage he had. In addition to the valet, Bubber had arrived in his own automobile—the first ever to roar through the quiet streets of Pellagra—and a perfect caravan of luggage. Always a natty dresser with a consuming interest in clothes, Bubber was now possessed of a wardrobe that would have done credit to an actor-manager. Coats of every color, with linings and collars of sable, astrakhan, beaver, and seal; toppers and bowlers of every shade from black to white; suits and capes and cloaks and waistcoats enough to dress a regiment. How had he acquired them? [2]

Covering his face with my happy tears and my kisses, I asked my beloved baby brother a thousand questions: Where had he been? Why had he stayed so long? Why hadn't he written? What had brought him home at that particular moment?

With his Oxford [3] accent, Bubber replied eagerly to my last query, "Why, to slice up the pater's melon with you, old thing. I say, a bit thick of you not to have told one that you'd found the mater's last will and testament. Rah-ther!

"A stockbroker chap—rather decent, for a man in trade—whom I met at Baden-Baden with the P.W., took a frightful shine to me when he heard that I was one of *the* Dinwiddies. *He* had to tell me what Dinwiddie-Butterfield meant in cold pounds and shillings—do forgive, dollars and cents; you Americans have such odd ways—and so here I am to pay my regards to the pater and collect every farthing of my share."

Pappa-daddy's face was a study when he returned home to find his only

---

[2] Although no definite facts are available, well-substantiated rumors have it that young Mr. Dinwiddie's bills from 1890-93 were paid by a prominent Parisian hostess; from 1893-94 by an Italian princess residing in Rome; for three months during 1895 by a Hungarian countess in Budapest; from 1895-97 by an English marchioness; from 1897-99 by her husband; and for the first half of 1899 by a Viennese actress. P.D.

[3] By which, Mrs. Butterfield refers to Oxford University, Oxford, county seat of Oxfordshire, England, and not to Oxford, Mississippi. P.D.

Bubber returns!

No-a-Count and Yankee Wife Held at Ellis Island

attempt
Continue

Indic
To (

NEW L
Governmen
that arn
rushed to
ern India
against the
continued to spr
The latest o
last night and
ing in Jamshe
in the southe
the state of
toll there
51, accor
Four p
have been
lice opened
Twenty-one
jured and
in to T
tot

"Count" Stanislaus Przyzplätcki and his American-born wife, the former Clytie Dinwiddie of Pellagra, Georgia. The "Countess" is the daughter of Beauregarde Dinwiddie, sole owner of the Loboola C nora

son stretched out in the conservatory wearing a brocade dressing gown and sipping champagne. So affected was that fine old gentleman that he was quite beyond speech. Not so Mammy! Her baby had returned, and to celebrate this once in a lifetime event she prepared one of her most sumptuous and overpowering meals. No one in the family could stir for several days.

But good things, they say, come in threes, and no sooner had Bubber settled in one of the guest rooms, ordered his valet to unpack, and summoned a firm of Atlanta attorneys to negotiate with Pappa-daddy and George for his share of Mumsie-love's bequest than a strange and startling telegram was delivered—collect—to Dinwiddiewood on a snowy December night. It had been sent from Ellis Island, New York, and the sender was none other than Countess Przyzplätcki—precious Clytie *and* Stanislaus! It seems that they had run into trouble with the immigration authorities while planning a surprise visit to us, and they were stranded at Ellis Island. Certain snide newspaper reporters made much capital of my poor, aristocratic sister's plight, using the word "phony" (the first time I had ever encountered such an epithet) and writing most unkindly about the "No-a-Count." Poor little Clytie! To think that a delicate Southern belle such as she, a noblewoman born to the purple, could be herded onto Ellis Island with ignorant, illiterate immigrants!

As I had planned to go to New York for a bit of Christmas shopping anyway, I left ahead of schedule, taking with me Mammy, a first-aid kit, and Bubber, who professed to have business in Gotham.

It was, alas, all too true. There, thrust in with some wild-eyed Balkan peasants and given a number like a common criminal, was none other than my devoted little sister, looking lovelier than ever but wearing a travelling costume I recognized as one she had bought in Paris a decade earlier, and quite penniless! The matter of her dowry had entirely slipped Pappa-daddy's mind. But poor as she was, dear, openhanded, generous, extravagant Clytie had not forgotten to bring her big sister a tiny little remembrance. There, sitting in a large wet puddle on Clytie's lap, was a soft white bundle of fur no bigger than a lady's handbag.

"Is that your muff, Clytie?" I asked.

"Muff, hell!" Clytie said. I should have been shocked, but after all that Clytie and Stanislaus had undergone at the hands of officialdom, I could understand her short temper.

"But what is it?" I asked.

"Here," she said, thrusting the squirming ball of fur toward me. "It's for you."

It was the cunningest, sweetest, friendliest little lap dog I have ever seen! "Oh, thank you, dearest," I said. "Just what I've always wanted, and I'm going to call it Fluffy."

I quickly vouched for the count and countess, and moved them into a suite in the Waldorf-Astoria on Fifth Avenue. I had fully expected poor Clytie to be so exhausted that she would need hospitalization, but as soon as she had availed herself of a hot bath and a good meal and borrowed my sable cape, she was off on a shopping spree, replenishing her wardrobe from the soles of her feet to the new tiara that she bought directly from none other than kindly old Mr. Charles Lewis Tiffany himself, then in the very last years of his long life. "Just send the bill to Lohocla," Clytie kept saying to the attentive shopkeepers of Fifth Avenue.

What a Christmas we had that year! The whole family reunited under the hospitable roof of Dinwiddiewood, although poor Pappa-daddy seemed to suffer a sort of sinking spell, brought on, I feel sure, by emotion at having his favorite child brought safely home to roost. We sang carols, posed

Huggie puppy
(*With my "pal" Fluffy*)

graciously for the Pellagra *News & Sentinel* (for Clytie and Stanislaus were the first European "titles" ever to have set foot in Pellagra County), and entertained all the Lohocla executives and their families at a New Year's Day reception.

Clytie, despite expectations at the time of her marriage, had never been blessed by little ones to carry on the royal name of Przyzplätcki, but so happy was I to see her that I impetuously offered to share little Alice with her for the gladsome holiday season. Clytie thanked me but said that, on the whole, she'd rather I didn't, bravely fighting back the tears of a mother unfulfilled.

We were all living at Dinwiddiewood until Clytie's and Bubber's lawyers could hack away the Gordian knot of red tape surrounding Mumsielove's last will and testament and the mighty empire that had been spawned of her simple formula. The process took more than a year.

To while away the time, I taught myself to operate Bubber's automobile, which I found a never-ending thrill, and became quite proficient at the new sport of driving.

Together we were—all the Dinwiddies, the Butterfields, and the Przyzplätckis, wealthy, secure, and utterly, utterly happy—to drink a toast to the birth of the Twentieth Century. How peaceful it all was in those dear, dead days, when we led the pleasant, indolent lives of the rich, thinking not about politics, world affairs, or social conditions. But it was not to last for very long. On a balmy September evening, while playing croquet on the green velvet tapis that was the lawn of Dinwiddiewood, the word came to us: President McKinley—that distinguished and kindly man—had been shot at the Pan-American Exposition, in far-off Buffalo. Little did I know at the time, but the shot fired by sick, demented Leon Czolgosz was the starting gun for my husband's entry into the political race. The Nineteenth Century was gone, and with it the life of simple pleasures, as my George—a born statesman—stepped into the political arena.

A narrow escape

X

George Enters Politics

1902–06

Mean Mr. Roosevelt. . . . Presidential tampering with Din-widdie-Butterfield Enterprises. . . . Proof positive that Theodore Roosevelt founded the Communist Party. . . . Drastic Steps. . . . George runs for mayor of Pellagra. . . . Masterminding George's political career. . . . Bubber as campaign manager. . . . Dirty work at the polls? . . . Victory! . . . A new statesman is born.

he fatal bullet that brought a slow and agonizing death to dear President McKinley brought also a reign of radicalism and terror, when brash young Theodore Roosevelt became our twenty-sixth President, in a hurried—and *I* say illegal—inaugural ceremony, performed in the private house of Ansley Wilcox, on Delaware Avenue, in Buffalo, New York. Gone were the happy, carefree days when honest businessmen like Pappa-daddy and my George could earn an honest million dollars without the *unconstitutional interference* of a "buttinsky" government. It is my considered opinion that "T.R."'s delicate health as a child and the violent exercising that followed in some way damaged his brain, and a number of distinguished older gentlemen, who are my fellow-guests here at Bosky Dell Home for Senile and Disturbed, agree with me.

"Roughrider" was indeed a splendid sobriquet for "King Roosevelt I," as he certainly rode roughshod over every respectable large corporation in the United States, beginning with none other than the Dinwiddie-Butter-field Enterprises! One should have seen the handwriting on the wall when, as Governor of New York State, that madman began taxing corporations! This was a totally illegal act, which had been unheard of in the good old days of such dignified and coöperative presidents as Andrew Johnson and Ulysses Simpson Grant, who, unfair as they may have been to the gallant old Southland, were at least *gentlemen!* And for my younger readers who, in their ignorance of *true* conditions at the time, may accuse me of personal prejudice, may I also point out that we were not the only large combine to suffer, but such spotless corporations—firms whose very names call to mind "honor," "decency," "honesty," "liberalism"; the very bedrock upon which our mighty democracy is founded—as United States Steel and Standard Oil (completely under the control of that reverent churchgoer John D. Rockefeller) were also taken to task, their closed books pried into, their private affairs meddled with and aired by a muck-raking administration.

Naturally, everyone knew about Senator John Sherman's Anti-Trust Act of 1890, but, just as naturally, few important executives paid any attention to it. "After all," as Pappa-daddy said, "them politicians up in Washington have to do something with their time and the taxpayers' money." But, as Secretary of State under the iniquitous Teddy Roosevelt,[1] how typical of that snake—and brother of General William Tecumseh Sherman, Defiler of Dixie!—to thrust his largely ignored and long-forgotten piece of crooked legislation to the fore! And what better collaborator could he have found than a damnyankee like Theodore Roosevelt?

That Roosevelt simply could not keep his nose one of other people's business! Look, for example, at the anthracite miners' five-month strike of 1902, a mild difference of opinion between the owners of the mines and their perfidious employees, which would have settled itself in short order through the simple expedient of hunger had not T.R. intruded his unwanted self into the controversy. As Pappa-daddy always said of the working man: "If they don't want to do an honest day's toil, let 'em starve!" Harsh words, perhaps, for such a kindly man, but nonetheless true. *We* never had any labor troubles before T.R.

And, not content to confine his infernal and eternal meddling to the continental limits of the United States, was it not Roosevelt who insisted on interfering as mediator of the Russo-Japanese War in 1904, thus bringing about peace and the upsurge of the Communist Party? How my heart

---

[1] Mrs. Butterfield has confused certain facts here. Mr. Sherman died in 1900, more than a year before the inauguration of Theodore Roosevelt. Secretaries of State were John Hay and Robert Bacon. P.D.

bled for poor Czar Nicholas II and his lovely Czarina Alexandra Feodorovna, who were invited by me so many times to visit the Executive Mansion. The invitations were never acknowledged, and I know now that it was because of Communist tampering with the Imperial Russian Postal System! You can thank Teddy Roosevelt for the mess the world is in today!

As for President Roosevelt's manners, *that* is a topic I shall take up in full in a later chapter.

It was one thing for Theodore Roosevelt to break up proud monopolies such as Northwest Securities, Standard Oil, Lohocla, and dozens of others; it was one thing for him to tamper with Venezuela and the Panama Canal; it was one thing for him to keep the Open Door in China (and, pray, look at China *now!*—far better if he had slammed it shut!); it was one thing for him and his henchmen to rig the Presidential election of 1904, so that this upstart was swept into office once again whether the common people wanted him or not; but the single greatest crime of this madman's corrupt administration was the Pure Food and Drugs Act of 1906. How this dictator, who knew nothing whatever of medicine, dared to swoop down upon an honorable old family firm such as Lohocla, confiscating thousands of cases of this strength-giving elixir, and claim *in print* that it contained wood alcohol and numerous other poisons will remain one of the darkest mysteries of all time. But raid he did—T.R. and his infamous "Dr." (I put the title in quotation marks as he was no more a doctor than I am)[2] Harvey Washington Wiley, Chief Chemist of the Department of Agriculture—a purely political sinecure if ever there was one. To make matters even more galling, "Dr." Wiley had been a professor at Purdue and state chemist of Indiana, my George's own birthplace! That is the sort of loyalty to a fellow-Hoosier a man of Wiley's stripe had!

"Walk softly and carry a big stick" was the maniacal Roosevelt's motto, and that is just what he did. He carried a club that very nearly crippled the source of my family's livelihood. Fortunately, George had rearranged certain papers and documents of the Lohocla firm, so that when persons responsible for what the government termed "fraudulent claims" were arraigned before the Senate, his was not one of the names called. Instead, he remained loyally behind in Pellagra, to look out for the family's interests, while Pappa-daddy and more than a dozen of the other leading Lo-

---

[2] Not entirely correct. Dr. Wiley received his medical degree in 1871 but never practiced as a physician, becoming, instead, a professor of chemistry. Mrs. Butterfield, however, feels very strongly about this. P.D.

hocla executives went to Washington to fight the good fight against Attorney General Philander Knox for family honor. Appearing before a "rigged" tribunal, Lohocla naturally lost the case. The firm was forced to change not only its advertising and its claims but *even its very formula!!!* In addition, poor Pappa-daddy was fined many hundreds of thousands of dollars. Darling George, completely baffled and mystified, said that it was a wonder that Pappa-daddy hadn't been sent to prison! Imagine!

The whole sordid affair so undid my poor father—both physically and mentally—that he would not even speak to George, *his own son-in-law,* when he returned from his ordeal in Washington!

All very well for some to sit back and take this sort of abuse from a despot such as Roosevelt, but for men of *action,* like my George, the time had come to *act!* In order to protect our basic human rights, my beloved husband went into politics.

Wisely deciding to start on a small, localized scale, George chose Pellagra's mayoral election in which to test his wings. Like some dynasty of yore, the position of mayor of Pellagra had always been held by a member of the Eubanks family. They were one of the oldest families in the county and in the state, having come to this country in the days of the thirteen colonies to settle in Pellagra. While the Eubanks family was very nice, and while I would never say a word against any of them, they did seem to have outlived their usefulness as civic leaders of the town. All very well to have one Eubanks after another occupying the mayor's office in the town hall when Pellagra was but a sleepy little Deep South village. But now, thanks almost solely to Lohocla and the additional industry and citizens it had brought to Pellagra and environs, what had once been a hamlet was a thriving metropolis, with a crying need for all the enlargements and improvements that go with a city's status. This concept was simply too much for Wade Eubanks, the present incumbent (and the *sixth* Eubanks generation in direct succession!), to grasp. As no one had ever run for mayor against any of the Eubankses, the elections had been little more than formalities, and so you can imagine the surprise and general consternation when my George tossed his hat into the ring and announced that *he* was going to run for mayor, on the Up-and-At-'Em Ticket for a *new* Pellagra.

His decision met with a great deal of disapproval. In the first place, George was a yankee and a newcomer, having been a part of Pellagra only since his marriage to me, while the Eubanks family had been heart and soul of Pellagra as long as it had existed. George represented the future—modernization and change—and a great many of the old residents resisted any change (resented even Lohocla, which had brought prosperity and fame to the town!). And, surprisingly enough, there was even a certain amount of ill will against Pappa-daddy and the whole Dinwiddie family, even though we had always lived in the vicinity and could hardly be classified as new. Although I had quite expected George to sweep into office with only a token resistance, I was quite taken aback by the heated battle waged by Wade Eubanks to hang on to a job that paid only a pittance. But battle he did, and to such an extent that George felt it wise to

Wade (r.) and Thurmond (l.) Eubanks

employ a campaign manager, if only to spare himself from becoming, in case of defeat, a laughingstock in the town that he and Pappa-daddy virtually owned.

Fortunately, like an extremely dapper *deus ex machina,* Bubber returned quite unexpectedly from an interrupted season on the Côte d'Azur. (The corrupt Eubanks forces even tried to spread word around the town that he had been *asked* to leave Nice! But that just showed what low minds they had and how frightened they were by the threat of George Butterfield and clean, progressive government!)[3]

Bubber's homecoming was most timely. What could be more useful to an aspiring politico than a young, energetic, forward-looking campaign manager, well versed in the ways of the world? And as Pappa-daddy preferred to have Bubber occupied while in Pellagra or out of it altogether, the collaboration seemed a godsend for everyone concerned.

For one so young and for one whose formal education had been halted at such an early age, Bubber displayed an amazing grasp of statesmanship. While I worried about the votes of the fine, old, substantial families of Pellagra, Bubber pointed out that each person—no matter what his background or lineage—had but one vote and that it would be a great deal more expedient for George to go after the votes of the poor, as there were so many more of them. How right my brother was!

George was a born public speaker, rivalling even William Jennings Bryan, the Silver-Tongued Orator, and naturally he made himself available for any and all speaking engagements. However, this activity had to be sharply curtailed when hooligans, obviously in the pay of the Eubanks faction, took to throwing tomatoes, rotten eggs, and even bricks at the podium while my husband was addressing the multitudes! Thank heav-

---

[3] As a matter of fact, young Mr. Dinwiddie was not asked to leave Nice. He was told to leave Monaco by Prince Albert on August 18, 1906. P.D.

ens *we* never had to stoop so low in our contest with Wade Eubanks! As we owned the only newspaper in town, we simply ignored the slanderous speeches he was brazen enough to make against George. But the Eubanks family had connections with certain other newspapers in neighboring towns, and, just to show you to what depths they were willing to sink in order to win so trivial an election, they even photographed Bubber (unbeknownst to him) when he was counting the money in his wallet with a group of workingmen, and had the audacity to claim that he was *buying* votes for George!!!

However, Wade Eubanks had been too stupid to reckon with the loyalty of our thousands of employees. At the Lohocla plant, at our two hotels, at our stores, at the newspaper, at the traction company, at the offices of Dinwiddie-Butterfield Enterprises (no matter how mighty the firm became, loyal Pappa-daddy always maintained his headquarters right at home in Pellagra), the employees *worshipped* George, just as they adored Pappa-daddy. To remind them of their love for George Butterfield, Bubber had leaflets especially printed and handed out to each employee at closing time on the eve of the election.

A REMINDER

DINWIDDIE-BUTTERFIELD WORKERS

TOMORROW (TUESDAY) IS ELECTION DAY

George Butterfield

IS RUNNING FOR MAYOR ON THE UP-AND-AT-'EM TICKET

IF HE IS NOT ELECTED, DON'T REPORT FOR WORK ON

WEDNESDAY

The Management.

No wheedling, no begging, no high-pressure sales talk—just a simple reminder of the citizens' duty to vote.

Bubber was up at daybreak. He had fortuitously managed to have the polling place moved to a spot equidistant from the Hotel Dinwiddie and the Lohocla House, and he saw to it that the bartenders in both establishments were kept busy pouring out free drinks to all the males of voting age on that excitement-fraught day. In addition, he had arranged for our trolleys to carry voters from outlying neighborhoods to the polls at no charge, to give them a free meal at either one of our hotels, and to return them to their homes. (Many, I am sorry to say, were all but unable to walk from having taken unfair advantage of our thoughtfulness and generosity.) The fleet of Lohocla wagons also brought in hundreds of our workers, and it marked the first time that Negroes had ever voted in our state. However, the colored employees of Lohocla were so anxious to show their loyalty to George that they abandoned their usual indifference to politics and came flocking to the polls in armed Lohocla wagons, under the protection of a squadron of private policemen hired for the occasion by loyal Bubber. Wasn't that a touching tribute!

I was on pins and needles all during that eventful day, and poor George, after having cast a vote for himself, felt that it would be the better part of wisdom to appear at both hotel bars and have a few last words with any voter whose mind might not have been made up. It was after midnight when he returned home, so exhausted that he could barely make it up the stairs. Poor Bubber, who must have been all but dead of fatigue, was still off at election headquarters helping to count the vote, which was unusually heavy that year—the heaviest, in fact, in all of Pellagra's history before or *after* the Butterfield-Eubanks election!

Bone tired, I finally drowsed off only to be awakened by a great commotion going on on the lawn outside. Rushing to the window, I pulled aside the lace curtains to see the first pearly-gray light of dawn in the sky and on the grounds of Dinwiddiewood all of George's loyal campaign workers. The cheering was deafening.

Baby Alice dashed into our room, terrified out of her poor little wits at the noise. "Don't fret, honey child," I said, clasping her to my bosom. "It's simply that your wonderful daddy is the new Mayor of Pellagra and your mummy is Pellagra's first lady!"

Then, together, little Alice and I half carried poor, exhausted George down the great staircase and to the porte-cochère, to receive the ovation that was so rightfully his. The *News & Sentinel* photographer was on hand with his powder flash mechanism, taking pictures of us. The shouting was tremendous. But to show what poor losers the Eubanks faction were, there were even some rowdies in the crowd shouting "Fraud!" and asking for a recount!

George had won, fair and square, by a landslide margin of 50,000 votes, while the Eubanks census listed only 25,000 souls! My beloved husband was on his way at last—on his climb onward and upward to the highest office in our land!

NEW MAYOR ELECTED

GEORGE WASHINGTON BUTTERFIELD, son-in-law of H. Gaylord Dinwiddie, president and founder of the Lohocla Corporation, was elected mayor of Pellucra by a majority of more than 25,000 votes in

XI

The Birth of a Statesman

1908

George proves his worth in public office. . . . A smoke-filled room. . . . Pappa-daddy founds the Bullfinch Party. . . . Enter Miss Gladys Goldfoil. . . . Deadlock. . . . General Lucian Lushmore, that grand old man. . . . A thrilling political convention. . . . George accepts the Vice-Presidential nomination. . . . Lushmore-Butterfield, that's the ticket!

y husband, George Butterfield, that man for all seasons, proved once again, as Mayor of Pellagra, his great versatility, adaptability, talent, and intelligence. For a man of such humble beginnings and so little schooling, he was a marvel of poise, charm, grace, and executive ability. As he had taken over the administration of the Lohocla firm, so did he take over civic administration, while easing up on none of his multitudinous duties toward our own private enterprise.

No sooner had he been sworn in as Mayor than he condemned the old town hall, had it razed, and a magnificent new structure erected in its stead, on some land that the Butterfield brothers had been farsighted enough to purchase during the mayoral election campaign. Although the poor losers of the defeated Eubanks contingent made wild claims of "graft" and "kickbacks," these were purely sour grapes. True, the Butterfields had bought the land—formerly the site of some disgraceful Negro shanties—very cheaply, but I do not consider the half-million-dollar profit they made on its resale excessive. After all, being businessmen, they deserved some modest markup. They had held on to the land for nearly ninety days, and it had been their sole responsibility to evict the tenants from the unsafe, unsanitary hovels and condemn the whole block. No easy task.

As for the new Pellagra city hall and community center—a structure that would house not only the town's executive offices but also the police and fire departments, as well as an auditorium, billiard and bowling facilities, and other services to the citizenry at large—many architectural sketches were submitted. We saw numerous examples of Queen Anne, baroque, William and Mary, Georgian, Greek revival, and gothic, but none of them seemed quite to capture the spirit George had in mind. Suddenly, however, while perusing an old photograph album, George came across some studies of Schloss Przyzplätcki, and the suitability of it as an edifice to grace the new Butterfield Plaza struck him at once. It was then suggested by one of George's younger brothers, Abraham Lincoln ("Honest Abe") Butterfield, that Clytie and Stanislaus might be persuaded to part with the authentic castle at a reasonable price and that it might be transported, stone by stone, from Bosnia-Herzegovina to Pellagra, as Mr. William Randolph Hearst was just beginning to do with many European architectural masterpieces. A brilliant suggestion!

A pioneer suffragette

Although it broke poor Clytie's heart to forsake that building steeped in history, romance, and folklore—the seat of the Przyzplätckis since the Crusades—she saw her duty to the old home town, and she and Stanislaus reluctantly parted with Schloss Przyzplätcki for two million dollars. Martin Van Buren Butterfield was placed in charge of razing and wrapping the ancient castle, and the twins, "J.P." and "J.Q.," were to oversee the removal, by burro, train, ship, and again train, to Pellagra.

Needless to say, we were *severely* criticized by the forces of reaction, and the ugly word "nepotism" began to be bandied about by George's detractors. As for hiring his brothers Martin and the twins to oversee the delicate and highly technical job of dissasembling Schloss Przyzplätcki, moving it, and reassembling it, why would George not turn to those he knew and could trust, instead of to some mediocre firm of strange contractors who took little or no personal interest in a structure of such immense historical and sentimental value?

Likewise, my poor George was verbally crucified when he appointed his brother Rutherford as Chief of Police; when Zachary Taylor Butterfield's new firm won the paving contract for the whole township; when Millard Fillmore Butterfield became Tax Collector, and so on, and so on. It was *not* nepotism, nor was it favoritism! George simply gave each job to the man he felt would do it best.

But fame and power do breed enemies, and thus trouble and dissension seethed around the clean, progressive government that George tried so manfully to install in Pellagra. The fact that appointments and contracts were granted to all of George's brothers or to subsidiaries of Dinwiddie-Butterfield seemed especially to incense his detractors. Happily, our family owned the Pellagra *News & Sentinel* outright, so that there was at least one public organ to point out the worthwhile things that were being done for the taxpayer, but when George's enemies planted derogatory—derogatory indeed, *libelous!*—stories in the newspapers of nearby towns and when even the Atlanta *Constitution* began regularly to mention civic affairs in Pellagra (as though it were any of Atlanta's business!), I felt that the opposition had stooped *very* low.

Nevertheless, during my husband's one term as Mayor the town was supplied with a new city hall (and a structure unlike any other in the United States, although poor Tom Butterfield's newly organized contracting firm had great difficulty in getting Schloss Przyzplätcki back together again in Butterfield Plaza, since bits of the ancient keep persisted in falling and there were five or six large rooms that seemed to go absolutely nowhere); with brand-new streets and sidewalks even in the parts of the township where no one lived (but this was merely foresight); with new lighting; with a telephone system; with a fifty-man police force; with a fire department; with a sanitation department; with a broad, straight, proud new highway, leading directly to the Lohocla plant; with the Martha Dinwiddie Butterfield Girls Elementary School (at the opening of which I proudly officiated); and with the Countess Clytie Przyzplätcki Wing of the Judah Benjamin Memorial Hospital.[1] That many of these new projects soon disintegrated cannot be blamed so much on faulty construction (as our enemies would have one believe) as on lack of proper maintenance and out-and-out sabotage!

In addition to opposition on a purely local level, President Theodore Roosevelt and his Communistic government, with its pat Red palaver about the "rights of the little man," was a constant thorn in the sides of Pappa-daddy, George, and the Board of Dinwiddie-Butterfield Enterprises. Not only did the government thwart and frustrate the over-all plans of the mighty combine at every turn—no matter how minor—but various muckrakers, such as Upton Sinclair and Lincoln Steffens (obviously in the secret employ of T.R.), were forever bringing up scandalous stories about members of the Board of Directors, most of them, needless to say, totally fabricated, and those tales with any vestige of truth to them simply overblown accounts of youthful peccadilloes better forgotten and ignored.

With the passage of the Pure Food and Drugs Act in 1906, and with poor Pappa-daddy's public humiliation in Washington, which I have described in the foregoing chapter, the very foundations of our family's living were threatened. T.R. and the perpetrators of this reign of terror so suddenly foisted off on the innocent American public even had the temerity to claim that Lohocla, which had done so much for so many, had actually *killed* some of its more ardent devotees!!! What a libel! If some of the users of this strength-giving emulsion did pass away, let us bear in mind that they were sick people whose life spans could not be judged *ex post facto* and that, like all of us, they had to go sometime. How fortunate, then, that they had at least the comfort of regular dosages of our medicine to sustain their last precious moments on this earth. The alcoholic content of Lohocla was also strongly emphasized in the government's vicious denunciation of our product, and poor Pappa-daddy, instead of be-

---

[1] A four-bed addition so modern and revolutionary in concept that it was the first hospital wing in the United States to cost more than $20,000,000. P.D.

ing shown the respect due a man of science, was treated like a common moonshiner! True, Lohocla contained a certain percentage of alcohol, but so, may I point out, did the famous vegetable compound manufactured by that pious New England lady Lydia Pinkham, our closest competitor. But if Lohocla incorporated a small percentage of alcohol,[2] it was there for a definite purpose, and that was—to borrow a contemporary word used so often by the physicians here in my present place of residence—to "tranquillize" the poor, suffering souls, often sick in both mind and body, who had dire need of the comforting effects of our product. Modern science, of course, understands this, whereas the superannuated old "sawbones" employed by that radical Roosevelt did not.

Wise old Pappa-daddy understood only too well that a menace like T.R. could not be combatted on a purely local level, but that the beast must be fought in his own arena—politics, and politics on a *national* scale. Carefully biding his time, Pappa-daddy waited until the 1908 political conventions were in the offing, and then approached both Republican and Democratic parties. For some unknown reason, neither could be made to see the real dangers that confronted our mighty nation, and while both parties listened courteously to Pappa-daddy, and even suggested contributions to their campaign chests, they lacked the spirit of *quid pro quo* that Pappa-daddy felt suitable. To consider the Socialist Party at all was, of course, out of the question. Therefore, it behooved my ever-resourceful father to create a party of his own. So, with the aid of the many influential members of the Dinwiddie-Butterfield Enterprises, and with some of his other business associates who had been especially damaged by Roosevelt's harmful "trust-busting," a glorious new political entity—called, for lack of a better name, the Bullfinch Party—was born right in the library of Dinwiddiewood, which became *the* smoke-filled room of the year 1908. In fact, so smoky did it become during the third day of negotiations (for seventy-seven hours Pappa-daddy and the co-founders of the Bullfinch Party remained closeted, interrupted only by faithful Mammy—none of the other servants was trusted—who kept up a constant supply of sandwiches, cigars, Lohocla, and other liquid refreshments) that when one of the stained-glass windows was finally opened in the interests of ventilation, Andrew Jackson Butterfield, at that time Chief of the Pellagra Fire Department, was summoned by a distraught neighbor, and the entire west,

---

[2] The actual amount in 1882, the first year of its manufacture, was 95 per cent. Later reduced (in 1906) to 70 per cent. P.D.

or Renaissance, façade of Dinwiddiewood was sprayed by pressure hoses, resulting in a great deal of broken glass and the drenching of valuable carpets and hangings before the misunderstanding could be explained. Finally, Pappa-daddy, triumphant but exhausted, was helped out of the library by George. The Bullfinch Party and its platform had been established. It was to be a party designed to appeal to the Solid South (not entirely unlike the Dixiecrats of half a century later), to the businessman, both large and small, to the farmer, to the workingman, *and* to the unemployed.

As the Republicans that year were holding their convention in Chicago and the Democrats in Denver, George—who had just constructed the Butterfield Coliseum, facing Butterfield Plaza, and the luxurious new Hotel George I, directly opposite—suggested that the Bullfinch Party hold its convention right in Pellagra. It was the first time a Southern city had been chosen since the Democrats convened in Charleston in 1860, which, of course, would please the South.

You can imagine my excitement on the eve of the Bullfinch convention, when the delegates—all personally picked by Pappa-daddy and his steering committee—began pouring into Pellagra from every state in the Union, as well as newspaper correspondents and reporters from all corners of the globe. As the town's social leader, as the wife of its daring young Mayor, as the daughter of the founder of the Bullfinch Party, I was very much on hand as official hostess to the many delegates, their wives, and their families. How nervous I felt and how I longed for darling Clytie, with her years of experience in court circles, to be at my side to guide me. But Clytie, after recovering from the loss of her beloved family seat, had leased a magnificent apartment on the Champs Élysées, as well as a perfect jewel of a Georgian house in Mayfair's Park Street, and was head over

A smart campaign outfit

heels in the social swim of both Paris and London (where she was a *great* favorite of King Edward VII), with so many side trips to Deauville, Cannes, Biarritz, Vichy, Baden-Baden, and numerous stately homes and châteaux scattered across the English and French countrysides that I rarely knew where to write to her.

The family circle was, however, enlarged by the arrival of Bubber, accompanied by a woman—I *cannot* use the word "lady"—who was obviously, even to naïve me, more than just a friend. His timing could not have been worse, and, love him though I did, I had to admit that he created anything but a desirable impression for the earnest young Bullfinch Party. Just as the delegates were parading in Butterfield Plaza—state by state, in alphabetical order—Bubber appeared in the tonneau of a costly French motorcar, driven by a Senegalese chauffeur with such recklessness that two members of the Massachusetts contingent were quite badly injured and had to be hospitalized. Bubber, monocle in one eye and his usual cigarette in a long jade holder, was dressed like a coxcomb in the palest of pearl gray, with an orchid in his buttonhole and, perched on his shoulder, a tiny, gibbering marmoset! Beside him on the seat, brazen as brass, sat his voluptuous blonde—*blondined,* if you were to ask *me*— woman friend, Miss Gladys Goldfoil, a common woman of the stage, who had, until her association with my innocent younger brother, been a member of the ensemble of Mr. Ziegfeld's fast new "Follies"! Wearing lavish furs and a gown far too revealing for any hour of the day or night, *she* was smoking a *cigar!* Can you wonder that the simple townspeople of Pellagra and the conventioneers and their wives were horrified?

Angry as Pappa-daddy had been because of Bubber's untimely appearance, he did unbend in the presence of Miss Goldfoil, laughing at her coarse witticisms and even deigning to sip champagne from her slipper, as did my George. But that was only because they were Southern gentlemen and that woman was a guest in our house. I am *not* ashamed to say that *I* could barely be *civil,* and I gave *strict* orders that precious Alice was *never* to be allowed in Miss Goldfoil's company.

Meanwhile, the convention raged on, both day and night. Many fine candidates were considered, Pappa-daddy among them, at the suggestion of an independent rooting section of Lohocla employees. However, as sterling a man as he was, my father was regretfully rejected as being too wealthy, in failing health, and the recipient of much unfortunate publicity, brought on not only by Bubber and Miss Goldfoil but by his recent ordeal at the hands of T.R.'s unsavory crew of inquisitors. A Mr. Kruschner of Mauch Chunk, Pennsylvania, was likewise passed over, as were several other promising candidates. Finally, the convention was in a complete deadlock. Something had to be done.

It was then that Pappa-daddy, disappointed but far from bitter over his own defeat, brought into focus that grand old gentleman of the Confederacy, General Lucian Lushmore, long a citizen of Pellagra. General Lushmore, who had had a lengthy and distinguished career as commanding officer of the Quartermaster's stores at Mobile during the War Between the States, had held various positions in the Pellagra County government with honor and distinction. As Purveyor of Deeds, Pappa-daddy had found him more than cooperative in many, many negotiations with the Lohocla firm and with Dinwiddie-Butterfield Enterprises. Although in his eighties, he was in excellent health. He came from a fine old Southern family of the Protestant persuasion, as did his gracious wife, the former Amaranthine Glottis of Savannah. A born public speaker, General Lushmore could discourse on any given subject for more than an hour at a moment's notice. He also had great presence and a noble bearing—the mark of aristocracy so important in a Presidential candidate. As he had

General and Mrs. Lushmore

been retired for the past five or six years, serving in an advisory capacity to Pappa-daddy, occasionally arranging the sale or purchase of lands or smoothing the way where political matters were concerned, he had nothing better to do. On the fifth night of the convention, therefore, General Lushmore was hastily got out of his bed, dressed in his finest, and "sprung" as a complete surprise to the weary delegates.

I will never forget his speech, completely impromptu and unrehearsed. It began at eleven-thirty and continued until four-fifteen the following morning. Those still present at the convention were so stunned at the finish of it that they were not even able to applaud. General Lushmore was indeed a "dark horse."

As to the question of who the Vice-Presidential candidate would be, certain irregularities arose. Because of my frail grasp on politics, I do not quite understand the ins and outs of nomination, but it seems that none of the possible candidates was even to be considered. At half past four in the morning, after General Lushmore's memorable speech, George jumped to the podium and called for silence. It was very quickly his, as only a handful of delegates remained in Butterfield Coliseum. Then, raising his golden voice, he began to speak to those who still occupied the convention hall. With all the smoke, the week of hectic ever-on-the-go social activity, and the extreme lateness of the hour, I felt my eyelids growing heavier and heavier. Fight it as I would, I must have dozed. When I awoke, it was broad daylight and there were hardly one hundred people in the vast auditorium. Dimly I heard the end of the roll call of states . . . Texas . . . Utah . . . Vermont . . . Virginia . . . West Virginia . . . Wisconsin . . . The conventioneers seemed more exhausted than I was. I was vaguely aware of voices drugged with fatigue saying hoarsely, "Lushmore-Butterfield." The delegate from Wisconsin—the only one remaining in his entire section—even added, "For God's sake, anyone!" I fell back into a sound sleep again.

When next I awakened, George was tugging at my arm. "Wake up! Wake up!" he kept shouting. "Lushmore's running for President on the Bullfinch ticket, and I'm running for Vice-President. You're the only one left to listen to our acceptance speeches."

TIME TO RETIRE?

XII

A Gruelling Campaign
1908

We all pull together. . . . Bubber shows his true worth. . . . Whistle-stopping coast to coast. . . . Reënter Miss Gladys Gold-foil! . . . A shocking anonymous letter. . . . Can George be un-true? . . . Alice's disaster. . . . A tragic death. . . . Vile practices of the opposing parties. . . . The great day. . . . Disguised as a man, I cast America's first female vote. . . . Dirty work at the polls—the mysterious disappearance of the New York City vote. . . . Six unendurable days of tension. . . . The miraculous victory of the Bullfinch Party. . . . Tragedy in triumph—General Lush-more dies of shock. . . . George is President-elect of the United States!

f I had thought that one week of the Bullfinch convention right at home in Pellagra was physically and mentally taxing, I had no idea what the months of August, September, and October held in store, for it was then that the real work took place. In those faraway days before the advent of radio and television, campaigning meant travelling from one end of the country to the other, and travel we did!

While dear General Lushmore had many, many of the qualities that make a great President, he did not have the one attribute that is vital to a successful Presidential campaign—*money*. The Lushmores lived comfortably but in extremely modest circumstances, in a medium-sized frame house of Federal vintage in a declining neighborhood, and it was only through the kindness and generosity of Pappa-daddy that they had been able to live there at all and not in a home for indigent Confederate officers. This, of course, was turned into an advantage, by showing the rest of the nation that as aristocratic as their lineage may have been, Amaranthine and Lucian Lushmore were "just plain folks" like the average voter, whereas the palatial milieu of Dinwiddiewood might well have dissuaded the common man from sending to the Executive Mansion a candidate who already occupied so opulent a residence.

As for the thousands and thousands and thousands of dollars that the Lushmore-Butterfield campaign cost, they were unstintingly supplied by the corporation and several forward-looking industrialists, who had suffered no few indignities from the reign of terror laid on by the Roosevelt administration.

Bubber, for all his foppishness (just a phase the poor, misguided boy was going through), had done a truly remarkable job of masterminding George's mayoral campaign against the long-entrenched Eubanks family. Through Bubber's unwholesome friendship with the unspeakable Miss Goldfoil, he had met a number of public-spirited New York citizens who belonged to an organization known as Tammany Hall, and as he said modestly, "With the things I learned from the Tammany boys, I could put an orangutan in the White House—and that's just what I'll be doing."

As we were complete tyros in the political world and as Bubber had successfully advised George when he ran for mayor of Pellagra, he seemed an ideal choice as manager of this dramatic nationwide campaign. He was someone we could trust. Independently wealthy now and generous beyond belief, Bubber refused to accept a penny for his services! Instead, he said, "I'll collect my reward *after* the election's won."

It was just after this that Cris Alexander, the aspiring photographer friend of George's boyhood, appeared to apply for the post of Official Photographer. Bubber put him to work immediately, taking pictures of General and Mrs. Lushmore sitting in their modest parlor, puttering in their garden, reading, dining, and so on. There were also photographs of George and me strolling on the lawns of Dinwiddiewood; of me and Fluffy, my "lap dog";[1] of George dandling Alice on his knee, although she was now quite large and burgeoning into womanhood; and of many other folksy activities, "to build," as Bubber said, "the right public image." Such complicated new terms!

---

[1] Mrs. Butterfield's pet, Fluffy, turned out to be a Great Pyrenees, inexplicably born in the mountains of Bosnia-Herzegovina. P.D.

But as time was of the essence and as Bubber wished George and the General to cover as much territory as possible prior to the election, he got to work immediately on lining up the Bullfinch campaign train—a magnificent private train lent to us by a rail magnate who had good and sufficient reasons for wanting the lawless Trust Buster and any possible successor out of office. In addition to a luxuriously furnished observation car, from which the General and George could address the adoring multitudes across the country, there was a private car for the Lushmores, one for us, two dining cars, a press car, several baggage cars, to accommodate the mountains of luggage necessary for such a journey, and—to my great surprise—Bubber's *own* private car! (Since the question of our inheritance had finally been settled, Pappa-daddy, Clytie, Bubber, and I each had equal fortunes, and how like extravagant Bubber to squander so much of his on a railway car containing living, dining, and sleeping quarters, as well as a bar.)

As I was loath to be parted from my precious Alice, I spoke to her headmistress, Miss Beaufort, about the advisability of having my little girl miss so much of her schooling in order to accompany us. Alice was getting on to college age, and I nurtured private dreams of Vassar, Wellesley, Radcliffe, or Smith. However, Miss Beaufort assured me that Alice would certainly get more out of so long and comprehensive a trip than she ever had from school. "After all," as she said, "travel *is* broadening." The other constant companion I refused to leave behind was Fluffy. Although he had been a dear little ball of fur no bigger than a man's hand when Clytie handed him to me at Ellis Island, Fluffy had grown and grown until, at the time of the campaign, he weighed one hundred and seventy-five pounds and consumed more than five pounds of meat a day! Bubber said that both Fluffy and Alice were a good idea to impress the Lushmore-Butterfield image on the minds of the voters, as no one who had ever seen either could forget them.

Our train set out on a steaming day in August with the bands of the Police Department and the Fire Department playing and with the entire citizenry of the town turned out to bid farewell. ("We hope it's forever," many said, showing the great faith they had in our ultimate victory.) General Lushmore and George each delivered long and stirring speeches from the rear platform. It was gala. However, I was in for a rude jolt. If I had been surprised by Bubber's private car, I was *horrified* by what was *in it*—Gladys Goldfoil!

"George," I said firmly as we rolled northward through the scorching countryside, "with Alice on board it is your duty as a father to go to Bubber's car and demand that he remove that woman." Reluctantly, George went to do my bidding, and he was gone for hours. At the first stop, he still had not reappeared. I watched from a window of the observation car, fully expecting that Miss Goldfoil would be put off the train, but I saw nothing. In the meantime, General Lushmore spoke stirringly to the crowds. As the Atlanta Limited was due to come racing through at any minute, the train moved unceremoniously on with General Lushmore still speaking. A hideous accident was narrowly averted.

An hour passed, two hours, and still no sign of George. Dinner was announced, and Alice and I dined in lonely splendor, the silver and crystal jingling rhythmically at the empty place set for my husband. Several more hours passed, and still George did not put in an appearance. Not wishing to create an incident, I did not ask the porter to fetch him from Bubber's car, but when we reached Chattanooga, Tennessee (one of the South's leading consumers of Lohocla), where we were to stop, be interviewed by the press, attend a reception given by the Chattanooga Bullfinch Party, and spend the night, and where General Lushmore and George were to speak at a citizens' rally the following morning, I knew that something must be done.

La Goldfoil

Horribly conscious of Mrs. Lushmore's even gaze, I excused myself and strolled forward to Bubber's private car at the very front of the train. It necessitated passing through the noisy press car, where many of the journalists had obviously had a drop too much to drink, and I was sorely embarrassed. But when I reached Bubber's car, the sight that greeted me nearly broke my heart. Instead of having sent that Goldfoil creature packing, George, in his shirtsleeves, was seated next to her on a divan drinking champagne, laughing at her lewd jokes, and giving every evidence of having already consumed far more than was good for him! Summoning all the dignity at my disposal, I helped George into his coat and tried to assist him back to our own car, explaining lamely to the gentlemen of the press that Mr. Butterfield had got hold of a bit of bad fish. (Dinner that night had been leg of lamb!) He was unable either to be interviewed by the Chattanooga papers or to attend the Bullfinch reception. And when, the next morning, I asked if Miss Goldfoil was planning to leave the campaign train at Chattanooga, he explained that she had been given a run-of-the-campaign contract as Bubber's secretary, and would be a permanent part of the entourage!

Thus my troubles began.

Life at best was difficult enough, being on display during every waking hour; answering the questions of reporters; changing from one costume to another; shaking hands and making conversation with hundreds—nay, thousands—of strangers; moving from railroad car to strange hotel suite, and from hotel suite back to railroad car, at all times of day and night; sitting erect and uncomfortable on platforms in the blaze of limelight; eating heavy meals at countless banquet tables; and constantly smiling, smiling, smiling whether I meant it or not. Alas, many times I did not. The Goldfoil creature, cocksure and cheeky now that she was certain of her position, became more and more forward, presuming to call me "Marty" —of all things!—and even making herself and her reeking cigars welcome in my private car! As for keeping my innocent baby Alice free from the contamination of this trollop, it was impossible. "Kid," Miss Goldfoil would say to her, "there's nothing wrong with you that a little rouge and a pair of gay deceivers couldn't cure."

At one time, when Amaranthine Lushmore and I were guests of honor at an important luncheon given by the wives of leaders of the Bullfinch Party in Chicago, I returned to our rooms in the Palmer House to find my baby Alice tightly corseted, dressed in a cloth-of-gold negligee, painted like a harlot, and *smoking a cigarette!* My heart nearly stopped beating. It was the work of none other than Miss Goldfoil! But when George returned from the Bullfinch smoker, where General Lushmore had spoken for three hours, and I pointed out the disgraceful sight of our little girl in her tawdry paint and tinsel, George simply said, "She looks a lot better," and *poured himself a drink of whiskey* right before his wife and daughter!

August faded into September and September into October, and still the campaign train charged onward. It was in San Francisco, where the blow fell. Alice and I had just returned to our hotel from a tour of the city, marvelling at how quickly that valiant town, just two years earlier razed by earthquake and fire, had sprung back to lusty life. I was in a hurry to change into a splendid new gown for an important reception to be held in our honor, on Nob Hill, in but an hour's time. I hurried into my bedroom, where my new creation was carefully laid out on my bed. Pinned to its bosom was a plain envelope addressed to "Mrs. Butterfield."

Mystified, I opened it and read a note carefully printed in a painstakingly disguised hand:

YOU FOOL CANT YOU SEE THAT YOUR NOGOOD HUSBAND
IS FOOLING AROUND WITH THAT BLOND CHIPPY!
A FRIEND.

Campaigning

I felt as though I were going to faint. Brave are the anonymous, but who could it be? I read the note again and again, and, clad only in my corset cover, I was still holding it when Mrs. Lushmore let herself into my bedroom. "A note from an admirer, Martha?" she asked, her green eyes glittering.

"Yes, yes. That's what it is," I said, trying to laugh at her witticism. "From a friend."

"Well, get a move on. Would you like me to hook you up the back?"

How I got through that reception or the dinner that followed or the political rally that was held after that, I shall never know, moving, smiling, and speaking mechanically with no idea or no recollection of what I said.

After I had undressed that night and brushed my hair, I decided to confront George with the note still warm from my bosom, still damp from my tears. Hesitantly, I knocked at his bedroom door. (Because of the extreme irregularity of his hours during the campaign tour, George had suggested separate bedrooms so that my sleep would not be disturbed.) There was no reply. I opened the door timidly. The room was empty. That night and every night afterward for the rest of the trip, there was no rest for me. Could it be true, or was this merely the work of a malicious prankster? It was many months before I would know for sure.

But this was not the only heartbreaking occurrence of the nationwide tour. On our way back from the farthest western point, and still stopping at every town and village along the railroad tracks, poor young Alice grew decidedly restive. And who could blame her? She was, after all, still just a girl, and two months cooped up on a private train and in various hotels, with no one of her own age to amuse her, had begun to tell. Alice longed for action, and just as we were approaching Kansas City, she decided that the one thing she wanted to do most was go forward to the locomotive and visit the engineer, with whom she had sometimes whiled away the waits at various railway stations along our circuitous route.

The engineer greeted Alice and me and, to my amazement, even consented, after much pleading and teasing on the girl's part, to let her take the throttle and "drive" the campaign train for a few minutes before we reached Kansas City.

"But is it safe?" I inquired.

"Surest thing in the world, ma'am," he assured me. "An idiot could run this train. That's why I'm lettin' the girl, here, do it."

With a squeal of joy, Alice took over the controls while the engineer explained the various mystifying knobs and buttons and gauges to her.

But before I knew what was happening, the train started to gain speed. Faster and faster we went, Alice laughing wildly as she pulled the whistle cord and clanged the bell.

"Hey, there," the engineer said, "not so fast." But when he tried to undo whatever it was that Alice had done, he found that something had jammed.

"Alice, darling!" I cried.

"Faster! Faster!" Alice shouted.

"Don't panic, ma'am," the engineer said. Then he yelled, "Oh, my God! Jump!" It was too late. The air was rent by a terrible screaming of iron and steel. I reached out for Alice, grabbing her plump little hand. I felt the strange sensations of coldness and wetness and blackness, and the next thing I knew both Alice and I had bobbed to the surface of the Missouri River. Somehow, Alice had managed to run the whole train off the track! The result was pandemonium.

There was but one victim—that splendid, patrician Southern lady and my dear, dear friend, Amaranthine Glottis Lushmore! Her lifeless body was dredged up the following day, the jewel box belonging to Gladys

Goldfoil—of all things!—clutched to her breast. Totally unhinged by the shock, I was put to bed for several days.

Bubber, however, was his usual cheerful self. He assured me that the whole train had been insured and that the dreadful accident had won more notice for the Bullfinch Party than the entire tour had. He also added that sympathy for General Lushmore's bereavement might even win a few votes. Somehow, though, it did not seem adequate reward to me for the loss of so splendid a noblewoman as Mrs. Lushmore.

Back home in my bedroom at Dinwiddiewood, where I was sent for a brief convalescence, I had ample opportunity to study the newspapers from every part of the nation. Oh, the low, vile tricks the opposing parties resorted to! There were vicious cartoons depicting General Lushmore as a marionette being controlled by a monster whose features closely resembled Pappa-daddy's. There were unfair stories—surprisingly accurate in their factual content—listing the exact contributions to the Bullfinch Party made by the corporation and by other influential men ("big bosses," as they were called). George was mercilessly ridiculed and caricatured, and there were even cartoons of Bubber, innocent little Alice, and me! The unfairness of it! The entire press seemed to be against us, and—most insulting of all—certain papers such as the New York *Times* did not even

see fit to take the Bullfinch Party seriously, lumping it with such minor organizations as the Socialists, the Prohibition Party, the Vegetarians, and other political nonentities.

But the show must go on, as they say, and, sick in both body and spirit, I left my bed and somehow staggered onward.

General Lushmore, far from broken by his wife's untimely passing, seemed almost inspired by the tragedy, and spoke extemporaneously for sometimes as long as four and five hours at a time.

Having read all of the newspapers available during my convalescence, I had but little faith that the Bullfinch Party would make any showing at all, but then I had not put sufficient faith in my young brother.

Finally, Election Day dawned, bleak and rainy. We had done all that we could; there was nothing to do but wait. However, there was one last thing that I could do to prove my love for my husband and for freedom. As Bubber was in New York City, I would vote *in his place!* Mine was the last vote cast in Pellagra, but it was the *first* female vote ever cast in the United States. Waiting until dark, when the polls were just about to close, I put on one of Bubber's more subdued suits, tucked my hair up under his bowler hat, pencilled a mustache on my upper lip, and, wrapped in his voluminous Inverness cape, went to the polling place and claimed to be John Sappington Marmaduke Dinwiddie. Keeping my head lowered, I went into the voting booth, voted straight Bullfinch Party, and hurried out, followed by a low whistle.

I was fully prepared for a quick and ignominious defeat. What I was *not* prepared for was the hideous period of waiting. In those days, there were no magical machines to foretell the fate of an election. Votes had to be gathered and counted by hand, and then the totals telegraphed to the Electors.

I went to bed on the night of the election convinced that I would awaken to the news of disaster. Instead, on the following morning word of the election was still incomplete. No one seemed to be leading. The next day and the next and the next, the news was the same—nothing. It was unheard-of in the history of American politics. The Electoral College was at a loss to explain such a delay, and then, bit by bit, the rumor began to spread—*the entire New York City vote was missing!* It was true. What had happened to the millions of votes cast by New Yorkers, no one could say. They had simply disappeared. And then, at midnight on the sixth day, the word reached us. Miracle of miracles, *we had won!* Won by a hair's breadth, perhaps, but the Bullfinch Party had been victorious!

George and a loyal group of Bullfinch Party members rushed to the humble home of General Lushmore to notify him that he had become President of the United States. Bubber and George rang the old-fashioned doorbell many, many times. (General Lushmore was elderly, and quite hard of hearing.) Finally, the old gentleman appeared in his nightshirt, half asleep and quite bewildered. After he had opened the door to them, a great cheer went up that he could not avoid hearing. Then Bubber stepped forward and shouted, "General Lushmore, it is my honor, sir, to inform you that you have just been elected President of the United States!" So deaf was the General that Bubber had to repeat his message again. Then, losing patience, Bubber wrote it down on a slip of paper and handed it to him. The General took one look. His hand flew to his heart, and, letting out a terrible cry, he died of shock.[2]

This, too, was unknown in the annals of American history, but one thing, and one thing only, was clear—the Bullfinch Party had won the election, and the Vice-President-elect, George Washington Butterfield, replacing the late President-elect, Lucian Lushmore, was the future President of the United States! My husband was to be our next President, and I would be First Lady of the Land!

---

[2] Had General Lushmore survived, he would have been our only President with twelve toes. P.D.

Dancing for joy (with my sweetheart)

XIII

Preparing for the White House

1908–09

*Many moods. . . . Clytie. . . . I travel to Washington incognito.
. . . Archie Butt. . . . Mrs. Roosevelt's unspeakable rudeness. . . .
Rebuffed at the White House. . . . I acquire a Press Secretary.
. . . A strange encounter with Gladys Goldfoil. . . . George's
mysterious appearance. . . . The Butterfield Cabinet is formed.
. . . Secret plans of my own. . . . Preparing Alice. . . . My offi-
cial portrait. . . . Waiting.*

fter the shock of that anonymous letter suggesting George's un-
faithfulness (its author will always remain a mystery), after the
shock of the dreadful railway accident, after the shock of victory,
after the shock of dear General Lushmore's sudden death, after the shock
of realizing that George, Alice, and I constituted the First Family of the
Nation, I was—to put it mildly—in a state of shock.

During the first few hectic days, when our doorbell and telephone were
never silent, when we were beleaguered by the press, inundated with
congratulatory letters and telegrams from all over the world, I was too
stunned, too swept up in the whirlpool of activity to sit down quietly and
take stock of what had happened to us—to *me*. But after the initial
frenzy had died down sufficiently for me to have some few moments to
myself, I began to consider the immediate past and the immediate future,

and both depressed me. On the one hand, there were the hundreds of cruel cartoons and articles that—before the surprising outcome of the election—had shown us in the most unflattering light, holding us up to ridicule as bumpkins, know-nothings, parvenus, and political opportunists at best. At worst, we were treated like common criminals or ignored entirely. But now reporters from the very periodicals that had made such sport of us and our close-knit family life, our simple Southern ways, were fawning upon us, begging for exclusive interviews, hanging on my every word when they asked such questions as how it felt to be the President's wife, what I planned to do in the White House, whom I would choose to entertain, and so on. And yet when these interviews were printed word for word, they reflected nothing of my sincere replies to the reporters' questions, but were almost a mockery of the things I had actually said. Nor did the many interviews granted by George seem entirely friendly. Instead, they exuded a quality of "wait and see."

As for the letters, there were thousands of them—mostly from people I did not know and many from people I did not know knew *me*—all asking favors. Mildred Eubanks, whose husband, Wade, had so vilified my George before, during, and after his mayoralty of Pellagra, reminded me that she was "one of my closest friends," that she would love to visit me in Washington, and that Wade, with his many years of political experience, was highly qualified for any number of appointive posts! Dressmakers, hairdressers, photographers, furriers, jewelers, all deluged me with their letters—some even sending representatives to camp on the doorstep of Dinwiddiewood. Everyone wanted something, and I was sorely distressed—happy because of my husband's victory and yet miserable because of the clutter of fair-weather friends, importuning for my favors.

Finally, I received a letter from darling Clytie—the first in years—which helped me no end. A sister always understands. It was written with violet ink on her lovely lavender writing paper, embossed with the Przyzplätcki crest and scented with Violette du Parme.

Paris
12 *Novembre,* 1908

Ma chérie—
Je suis dans un orgasme de joie at the amazing news! Georges Butterfield President of *les Etats Unis! Zut, alors!* Who could ever believe it? All Paris is in an uproar over *les élections Américaines,* and even now so many *arrivistes* are all but butting down *les portes* of my *appartement,*

trying to get in with the sister-in-law of the new President. Social climbers! One must beware of them.

If only I could be by your side to point out the ones worth cultivating and those who ought to get the bum's rush. *Mais, malheureusement,* I have promised to spend the long *vacance du Noël* with Friedl and Otto von Achtung-Mecklinberg (*she* was a von Fuerstenberg and *he* is a cousin of the Kaiser's). But the minute you're in the White House, I'll be there with you. I've had more experience *du monde* even though I'm so much younger.

And now that Georges is really President, could I have his and your photograph to put on the piano next to King Edward, *le Prince de Monaco,* and one or two other *copains intimes? Tous les deux ensemble avec une dédicace*—making it very clear that we're sisters. It is all I ask for Christmas, *mon Ange.*

Au revoir, au revoir, ma sœur, je t'embrace de tout mon cœur et t'aime tendrement.

Clytie

P.S. Until I can get there to run things and tell you what to say and who to, you better find somebody who can. *Bons baises.*

C.

Darling Clytie! How well she saw the problems ahead of me.

After the hectic pace of the political campaign, the tense days of waiting, the whole distasteful dog-eat-dog existence of sordid party politics, I looked forward to four years—and more likely eight—of peace, prosperity, and gracious living in our nation's Executive Mansion. Instead of turning the White House into a place of roughhousing, into something little better than a prize fighters' gymnasium (T.R. was forever entertaining men like John L. Sullivan and Jake Kilrain), I wanted to establish a residence of charm, culture, and taste.

Realizing that from now on my life would be radically different, I understood that I could not simply move into the White House naïve and unprepared. I would have to sniff out the territory and lay a bit of groundwork if I were to help George in my new role as Number One Hostess of the Nation. Therefore, right after New Year's Day, I went quietly and without fuss or fanfare to Washington, accompanied only by my faithful dog, Fluffy—the only one at that moment of torment and indecision I felt I could trust.

Heavily veiled, I went directly to the lovely new New Willard Hotel, Washington's most elegant hostelry, built but a few years previously by H. J. Hardenberg, the architect of New York's Plaza Hotel. Not wanting my presence in the capital to be known, I registered under the alias of "Mrs. George Smith," but I'm sorry to say that my disguise and use of an alias did very little good. I was immediately recognized by the manager, Frank Hight, who, like much of the Willard's staff, had been lured away from the Waldorf-Astoria, where I had so often stayed. Instead of being given the simple, single room I had asked for (with an extra cot for Fluffy), I was immediately put into the hotel's most elegant suite (where Fluffy had a room of his own), surrounded by flowers, petted, and made much of. Although my only wish was for privacy and secrecy, the information soon appeared in the "Heard in the Hotels" newspaper column that Mrs. George Butterfield, the future First Lady, was staying incognito at the New Willard, home of the Gridiron Club and headquarters of the Republican National Committee—the last people on earth who should have been informed of my presence in Washington!

Although Mr. Hight and the staff of the Willard did everything within their power to protect me from outside intrusion, I was soon beset by reporters, lobbyists, and the usual parasites seeking favors and positions for themselves. When I walked through Peacock Alley with Fluffy on his leash, every head turned, and whenever I ventured forth from my suite to lunch or dine in the Pompeian Room, even though I requested a table in a faraway dark corner, my presence was soon ferreted out by the curious, and I bolted down my meals in misery, conscious of the stares, whispers, and giggles surrounding me.

As the purpose of my mission to Washington was to look over the White House and decide what arrangements could and should be made for our tenure there, I tried many, many times to reach Captain Archibald Butt, who had been installed by the Theodore Roosevelts as a sort of major-domo, *chef du protocole,* and a buffer between the Presidential family and the outside world—most *undemocratic!* As "Mrs. George Smith" I got nowhere, and, after telephoning more than *thirty times* as Mrs. George Butterfield, I still was not permitted to speak to this "great man." Finally, I wrote a letter introducing myself, announcing my presence in Washington, and begging for an interview. The interview was granted more than a fortnight later and not *in* the Executive Mansion but, if you please, in the offices of a law firm in the business section! Ignoring this slight, I dressed in my loveliest and, with Fluffy on his new leash, put on my very best manners. Fluffy took an immediate dislike to Archie Butt, which should have warned me immediately. *Dogs always know!* However, I carried on my half of the interview with all the dignity of a true daughter of the gallant old Southland. I informed Captain Butt that I would like to look over the Presidential mansion, with an eye to entertaining there during my husband's term or terms of office. He was very vague and noncommittal about this. I also said that I would like to meet Mrs. Roosevelt and discuss with her some of the many problems confronting a President's wife when it came to entertaining, housekeeping, and so on. As to this, he seemed most dubious, explaining that Mrs. Roosevelt was very busy, that she had very little time to receive callers,

Archie Butt (and friend)

that she was often away from the city, etc., etc., etc. Lastly, I offered him the same position under the Butterfield administration at—thinking that there must be some way to get around this ungracious man—double whatever salary he was receiving as steward to the Roosevelts. At this, he rose to his feet, said that he had other plans, and ended the rendezvous, pleading a previous engagement. That was the first and last time I ever saw the man, but if he was the sort of representative the Roosevelts chose, I don't wonder that they were so unpopular!

Not knowing how to cope with the rudeness of these yankee[1] Republicans, I decided to throw myself on the mercy of Edith Carow Roosevelt. Another woman always understands, and even though I had nothing but hatred in my heart for the Communistic T.R., I felt no rancor against his poor, long-suffering wife—*then*. At any rate, I wrote to Mrs. Roosevelt announcing—not asking—that I was coming to tea on the following afternoon to look over the premises and to discuss with her the attendant problems. This note I sent to the White House by the hotel's most trusted courier.

The following afternoon, again dressed to the nines, I descended upon the White House only to find an endless queue of the most common women waiting at the gate. Marching to the front of the line, I announced myself to the Irish guard.

"Get to the end of the line, sister," he said harshly.

Patiently, I explained to him that I had come to take tea with Mrs. Roosevelt, and the uncouth man laughed in my face. "Sure and I'll be going along to drink a beer with the King of England as soon as I'm off duty. Get to the back of the line."

At this, the uncouth collection of women began hooting and jeering at me—*me,* the future First Lady!

"My good man," I said coldly, "I will have you know that I am Mrs. George Washington Butterfield, the wife of your next President." The vulgar harpies waiting on line shrieked derisively.

"Oh, is that so, Mrs. Butterfingers?" he said. "Well, in that case, just let me make a quick tellyphone call, and I'm sure you'll be taken right to where you belong."

"Butter-*field*," I said, correcting his ignorance.

He disappeared into his little sentry box and was gone for a few moments. When he came back again, his manner was entirely different. "If

---

[1] Archie Butt was a native of Augusta, Georgia.   P.D.

Spurned

you'll wait here for just a moment, your royal highness," he said, "you'll be taken care of."

I was somewhat mollified, but not enough to forgive his rude manner. When I was mistress of the White House, no visitor—be it emperor or commoner—would be treated with such lack of respect. "Like Archie Butt," I said pointedly, *"you* must have other plans for employment during the next administration also."

"Oh, sure and I do, Miss Buttermilk. Archie and me is going to open a saloon together."

"Where you *both* belong," I said, getting in the last word.

At that moment, there was a clanging of bells. Before I knew what was happening, two policemen grabbed me and I was thrust into a patrol wagon and hustled off to the common *jail,* where they treated me as a lunatic! It was several hours before I could make my true identity known.

When I finally returned to the Willard (more dead than alive, cold, hungry, and frightfully bedraggled), screams of laughter went up as I made my way across the lobby. The story of my fearful encounter was on the front page of every newspaper.

So distraught was I that neither could I eat nor sleep. Rising, I got out darling Clytie's letter and reread it. The postscript was most edifying— "Until I can get there to run things and tell you what to say and who to, you better find somebody who can." How right Clytie was—as always.

It was through following her advice that I found the first First Lady's Press Secretary, who has been my close friend and adviser ever since.

But where to find such a paragon to guide me safely past the shoals and reefs of social and political intrigue? I did not even know, in my naïveté, what to call such an employee or what his or her salary or title should be. I decided, first of all, that I wanted a man, as I have always enjoyed leaning on men of the strength and wisdom of George, Pappa-daddy, or Bubber to guide an innocent such as I and also because I felt that a woman's place was really in the home and not out competing with the stronger sex.

Not knowing exactly what I did want or what to call him or how to find him, I placed a carefully worded advertisement in all the Washington newspapers:

> Prominent lady in public life desires male
> companion and adviser. Experience essential.

Perhaps my niche should have been in the hectic world of advertising, for I was simply *deluged* with men! But a great many of them had misunderstood my requirements *entirely*. Thank heavens for Fluffy! Without that loyal watchdog to protect me, I don't know what some of the applicants would not have tried in their disgusting attempts to impress me.

Finally, however, I received a letter from a Mr. Dennis that gave some indication of understanding what I had had in mind. Mr. Dennis had been a writer of sorts. He had also managed the social career of a Chicago meat packer's wife, who shall be nameless, and as the woman was known to me and was a fellow-expatriate and acquaintance of Clytie's, I granted him an interview. We hit it off beautifully from the very first, but what pleased me most about this sympathetic young man was the way Fluffy took to him. My dog simply would not leave Mr. Dennis alone during the whole interview, and so affectionate did Fluffy become that I had to lock him in an adjoining room so as not to embarrass both of us. Dogs always know, and it was largely because of Fluffy's obvious devotion that I chose Mr. Dennis from the many applicants. It was not until some years later that Mr. Dennis, who himself suggested the title of "Press Secretary," told me that the reason for Fluffy's overwhelming affection was that Mr. Dennis had been carrying a liverwurst sandwich in his trousers pocket! Anyhow, we became an unbeatable team.

What a change and what a relief it was for me to have someone to look out for my interests and to protect me from the harsh blows of an envious world. I noticed how much easier was my lot on the very first day. Arriving at my suite early that morning, my Press Secretary was able to drop ninety per cent of my mail into the wastebasket unread and unacknowledged by me, whereas I would have wasted half the morning pondering over each letter and answering it. He wrote a short, polite note to the I.W.W., stating that illness prevented me from leading their march on the Cleveland Lohocla plant, and explained patiently to me that I.W.W. stood for Industrial Workers of the World (the "I Won't Works"!) a dangerous Communistic organization, and not, as I had thought, the International Women Writers, a group of poetesses, the Southern chapter of which had once picnicked on the lawn of Dinwiddiewood. What a *gaffe!*

Before the day was finished, he had prepared a statement to the press for me on war and peace. I was to be, he said, *against* war and *for* peace. I began to dictate a few letters to him, but he stopped me in the middle of the first one and said that *he* would answer the letters for me, and that all I would need to do was to sign them. Such a relief! I spent the rest of the morning playing with Fluffy while my new Press Secretary dashed off my correspondence succinctly and tactfully, expressing my opinions on national and international matters in a way that would create no trouble.

"How wonderful it is to have you," I said as he left for the day. "Now I don't have to think before I say anything."

"That is as always, Mrs. Butterfield," he replied.

"Ah, but, Mr. Dennis, you give my every pronouncement a certain *je ne sais quoi.* I don't know what it is you add."

"Just basic horse sense and a modicum of intelligence," he said modestly.

"Flatterer," I said, wagging a finger at him. It was such a joy to have a *friend* in Washington—someone who understood my every thought, no matter how deep, and could express it for me far more beautifully than I could myself. It was amazing!

In addition to handling my relations with the press and creating what Bubber had mystifyingly called "public image," Mr. Dennis was invaluable at helping me plan for the day—now drawing nearer and nearer—when I would be chatelaine of the White House. What plans I had! I would be the new Dolley Madison, bringing to our doorstep all the great, the gifted of the earth to sample some real Southern hospitality.

Theodore Roosevelt did not care for the social life and preferred to entertain in the afternoons, health faddist that he was, so as not to interrupt his night's sleep. I decided that the Butterfield administration would entertain morning, noon, *and* night. Nor would I have the place cluttered up with old Roughriders, athletes, and popular authors. In their stead, I would introduce to the nation the leaders of society and culture, surrounded by settings of lasting beauty.

Totally unable to gain admittance to the White House and yet anxious to get some idea of its facilities, I purchased a telescope and set off with my Press Secretary one bleak, rainy afternoon to observe its rooms as best I could from the steps of the neighboring State Department Building. I was just remarking to Mr. Dennis on how tackily I thought Mrs. Roosevelt had done it over, during the White House restoration of 1902, when I heard a sharp click and discovered that I had been photographed in the very act of spying on my predecessors! I was scarlet with embarrassment, and ready to take to my heels, when I heard Mr. Dennis suavely explaining to the nosy newsman who had photographed us that I was a gifted amateur ornithologist, and planned to build a bird sanctuary on the White House lawn as soon as I moved in. Wasn't that clever? He turned a disaster into an advantage. Audubon Societies and independent bird-watchers from all over the country wrote the most enthusiastic letters to me—many of them pointing out that it would be a pleasure to have the White House occupied by someone who wished to *preserve* wildlife after a tenant who had done so much to destroy it. Needless to say, word of this wave of pro-Butterfield feeling "leaked" out to the national press through the discreet offices of Mr. Dennis. He also explained that like most of the announced intentions of Presidential families, this one could be quickly forgotten by me and would be even more quickly forgotten by bird-lovers of the nation once my husband started dealing with matters that concerned human beings.

In the afternoons, once my ever-growing correspondence was out of the way, my Press Secretary and I planned the gala entertainments that would take place almost nightly after I had installed my little family at

the nation's Number One address. Mr. Dennis lost no time in writing to such international celebrities as Anna Pavlova, Sarah Bernhardt, Moonyeen Mulligan the Irish Mudlark, Enrico Caruso, Julian Eltinge, Paderewski, Adelina Patti, and others, asking them to entertain on certain nights at their usual honoraria. In addition, I wrote charming letters of invitation to the crowned heads of Europe—Edward and Alexandra, Franz Josef, the Kaiser and Kaiserin, the Czar and Czarina and many others—asking them to come and stay at the White House.

I had been gone from home for more than a month, which, as I know now, is too long for a wife to be separated from her husband. Although I had written to George every day, he had been too busy to reply—that did not surprise me. What *did* surprise me, however, was the following:

Having studied photographs of the White House as redecorated by the Theodore Roosevelts, I felt there were many, many rooms that needed changing—all the rooms, in fact. I had been consulting in my suite at the New Willard with a gifted young interior designer, for the greater part of the afternoon, about doing over the public rooms as my surprise gift to the nation, and together we had reached some very dramatic conclusions. He was anxious to get to his drawing board and produce colored renderings for my approval, and so I let him out and paused for a moment in the open doorway to bid my adieux. As I did so, the door opposite opened and who should be standing there but Gladys Goldfoil! The musky scent, the reek of her cigar, the garishness of her costume all but made me reel. She seemed stunned to see me, too. However, she was the first to recover her speech. "Who's your friend, Marty," she asked impertinently, "Vesta Tilly?"

"Good afternoon, Cecil," I said to this truly gifted decorator. "I shall expect to see the sketches later in the week." Almost imperceptibly nodding to Miss Goldfoil, I was about to go back into my suite when I saw coming along the corridor none other than George.

"George!" I cried. "Darling, this is a surprise!"

"Surprise is right," the crass Miss Goldfoil said, and slammed back into her room.

George was almost as overcome by our reunion as I was, and gave the impression of being distant and distrait for much of the evening, but, naturally, I understood that he had a great deal—indeed, the problems of rebuilding our entire nation—on his mind. After I had changed into an exquisite dinner gown (one of many startling creations that I had ordered for important White House functions), we dined *à deux* in the Pompeian

Room, and *this* time I chose not a dimly lighted table hidden away in a corner but a table in the very center of the room, right beneath the brightest chandelier of all! How much I had learned from my Press Secretary! Instead of skulking into the room with lowered eyes, afraid to be seen, I strode in majestically on the arm of my beloved husband, my head held high and looking neither to right nor left. Owing to a badly placed chair, I tripped and turned my ankle quite painfully, but I doubt that anyone noticed. The room was all eyes, and this time I was proud to hear the buzzing of "Butterfield, Butterfield, Butterfield" as the head-waiter, bowing low, took our order.

George, it seems, had come unexpectedly to Washington to form his Cabinet. Under the Roosevelt administration, this august body had been woefully inadequate, comprised of but a handful of administrators—eight in all. It was George's plan to enlarge the Cabinet enormously. "A lot of obligations to pay off," he said. I was that proud of his executive ability!

The new Secretary of State was to be Bubber. I felt that this was a wise step, in that Bubber was so tactful and diplomatic and had such a splendid wardrobe for that lofty post. Pappa-daddy had been consulted and offered the position, but he refused, saying, "After all the money I sunk into the campaign, I'd prefer to be Secretary of the Treasury." And so he was appointed to that secondary post, which, in all modesty, he had chosen, leaving the more illustrious position of Secretary of State open for his beloved son. How like selfless Pappa-daddy! Personally, I would have preferred to see my father appointed Chief Justice of the Supreme Court, a position more fitting to his age and great dignity. Unfortunately, there were no vacancies on the Supreme Court at that time, and *my* husband, unlike certain subsequent Presidents whom I could but will not name, was above "packing" the highest tribunal in the land. Zachary Taylor Butterfield, who had always been an ardent philatelist, was given the Postmaster Generalship and the twins, "J.P." and "J.Q.," the positions of Secretary of the Army and Secretary of the Navy, respectively. Just so there wouldn't be too many Butterfields in the Cabinet, thus confusing the public, the embassies in London, Paris, Madrid, Berlin, Vienna, Rome, and St. Petersburg, were offered to—and quickly accepted by—George's other brothers.

The balance of the positions in the Cabinet were given to loyal workers and supporters of the Bullfinch Party. What a team they were! As H. L. Mencken wrote, in the Baltimore *Sun,* "Captain Kidd himself could not have picked a better crew."

George was always a glutton for work. On that first night when we were together again in Washington, I mentioned retiring just as the clock on the drawing-room mantel was striking eleven. But not my George! "That's a good idea, Martha," he said. "You need sleep. Me, I've gotta do a little more work on the diplomatic front. See you in the morning." Without even taking his hat or coat—although the night was bitter—he was gone. I was disappointed, of course, but I understood that George was in full command of the ship of state. It was nearly seven the next morning when Fluffy's furious barking awakened me, and George returned from his all-night session. The poor darling! For the rest of the time we were waiting to move into the White House, he was out working every night but, I am happy to say, showing the wise precaution of taking his hat and coat.

As to my "neighbor," Miss Gladys Goldfoil, she at least had the taste to move to different quarters the day after our first and only encounter. Not even the twelve-story New Willard Hotel was large enough to hold the two of us!

The new First Family was now complete all but for little Alice. How Fluffy and I missed her! (Her father, too, of course, although he was much too occupied with affairs of state to say so.) With only a few weeks left until March 4th—"moving day"—it seemed silly for her to be pining away all alone, save for Pappa-daddy and Mammy, back in Pellagra. Therefore, I instructed Mr. Dennis to write to her headmistress, Miss Beaufort, saying that as long as Alice would be transferring schools very soon anyway, didn't Miss Beaufort think that Alice might just as well come to Washington a little ahead of time, so that she might investigate Madeira, Mount Vernon Seminary, and one or two other exclusive girls' schools in and convenient to the District. Miss Beaufort replied by return mail saying, to my surprise and delight, that Alice had absorbed about all the learning she was going to and that it might be better if she gave up school altogether. (Say what one will in favor of public education—and, naturally, I am all for it—there is nothing quite like a first-rate private school under the guidance of a sympathetic headmistress or headmaster.) The very next week Alice was in Washington.

Girls—especially in the South—mature so rapidly. It seemed that I had left behind a child, and now, but a few weeks later, I was accosted by an almost fully grown woman, all but bursting out of her demure Peter Thompson outfits. "Isn't she stunning!" I said to my Press Secretary. He agreed wholeheartedly. "In the truest sense of the word," he said. He added that surely something could be done for her.

Seeing my tiny baby now as a fresh and lovely young woman, a thought occurred to me. For the past seven years, the nation had been plagued with the unladylike hijinks of Alice Roosevelt—she even had a color named for her[2]—culminating with her ostentatious wedding in 1906, in the East Room of the White House, when she became Mrs. Nicholas Longworth. If Alice Roosevelt could be the darling of the nation, why not Alice Butterfield? After all, my daughter had grace, beauty, breeding, charm, and talent; she was nearly of the age to make her début to society and, thinking back on my own brilliant season in New York, what better way to establish the Butterfield family in the hearts of the nation than to present Alice at a ball in the White House, as Mrs. Roosevelt had presented her Alice and Ethel?

Consulting with Mr. Dennis, he said that it was just possible. He could slip Alice's début into one of our few free evenings without too much difficulty. But, he added, the real onus would fall upon Mr. Alexander, the Official Photographer. Mr. Alexander, who was at that time engaged in setting up his studio in Washington, said that with candlelight, soft focus, and the use of "illusion" veils, Alice could probably be photographed to the best advantage, although the greatest challenge would arise in the darkroom. These were all technical terms about which I knew or cared nothing. "Then let's go!" I said with gusto. However, both gentlemen were adamant about giving Alice a certain amount of advance preparation. Mr. Dennis suggested a charm school, where walking, talking, dancing, eurythmics, and general aids to poise were taught quickly. Mr. Alexander suggested a surgeon in Paris, but there hardly seemed time for anything quite so drastic.

And so we began—more like sisters than like mother and daughter—giving every free moment to preparing for the time when the eyes of the nation would be glued upon us. Mr. Alexander stated that Alice would have to remove at least twelve inches from her waistline, and with that goal firmly in mind all of her dresses for the White House were made accordingly. I, too, wanted to be as svelte as possible, and a credit to George and the young Bullfinch Party. Therefore, we exercised and dieted stringently with Inauguration Day, March 4, 1909—now but a month off—as our target. In addition, Alice practiced her singing, danc-

---

[2] Alice blue. P.D.

ing, painting, and sculpting, and two Secret Service men were hired to keep her from popping into every confectionery she passed on the way to and from her exercises.

And so the glorious, fun-filled days of togetherness passed. As I sat for my official portrait, which I had envisioned hanging in the Blue Room,[3] I dreamed beautiful fantasies of the rich, exciting, the glamorous, the constructive new life that was to be ours—George's, Alice's, and mine— once we crossed the threshold of the White House. There was nothing to do now but wait.

[3] Mrs. Butterfield's official portrait came to light after more than four dacades, in the subbasement of the White House during the Truman restoration in 1950. It disappeared immediately thereafter and was not unearthed until Mrs. John F. Kennedy's search for important antiques in 1961. Scheduled to be restored, the portrait was inadvertently misaddressed and was not seen again until 1964, when Miss Alice Butterfield miraculously discovered it in a suburban branch of the Goodwill Industries. It hangs now in Mrs. Butterfield's suite at Bosky Dell Home for Senile and Disturbed, awaiting delivery instructions from the White House. Surely one of the most romantic of all stories of lost and found art treasures! P.D.

With Alice—preparing

Fittings, fittings, fittings

LEFT: *My official portrait
by Dame Edith Amelia Plunkett,* R.A.

ABOVE: *A cruel stab in the Hearst press*

XIV

A First Lady's First Day

1909

George's mysterious absence on Inauguration morn. . . . Inauguration in the teeth of a blizzard. . . . My triumphal drive to the White House. . . . Carried over the threshold. . . . My official reception. . . . George's mysterious disappearance. . . . A gala Inaugural Ball. . . . Gladys Goldfoil appears in my box! . . . George's mysterious disappearance. . . . A lonely night.

So excited was I on the eve of the Inauguration that I drank several glasses of warm milk, and still sleep would not come. Finally, at midnight, George took pity on me and gave me three pills, which he assured me would induce a sound, sound sleep. They achieved a miraculous result, and my head was no sooner back on my pillow than I felt my eyes grow heavy.

"Good night, sweet prince," I said to George. "Not coming to bed?"

"I'll read for a little while," he said. That was surprising, as George never picked up a book, and staunchly refused to read any letter longer than one page in length. Then I closed my eyes and all was blackness.

The following morning, I was all but pummelled awake by Alice, my Press Secretary, and the Official Photographer. It had been Mr. Alexander's brilliant idea to record the whole day of the First Family on film, thus anticipating *Life, Look,* and other magazines dealing in photographic reportage by more than a quarter of a century. When I finally forced my eyes open the room was bathed in an unearthly whitish light. A blizzard was whirling its gigantic flakes past my window. I gulped down a cup of coffee, Mr. Alexander clicked away with his camera under the special lights he had set up in my hotel suite. I blinked several times, ran a comb through my hair, and then suddenly realized that something was missing. George's bed was empty and obviously had not been slept in!

"Where is your daddy, dear?" I asked Alice.

"I don't know, Mummy," she said. "I've been up since six, and there hasn't been a sign of him." Poor little Alice was so excited that she could hardly sit still, and kept rushing to the mirror, preening in her first "grown-up" dress, which had been ordered especially for the Inauguration.

Mr. Alexander took several photographs of me in my peignoir, doing up my hair, eating my breakfast, selecting the dress I would wear for the great occasion, chatting calmly—*calmly,* I was nearly beside myself! —with Alice, and other more or less candid studies. But where could George be? With my heart like a lump of lead, I kept glancing at the little clock on the mantel. He had said nothing about going out, and as I had drifted off to sleep the night before, I had fully expected that he would join me as soon as he had accomplished whatever reading it was that he found so important. As the minutes first crept and then raced, a number of horrifying thoughts came into my mind. What if he had been kidnapped? From the way the Republicans and Democrats had acted toward the Bullfinch Party during the campaign, I would put nothing past them—not even murder! Could it be possible that a President would miss his own Inauguration?

Bubber appeared wearing a splendid morning suit, silk topper, and a coat lined with sable. With him was Pappa-daddy, looking only a little less magnificent. Neither of them had seen or heard from George. As the time for the procession drew nearer and nearer, I was ill with worry and anguish. Suddenly, just as I had given him up, George appeared in the same clothes he had been wearing the night before, looking haggard and bleary-eyed. There was no time for explanations. With Bubber to help him, he got into his morning coat and silk hat, grabbed up his speech, and pounded down the corridor to the carriage that was awaiting him.

The blizzard that was raging outside had now reached staggering proportions, with snow falling so thickly that one could hardly see across the street. However, with a good bit of slipping and sliding, of losing the way, and of being stuck in the heavy Washington traffic, our carriage finally fell into the procession and, after a long, slippery, hazardous ride, reached the reviewing stand.

As befits a young republic, the Inauguration ceremonies are notoriously short and simple. But through the pelting snows I could scarcely hear a word. A crowd was assembled to take in this historic event, but it seemed strangely hostile. This I put down to the freakish weather, and before I knew it, the Inauguration was over and we were back in our carriage for the triumphal procession to the White House. Caring naught for tradition, *former* President Roosevelt declined to ride back to the Executive Mansion in the carriage with George, and broke all precedent by going immediately from Inauguration platform to railway platform. A direct slap in the face, if ever there was one! However, T.R.'s unspeakable rudeness gave me the opportunity of being the first President's wife ever to ride directly to the White House at her husband's side. How proud I felt! The snows had let up momentarily, and I was able to see the throngs of people lining the curbs on both side of the street. George and I smiled and waved graciously, and the only untoward event that occurred was when a low urchin threw a large snowball, catching poor George full in the face.

With Mr. Alexander and his camera never far away, we mounted the steps of the White House all ready to take possession. Just as George was about to march in, I said, "Georgie, carry me over the threshold, please—like bride and groom."

This he proceeded to do, but the marble floor at the entrance was so wet and slushy from the many snowy feet that had passed over it that George lost his footing. He just barely managed to save himself, but I was dropped quite painfully on the great seal of our nation.

Luncheon was a hurry-up affair, comprised of just George, Alice, Bubber, Pappa-daddy, and me, in the Family Dining Room. We raced through it as though we had to catch a train, for a great reception was planned for that afternoon, and I wanted not only to rest and to change into a particularly memorable afternoon gown but also to tour my new place of residence and become really at home as soon as possible.

Again feeling like a bride in her first little nest, I said to my husband, "Georgie, dear, do come and explore our new home with Alice and me. It will be such fun now that the Roosevelts have gone." But George declined my invitation, although I was aching for him to come so I could explain how I had planned so many of the rooms to be completely transformed beginning the very next day. Pleading work, he went off in the direction of his office.

Together, Alice and I roamed the building so recently refurbished by the Roosevelts. "If you ask me," I said, "Mrs. Roosevelt's taste is all in her mouth." Alice went off into fits of giggles, and then, seeing the vast, empty East Room, asked to be excused.

Left alone, I wandered into the bedroom I would occupy for at least that first night—the room where Abraham Lincoln had slept. Suddenly overcome by languor, I stretched out on the bed and shut my eyes for just a moment. When I was awakened by one of the ushers, I discovered that they had allowed me to sleep until almost the last minute before the guests began to arrive for the Presidential reception.

I scrambled hastily into a sensational new dress, then searched high and low for George and Alice. Alice, bless her heart, had slipped out of her "grown-up" dress and was roller skating, of all things, in the East Room! Always a child at heart! As for George, he was nowhere to be found. Servants were dispatched all over the building, but there was no sign of the President. Once again he had simply vanished, and once again I had to undergo the long, tormenting waiting period. This I did in the Blue Room—mine, at last—but there was no pleasure in it without George at my side, and for the second time that day I had to endure

Alice—a child at heart

the torture of watching the hands of the clock—the lovely early Nineteenth Century French example presented to the White House by President Monroe—creep relentlessly forward. But from this agony of waiting there was no reprieve, no welcome sight of my beloved George rushing in at the last moment.

To my horror, what did appear were the earliest of more than two thousand guests who had been invited to our first reception in the White House. I had to go it alone. Naturally, there were loyal friends and loved ones to help me. Alice, Bubber, and Pappa-daddy were on hand. My Press Secretary gave me invaluable moral support, whispering, whenever he could, some intimate fact about each guest who was announced. Standing there in lonely splendor, an empty smile upon my lips, I wondered if the august flock of well-wishers knew of the anguish contained in my heart.

"And where is the President?" they would ask. "Oh, something very important has just come up that required his personal attention. . . . He'll be here immediately. . . . He had a slight twinge of indigestion and had to be excused. . . . Why, he's mingling with the other guests, haven't you seen him?" These were the gay, insincere replies that I invented. Finally, as the crowd began to thin and still there was no sign of George, I answered honestly and hopelessly, "I don't know where he is." What a beginning as *the* nation's hostess!

As soon as the last guest had made his farewells and the last soiled teacup was cleared from the mantels of the East Room, I excused myself, went again to Abraham Lincoln's bedroom, and, heedless of my gown, threw myself upon the counterpane and cried.

George arrived just as it was time to dress for the Inauguration Ball, and he was unmistakably intoxicated. "George!" I cried. "Where have you been?"

Giving me a sharp slap across the *derrière* (something he had *never* done before), he said brokenly, "Affairs of state, satchel. Big affairs!" With that, he dropped his elegant morning coat on the floor and wove to the bathroom. Picking up the coat, I saw the unmistakable traces of rouge upon one sleeve. There was a long yellow hair on one of the shoulders, and the whole garment smelled of cigar smoke and the heavy, musky scent that I could recognize at a hundred yards as belonging to no one but that vulgar adventuress, Gladys Goldfoil!

Again there was no time to remonstrate with my husband—to plead with him. The White House limousine was waiting at the door to trans-

Receiving

port George and me through the snow to the Bullfinch Inauguration Ball. Even in the car, separated by a sheet of glass from the ears of the chauffeur, I was not able to speak to George, as he was fast asleep, reeking of liquor!

"It's only the excitement that is doing this to him," I told myself. "He is too young. He started life with nothing, and in an unbelievably short time he achieved everything—me, a child, a fortune, and now the highest honor of all. It's simply too much for him to grasp all at once, but if I just give him a little time . . ." I tried so hard to convince myself that these comforting words were true, that as soon as the newness of George's situation wore off, everything would be beautiful as before.

The "Butterfield Brawl," as it was called, was the gayest, the most colorful, the most bacchanalian of all the Inaugural Balls in history—before *and* after. Even the rowdy routs of such *bons vivants* as Calvin Coolidge and Herbert Hoover were but pale and quiet affairs when compared to the Butterfield revels. Yet so benumbed was I by grief that I recall but little of it, and what I do remember of the evening contains no gaiety, no joy for me.

My Press Secretary circulated about, giving out typewritten descriptions of my gown, created especially for this gala evening and now gracing the Smithsonian Institution. The Official Photographer still hovered, as he had all day except for those few moments when I begged to be alone in order to cry my heart out in ignominious solitude. The guests of the ball—largely members of the victorious Bullfinch Party—all but stampeded us when we made our tardy appearance. The noise, the fawning, the adulation sickened me on this, *the* night of my life.

Although the company was distinguished and the *toilettes* brilliant, I can recall no specific detail of our entrance. When the noise died down, George—who could hardly stand—and I led off the grand march, and after he had staggered around the room twice, lurching and belching, piling insult on top of injury, we were led to the Presidential Box. Entering the box and approaching its rail, I was suddenly conscious of a great gasp arising from the multitude of guests at the ball. Could something have happened to my costume? Surreptitiously I fingered my necklace, my *décolletage,* my bracelets, glanced quickly down the front of my ball gown, touched my hair. Everything seemed in order. In a moment of panic, I thought of George and turned to see if—horror of horrors—he had collapsed. But no! Something even worse! Spinning around, I saw George entwined in the embrace of none other than Gladys Goldfoil

An uninvited guest

right in the box! What the guests could have thought I do not know. And what could they have felt for me, the faithful, loving wife who was being insulted publicly before an audience of thousands? Volleys of flash powder went off all over the gigantic hall as press photographers recorded my humiliation and George's disgrace for all the world to gloat and laugh over. Not even the fact that George sustained a severe burn from Miss Goldfoil's cigar gave me any comfort, any surcease from the agonies I endured. (Please bear in mind that all this took place before World War I, when morals and mores were far more rigid. Even today, such behavior on the part of the Chief Executive would hardly pass without comment.) There was nothing for me to do but withdraw as gracefully as I could.

With Miss Goldfoil monopolizing the Presidential Box, I gathered up my wrap and said, in as steady a voice as possible, "Excuse me. I have rather a headache. Will you see me home, George?"

"It's on Massachusetts Avenue," he said drunkenly. "You can't miss it." With that, he laughed boisterously.

"That's right, honey. Go soak your head," Miss Goldfoil bellowed, blowing an immense cloud of acrid cigar smoke into my face.

With hollow dignity, I made my way through the throng of merrymakers, some of them quite intoxicated, and all but collapsed into the limousine.

"No more pictures, please," I said to the Official Photographer as he scratched at the door of the Lincoln bedroom. But he, too, had drunk too deeply of the grain and the grape. There was a blinding flash as I reclined on the bed trying to undo my elaborate coiffure. Then I was alone—alone with none but Fluffy, to console me with his wet pink tongue—as I passed the first of many sleepless nights in the White House as First Lady of the Land.

A lonely night in Lincoln's bed

Nesting on Pennsylvania Avenue

1909

There'll be some changes made! . . . Installing Mammy as major-
domo of the White House. . . . My secret surprise. . . . Doing
things my way. . . . I bring Alice "out." . . . My gift to the
nation—a "new" White House. . . . The arbiter of taste.

n the morning after the Inauguration Ball, I could barely bring
myself to glance at the newspapers, but, gritting my teeth, read
them I did. The whole story of George's flagrant misconduct, accompanied by photographs, was on each and every front page.

Miss Gladys Goldfoil, being just the sort of common person who would
revel in sensationalism, had naturally capitalized on such undignified
publicity and, or so it was printed, had already been offered a starring role
in a touring musical extravaganza (little better than the most vulgar
burlesque show, if the truth were known) that was playing in Washington for a month prior to its New York engagement. Just how talented
Miss Goldfoil was as an actress, singer, or dancer was a matter of no importance. That she had once appeared in the "Follies" and was now touted
as the new President's "mistress" was apparently reason enough for star-
dom in the distasteful spectacle[1] that had employed her services to extend
its Washington engagement indefinitely.

---

[1] A musical comedy entitled "The Chicken Inspector." P.D.

Need I put into so many words what I, the President's lawfully wedded wife, was feeling? I breakfasted with Alice and my Press Secretary in the Family Dining Room. (George, although lord and master of the White House, had not deigned to return to it after the fiasco of the Inauguration Ball.) Except for the rattle of the morning newspapers—each printing a more scandalous account of the evening's occurrences than the last—we ate in silence. Alice, who was beginning a series of singing lessons with Signora Viola da Gamba (formerly of the chorus of the Metropolitan Opera Company), was excused and ran prattling from the room as though nothing had happened. Left alone with my mentor and confidant, I turned to him with welling eyes and said, "Tell me, pray, what are we to do now? After all our careful planning, the public image that you have created for George and me is shattered. I am today the deceived wife—a laughingstock or, at best, an object of pity and scorn. *Quo vadis,* Mr. Dennis, *quo vadis?*" [2]

"Mrs. Butterfield," he said to me, "you personally have nothing to fear. You conducted yourself as a true lady should have, and public sympathy will surely be on your side."

"Ah, but don't you understand?" I said. "I am not interested in the public's acceptance of *me*. I am not important. The President is. So is my marriage and my little family and the innocence of our little girl, Alice."

"As for Alice, Mrs. Butterfield, there is very little to worry about. She is

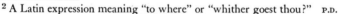

[2] A Latin expression meaning "to where" or "whither goest thou?" P.D.

One of Washington's loveliest monuments

not the most observant of young ladies, and I doubt very much that she even noticed what went on at the ball last night. In fact, she seemed quite taken with young Lord Lissom, who is a guest at the British Embassy. As for yourself, you are holding all the cards. Public sympathy is on your side. So are all the major weapons—*if* you choose to fight."

"Explain yourself," I said, at once fascinated.

"It is very simple. You are legally married to Mr. Butterfield, I believe. You are his wife, the mother of his child, and the First Lady."

"Yes, yes?" I said.

"Miss Goldfoil is an adventuress, your brother's castoff *como si chiamo,* without any legal claim, without position, and, I believe, quite without funds, save for what she has been able to—uh, wrest from the President and, before him, the Secretary of State.

"Therefore, it is up to you to continue to conduct yourself like a lady, quite above even noticing Miss Goldfoil's rather obvious intrusions. You have, after all, position, virtue, charm, breeding. . . ."

"Please, this is no time for flattery," I murmured, not entirely displeased.

"And, most important of all, *money.* With these weapons at your command, you can fight any adversary."

What my Press Secretary said was true. While George had risen a long way since our marriage, nearly twenty years earlier, but while he had done extremely well as a member of the Dinwiddie-Butterfield combine, his personal fortune was a mere bagatelle as compared to mine.

"The thing for you to do is to continue as though nothing had happened," my Press Secretary said, "until this unfortunate affair blows over. If that fails, we may even be able to hire some unemployed actor to pose as *your* lover to keep your name in the public—"

"*Never!!*" I cried. "My marriage was a *sacrament!*"

"Be that as it may, let us simply continue as scheduled—the White House redecoration, Alice's début, the series of entertainments—and see what happens. As President Butterfield is not free to marry Miss Goldfoil and, even if he were, not rich enough to fulfill her demands, she may very well pass him by for a more satisfactory protector. Now, as to your plans for the White House?"

What a blessing that man was and what sage advice! He had already, without even consulting me, started a rumor among the gentlemen of the press that Gladys Goldfoil was a mental case, unknown to our family, who had "crashed" the Inauguration Ball (indeed, her name was *not* on the list of those who had received invitations, for I had removed it carefully myself) and flung herself into the President's arms in order to achieve quick notoriety. The afternoon newspapers dutifully carried various versions of the story, some of them even going so far as to print the "F" to "H" sections of the invitation list to show that her name was not among those honored.

Although I had but little heart for the project, I got myself into a stylish but quiet *tailleur* and allowed the Official Photographer to do some studies of me with the Monroe gold *surtout de la table* in the State Dining Room as I laid out place cards for my first official dinner party. The menu, however, as sent up from the kitchen, depressed me with its dullness:

Blue Points on the Half Shell
Potage Mongol
Sole Bonne Femme
Baron of Lamb
Potatoes Anna
Petits Pois
Roman Punch
Hearts of Romaine
Bombe Martha[3]
Petits Fours   Savory   Coffee

and, of course, three wines, about which I knew little. An adequate meal, I suppose, but dreary and official-seeming, like the hundreds of dinners I had consumed in as many banqueting halls on our coast-to-coast campaign tour. I had wanted the White House menus to "sing" with their unusualness while I was chatelaine, and—even though I had no time to plan this one, what with the commotion of the previous day—here was the first state dinner in no way different from dinner menus of the last dozen or so administrations.

And then, as though Our Lord had read my thoughts, Mr. Alexander, the Official Photographer, burst back into the dining room. "Mrs. Butterfield," he cried, "the most *unusual* person, who claims to be your mother, is here. Wonderful features. If only I could get her in color."

"My *mother?* Impossible. Mumsie-love passed away when I was a child."

---

[3] Named for Martha Washington, not for Martha Dinwiddie Butterfield. P.D.

Mammy returns

"She keeps calling herself your mammy."

"Mammy!" I cried. In a trice, I was down the stairs, with Mr. Alexander at my heels. There, at the front door, fending off the White House guards with her umbrella, was Mammy, an angel sent from heaven!

"Mammy!" I cried. "Just the one to add a dash of originality to to-night's dreary dinner!" Embracing her, I led her immediately to the housekeeper's quarters and installed her as major-domo. From now on, the White House would be my *home,* in every sense of the word.

Dinner that night, instead of the tried-and-true dishes as old and as dull as history itself, consisted of the following:

Fisheye Surprise
Crème de Collard Greens
Catfish Arlesienne
Supreme of Possum
Yams in Drippings
Candied Okra
Deep Fat
Curried Orange Juice
Hot Sour Grass Salad
Bombe Martha[4]
Lump Cake
Squirrel Brains on Toast Points
Coffee

Mind you, this was but a spur-of-the-moment dinner. Mammy had scarcely time to take off her hat and remove her teeth before she was hard at it, bossing the shiftless kitchen staff around and sending out for the little-known delicacies she prepared so exquisitely. Although there was a great deal left over (like all true daughters of the South, Mammy believed that "plenty" was synonymous with "hospitality"), our guests pronounced it an unforgettable repast.

I was sick with apprehension at these first official entertainments, won-dering whether or not George would appear—and in what condition—and terrified that the unspeakable Miss Goldfoil would also arrive, but my fears were groundless. Miss Goldfoil was playing to standing room only at Dodge's Theatre, and George, rather contrite, or so he seemed,

---

[4] Named for Martha Dinwiddie Butterfield, *not* Martha Washington. P.D.

backed up by Bubber and Pappa-daddy, was more or less at ease with our guests, all of whom said that it was simply incredible to find a family like ours in the White House—high praise from unexpected sources! Of the whole family, Alice shone the brightest, her high-pitched giggle resounding through the rooms. And on no evening did her vivacity soar to such heights as the night the British Ambassador came to dine, bringing with him the courtly young Lord Lissom, a stunning young Englishman, whose fancy had been quite captured by my lovely daughter.

Meanwhile—often when guests were being entertained in adjoining rooms—workmen were toiling round the clock on my special surprise, a *new* White House. So many of the rooms seemed poky and old-fashioned to me that I had decided to have most of them entirely done over (paid for out of my own pocket, mind you, without bleeding the poor taxpayers, as was the custom of so many administrations both preceding and following ours). This was to be my little surprise gift to the nation, presented without any of the bothersome red tape of going through Congress and the Senate for allotments and permissions. With Cecil Lambrequin, my talented young interior decorator, I consulted each and every day, often at risk of life and limb as the workmen pounded and hammered over our very heads. In this brave new endeavor, I was busily introducing many exotic Middle Eastern effects, as well as the exciting *art nouveau,* a mode that had swept Europe (Clytie's entire apartment on the Champs Élysées was a breathtaking tribute to this new form) ever since the turn of the century but had barely created a ripple in United States decorating circles. The work was coming along splendidly, unbeknownst even to my immediate family.

George provided a gracious home for his darling mother

With Cecil—redecorating the Blue Room

However, my first really big undertaking as First Lady was to present adorable Alice to social, governmental, and diplomatic circles. This great event, scheduled for just one week after the Inauguration, was to be a "double" début, for it would mark not only Alice's emergence into society but also her début as a gifted coloratura soprano. Invitations had gone into the mail on the day of the Inauguration, and to make sure of having plenty of handsome young dancing partners for my little girl, I took advantage of George's position as Commander-in-Chief of both the Army and the Navy and ordered all the midshipmen at Annapolis and all the cadets at West Point to be at the White House, in full-dress uniform, punctually at nine o'clock on the evening of March 11th. They, plus the unattached secretaries and aides from the embassies and the young blades of Washington society, created a formidable "stag line." It was a glorious sight!

Alice, in a bouffant dress that had been ordered from Paris, was radiant as the honored "bud" of the evening. Her father, I am sorry to say, fell during the first waltz with her, but I feel sure that no one noticed. Instead, the Chief Justice chivalrously took over the honors. Just before supper (Alice never sang at her best on a full stomach), the dance floor was cleared, and, standing sweet and demure at the golden piano in the

East Room, she presented a full hour's recital. It was an all-Grieg program, and she even sang the lyrics in both English *and* Norwegian—a rare accomplishment in one so young. Her voice was so pure and high that it shattered no fewer than three hundred and seventeen champagne glasses (the East Room was a shambles), and many of the guests were forced to leave the room, as the intensity of her true, young voice was just too much for the human ear to endure! Unfortunately, Fluffy (also a vision, wearing a large rose-colored bow) got loose and howled piteously during the haunting "Solveig's Song," but it was the only minor flaw in an otherwise brilliant evening.

As mother of the débutante, I was kept busy greeting one distinguished guest after another, but I could not help noticing that of all the gallant young beaux at the party Alice seemed to have eyes for only one—Lord Lissom, the elegant young British nobleman who had so struck her fancy at the Inauguration Ball.

As I was feverish with curiosity about this young man—what mother, pray tell, would not be?—I asked my Press Secretary to find out whatever he could about the young man's antecedents. It would not do, I felt, to throw away my precious daughter on a lad who had anything save the bluest of blood flowing in his veins. My worries seemed for naught. The

Alice sings!

Lissom family had flourished in England since the Norman Conquest. Alice's suitor had already come into the title while at Eton, his father having met his untimely and inexplicable death while cleaning a gun at the Cavendish Hotel in Jermyn Street. Although impoverished, the family was one of great distinction, nobility, and looks, and Lord Lissom's six lovely sisters, Lavinia, Hermione, Solange, Lalage, Drucilla, and the boy's favorite sister—and perhaps the most exquistite of all—Griselda,[5] were noted throughout the British Empire for their aristocratic beauty and bearing. Even though I experienced all the pangs of anguish customary to a mother about to lose her baby, I was relieved to think that Alice had had the taste and wisdom to choose a gentleman and not some fortune hunter interested in her only for money.

As for my own heart, it was heavy, needless to say, but, following the

[5] All the Lissom sisters, save one, made brilliant marriages, becoming, respectively: Principessa Guttapercia, the Duchess of Gland, Gräfin von-und-zu Schmaltz-Geschlumpfert, Marquesa da Silva y da Costa y Congonhas, and the Marchioness of Bermondsey. Only the Hon. Griselda did not marry, finishing out her days as the sole companion of her brother, who also remained single after terminating his engagement to Alice Butterfield. P.D.

advice of my Press Secretary, I plunged ahead, trying as best I could to ignore the ominous presence of my rival and to be a First Lady worth noticing.

That, I can proudly say, I achieved. No sooner had the last guest filed out of the East Room after Alice's triumphal coming-out party than Cecil Lambrequin and his helpers surged in and, overnight, transformed the room into a vision *à la Turque*. The effect was electrifying! Mr. Alexander photographed all the new rooms, and the prints were released to every newspaper in the country. The furor that my renovations caused is still discussed in hushed tones on Capitol Hill. There was no doubt about it—from that day on, I was news. Everything I said, did, served, or wore was reported in minute detail. Not only was I First Lady of the United States of America, I was *the* arbiter of taste.

My gift to the nation—the East Room à la Turque

XVI

R.S.V.P.
The White House

1909

Parties, parties, parties! . . . Manners and menus. . . . Mammy's cuisine leaves its mark on diplomatic Washington. . . . Brilliant entertainments—Bernhardt, Pavlova, and others. . . . Social sabotage! . . . I replace the Postmaster General. . . . "Mad Ruth" of Ruthenia's terrible seizure in the Red Room. . . . Did her attack foretell the coming of Communism? . . . A cruel practical joke. . . . Mammy saves the day. . . . Bubber as Secretary of State. . . . Clytie's visit. . . . A disastrous period ball. . . . L'Affaire Goldfoil.

lthough my heart was heavy, my spirits were high. Of all the gay social butterflies in Washington, I was the gayest. Owing to the carefully laid plans of my Press Secretary and me, there was a party every day—sometimes two or three—in the White House. Within hours after Alice's début and my renovation of most of the public rooms in the Executive Mansion, I became the most talked-about hostess in the city—nay, in the nation.

For this rapid rise from being a quiet housewife in a little Southern town to the queen of Washington society, I had Mammy to thank in a large part. It was she who revolutionized the White House kitchen, ruling that office with a rod of iron. True, most of the kitchen and pantry staff resigned after Mammy's first day in power, but it mattered little to that implacable tower of strength. She simply put on her best hat, went to the Negro section of Georgetown, and recruited dozens of capable assistants at, may I add, far lower salaries but with "toting" privileges. Overnight, word of the White House table spread like wildfire. Both the United States Military Academy and the Naval Academy were forced to suspend all classes—and even watch and guard duty—for two days following Alice's début. Our enemies have snidely credited this amazing occurrence to "food poisoning," but I know better. It was simply greed. If there was anything Mammy loved, it was to see boys eat, and who could resist a groaning board piled high with braised sow, mountain oysters, delice of carp, moccasin eggs, and sorghum loaf? If guests at our table gorged themselves to the point where they were laid up for a day or so (and, in some cases, even hospitalized[1]) their lack of discretion should be blamed and not the cook!

I still have among my most precious souvenirs the Party Book that I kept religiously during our residence in the White House. What memories it recalls! In it I listed every guest, the seating plan, the menu, the entertainment (if any other than sparkling conversation), and my costume for each vibrant function, so that there would be no repetitions whenever a guest came back to one of *my* White House parties. Alas, few of them ever returned. But that is another story.

I will, however, endeavor to describe just a few of my earlier social triumphs. We were indeed fortunate to capture none other than Sarah Bernhardt ("the Divine Sarah") on one of the first of her many farewell tours. She was just sixty-five at the time, and the English translation of her autobiography was sweeping the country. She graciously agreed to appear at the White House—for quite a large fee, which Pappa-daddy paid directly from the ample funds of the United States Treasury, listing the expenditure as "spreading culture"—for an afternoon. I used the occasion to treat the leaders of Washington society to a tea party of sparkling Gallic wit and also as a sort of formal unveiling of the new East Room. The hand-picked audience was frankly as stunned by the décor as by la Bernhardt.

The Divine Sarah (although communication between us was difficult, I called her "Sally" right off, to put the lonely stranger at her ease) obliged with readings in full costume from "Hamlet," "Phèdre" and from Ed-

---

[1] Only three fatalities were reported immediately following White House dinners during the month of March, 1909. P.D.

With The Divine Sarah in the Green Room

mond Rostand's "L'Aiglon"—in French, of course. The afternoon went beautifully save for one unfortunate incident. During the Soliloquy from "Hamlet" (by William Shakespeare), the French Ambassador's daughter, who was seated just next to George, emitted a piercing shriek and fainted dead away. When revived, she kept moaning something in French, which, as well as I could figure out from her atrocious accent, had to do with "leg, leg, leg"—a statement I felt to be in the most dubious taste, considering the tragic afflictions of Bernhardt's limbs. Otherwise the occasion was one of the utmost brilliance, and the great tragedienne remained with us until she had received her check.

The Grand Duchess Sirene, a distant relative of the Romanovs, dined with us *en famille* while visiting the Imperial Russian Embassy. Delicate in the extreme, she was not able to touch any of her dinner. However, being introduced for the first time to Lohocla, she drank several glasses of it and felt so much better that she danced the entire length of the dining table, doing an amazing series of high kicks that destroyed all the Limoges imported by Mary Todd Lincoln.

Among other crowned heads, we were visited by darling little Ror-schach, King of Ocarina, accompanied by his wicked uncle, the Regent. My heart went out to the poor little boy, who was only six years old, just as it withered with revulsion at the sight of the evil "power behind the throne," his uncle. The purpose of their visit, although they had not made it clear at the outset, was to negotiate a loan with which the tiny nation could battle for its independence from the overbearing Ottoman Em-pire. Thin, pale, and wan—obviously in the last grip of a wasting dis-ease—the poor little tyke, in his trim uniform of field marshal, stood at attention for two hours in front of George's desk while his uncle ha-rangued my husband, my father, and my brother to advance twelve billion dollars toward a lost cause. When the child collapsed from exhaustion, he was carried to my boudoir, where I revived him with a bottle of Lohocla and with one of Mammy's most sumptuous afternoon spreads. The fol-lowing day, the little monarch was dead! "Acute indigestion" was the reason set forth in the official bulletin sent out by the government of Ocarina, but I, for one, will remain forever suspicious, sensing foul play on the part of the Regent in order to usurp the throne of that valiant little kingdom.

As Clytie was even now on the high seas (and how I looked forward to her help and guidance!), I had wanted, as I may have said, to build a sort of houseparty of monarchs around her, with dear old Franz Josef, long since widowed; Kaiser Wilhelm II and Augusta Victoria; Czar Nicholas and Alexandra; and Clytie's special chums from England, Ed-ward VII and Queen Alexandra as a nucleus, but, alas, affairs of state kept them from accepting. "Uneasy lies the head that wears a crown." I'm afraid that is all too true.

Still the parade of distinguished royalty marched on in never-ending splendor. "Zizi" and "Max," Pretenders to the throne of San Marino, were our guests for several days until it developed that they were wanted for fraud in Mexico. The Mexican government being what it was, I had little belief in the unjust accusations against this charming couple, but as our relations with that nation were not at their best, it seemed best to ask our guests to move on. Poor, petite sweet-tempered Zizi! Who can blame her for flying off the handle when I gave her the sad news? As for my missing necklace and earrings of flawlessly matched garnets, which fell out of her dressing case at the Canadian border, I feel sure to this day that the White House maid who did Zizi's packing simply made a mistake. "To err is human, to forgive divine."

H.R.H. the Maharanee of Ghozapore came to luncheon one day and very nearly caused an international incident because of the strange dietary laws enforced upon her by her religion. Course after course was sent back to the kitchen untouched by anyone at the table. (The Maharanee could not even remain in the same room with anything containing meat or meat stock.) Not knowing this, Mammy had prepared potage chitterling, sowbelly Marmaduke (in Bubber's honor), yams in drippings, and gizzard mousse. When the fourth dish was returned to the kitchen, Mammy herself appeared, wielding an enormous meat cleaver. "You black bitch!" she shouted. "You don't like the cooking here, just you drag your uppity self down to the Jim Crow hotel and eat your dinner there, nigger!" I was aghast! Alice giggled hysterically. Fortunately, the Maharanee was very deaf and spoke no English. She continued happily nibbling at the centerpiece of larkspur and carnations, quite unaware that Mammy was even in the room, let alone brandishing a lethal weapon just behind her. Bubber, the Secretary of State, got up quickly and hurried Mammy out of the room. He was the only one who could reason with her when she took one of her "spells"—the perfect diplomat. A crisis had been narrowly averted.

A mysterious and rather shabby visitor appeared at my *bedroom* door one day, introducing himself as the Aga Khan! So flustered was I at his sudden arrival that I had no time to consult with anyone. I simply wrote out a standard form of invitation for a reception that very evening, and had it telegraphed to the "A" and "B" lists all over Washington. The man spoke with an incomprehensible accent and seemed amazed when I showed him to a guest suite. As he had no luggage and as he was so rotund that nothing of George's would fit him, I telephoned Cecil Lambrequin, my decorator, and asked him to devise some sort of native robes that would blend in nicely with the new Turkish décor of the East Room. Imagine my embarrassment, however, when the British Ambassador unmasked the stranger as an impostor in front of several hundred guests! The Secret Service was called, and it took hours of intense questioning before we discovered that our guest was not the Aga Khan but a Mr.

Aaron Kahn, from the fur department of Woodward & Lothrop, who had come to call for my ermine cloak! How our detractors dined out on this unfortunate misunderstanding!

In spite of the spectacular job I was doing (or perhaps because of it) the enemies of the Bullfinch Party and others were doing their subtle best to undermine my attempts to make the White House a new Versailles. To anyone who knows the first thing about etiquette, an invitation from the White House is not a request; it is a *command*. Only severe illness or death can prevent one from accepting the honor of an invitation from the President and/or the First Lady. Yet many of my invitations to fellow-Americans were seemingly being ignored or, as I suspected, had met with foul play. For example, an invitation to Mrs. Stuyvesant Fish was returned from New York with "Deceased" written across the envelope, when the very next day there was a long description in the New York *Sun* of one of her more unusual parties. Similarly, Mrs. Vanderbilt, Mrs. Astor, and Mrs. Belmont were all dead, according to the envelopes returned to the White House.

When I planned an afternoon recital of *lieder* to be sung by Alice, five hundred engraved invitations were dispatched. Mammy had outdone herself with preparations, and Alice and I, dressed like duchesses, were waiting punctually at four o'clock on the big afternoon to receive our guests. At five no one had appeared. Six o'clock struck and still no guest had arrived. There was nothing to do but dismiss the accompanist. Poor Alice retired to her bedroom in tears.

It was then that I realized that someone was sabotaging the White House invitations. The very next morning, I marched into the office of the Postmaster General (my own brother-in-law, Zachary Taylor Butterfield). He was not alone. In addition to his enormous stamp collection, which had grown by leaps and bounds in the fortnight he had held office, a most vulgar young woman was *on his lap*. Zack explained that she was his secretary, but I discovered that she had not even taken a Civil Service examination!

"Zack," I said, "blood is thicker than water, but even though you are George's brother, I cannot endure the slipshod postal service we have been getting since you took over. Thousands—literally, thousands—of invitations to the White House lost, strayed, or stolen. This will have to stop, and it will the minute you resign and an experienced executive with some knowledge as to how the government mails should be handled takes your place. You will please dictate your resignation to this so-called

☆ [213] ☆

'secretary' now, and I will hand it to George at dinner tonight. Otherwise I shall be forced to report what I have just seen to Elvira." (Zachary's wife, Elvira, was a Tennessee girl who stood six feet two in her stocking feet and who was widely known as shot-putting and hammer-throwing champion of Cumberland County. More playful than belligerent, her slightest wish was Zachary's command.) Then and there, the crestfallen Zachary penned his resignation in longhand; the "secretary," as I had suspected, could barely write her own name.

My dramatic action did something to still the accusations of nepotism in the administration. Taking matters into my own hands, I telegraphed back home to Pellagra for dear old Miss Kunkel, the retired postmistress, to fill the vacancy, which she did with alacrity. The office of the Postmaster General was a different place once Miss Kunkel had installed her cat and her plants, had run up a set of gay calico curtains, and had taken over with a strong, if palsied, hand. It was Miss Kunkel, then, and *not* Frances Perkins who had the honor to be the first woman Cabinet member, although her tenure was extremely brief.

From then on, the White House functions were far better attended. For example, when I engaged Anna Pavlova to appear at one of my brilliant Wednesday afternoons, the East Room was thronged and even a few "gate crashers" had to be discouraged. And well they might have turned out in full force, for in addition to Pavlova, who had just begun her quarter century of world tours, I had the inconceivable luck to secure as her partner the vibrant young Boris Nijinski (a cousin of *the* Nijinski), who, at the age of sixteen, was the most promising dancer at the St. Petersburg Imperial Ballet. Indeed, it was an afternoon of quicksilver enchantment. And it was I, not Diaghilev, who introduced the electrifying name of Nijinski to the Western world!

Dame Moonyeen Mulligan the Irish Mudlark attracted something of a crowd as well, although not the crush occasioned by Pavlova. Her six-hour program of early-Gaelic songs was well and respectfully attended. Unfortunately, Pappa-daddy, who was *not* feeling his usual jovial self that evening muttered a number of remarks concerning the Irish and the Catholic Church, which Dame Moonyeen unhappily misconstrued. Still, the headline "DONNYBROOK BREAKS LOOSE IN WHITE HOUSE," which appeared in the Washington *Post,* was downright libel! Pappa-daddy's face was completely healed in a matter of days. Today, by an odd coincidence, Dame Moonyeen occupies the room just across from mine at Bosky Dell Home for Senile and Disturbed, and, save for the

Left, *Boris Nijinski;* center, *M.D.B.;* right, *Pavlova*

times when she has her little fits of anger or depression, we are the fastest of friends. Life, as I have so often said, *is* strange.

Another interesting anecdote concerning the important members of royalty who flocked to the White House during my tenure there concerns a vision I had regarding the coming of Communism. Our distinguished guest was Ruth of Ruthenia (often and *most* unfairly referred to as "Mad Ruth" of Ruthenia). This lovely, gentle Hapsburg princess was so exquisitely bred (sixty-four quarterings!) that she was naturally highstrung and of a quixotic temperament. So much so that, for fear she might do harm to herself or to others, her cousin the Emperor Franz Josef kept her confined in opulence, if in solitude, in a three-hundred-room pavilion, designed for her by her kinsman and fellow-patron of the arts Ludwig II ("Mad Ludwig") of Bavaria, in the Carpathian Mountains, where it was hoped that the high, clear air would have soothing effect. A great beauty, she was summoned to Vienna only once each decade, to celebrate the Emperor's birthdays at large parties that included the entire reigning family. That was, the Emperor seemed to think, often enough. However, with the advent of Sigmund Freud and the great success of his new technique known as "psychoanalysis," Ruth was allowed to move to the outskirts of Vienna in order to consult this amazing scientist (Carpathian Ruthenia being rightly considered too great a distance for a physician to cover on a daily house call), which she did for several years. Having shown some slight improvement since beginning her analysis, seven years previously, it was decided that Ruth might "test her wings" socially by paying a series of state good-will visits on such important political personages as the Queen of Tonga, the Emperor of Abyssinia, the Prince of Monaco, the Imam of Yemen, and us. I was thrilled.

Ruth arrived with an entourage of six doctors, a masseuse, two therapists, and twelve nurses disguised as ladies in waiting. Her personal luggage included twenty trunks, nineteen of which, according to Mammy, who witnessed their unpacking, contained only apple strudel. I waited to receive her in the Red Room with a dazzling array of carefully chosen guests. After a delay of several hours, Ruth of Ruthenia was announced. The Dresden beauty appeared in an original Magyar costume said to be one thousand years old! (Bubber opined that there was no reason to doubt it.) As I stepped forward to make the court curtsy at which I had become so proficient, Ruth glanced about the Red Room. Her lovely periwinkle eyes widened, and she let out a piercing scream. Tearing at her hair, she cried, *"Mein Gott in Himmel! Rot! Rot! Die ganze Welt zur Röte verwandelt ist!"* [2] With that, she collapsed and was removed in an ambulance.

---

[2] "My God in Heaven! Red! Red! The whole world is changed to red!"   P.D.

THE THREE KINGS AND SIX QUEENS

King Edward   Emperor of Germany   Queen Alexandra   King of Spain
Queen of Spain   Empress of Germany   Queen of Ruthenia   Queen of Portugal   Queen of Norway

A bevy of Swans—the Lissom family

Dame Moonyeen Mulligan

Pavlova and (Boris) Nijinski

The Maharanee of Ghozapore

Rorschach of Ocarina and Regent

Graf von-und-zu Schmaltz-Geschlumpfert

H. R. H. Ranavalona and Consort

The Eunuch of Angora

Generalissimo Junta y Flotilla

Max and Zizi of San Marino

Piua, Infanta of Brazil

Grand Duchess Sirene

Astrid des Loges—danseuse

The "Queen" of Bechuanaland—darling Mammy

How odd that this woman, living so near the Russian border yet so far from the sordid world of international politics, would have such a vision! I have always had a great interest in clairvoyance, telepathy, and matters of extra-sensory perception, being quite a "sensitive" myself. And I have been told that those of more delicate mental balance than most sometimes experience amazing psychic manifestations. I could not sleep that night for thinking of "Mad Ruth's" prophecy, which, despite the abortive Russian uprising of 1905, seemed impossible to us at the time. The following day, I had the Red Room redone in the popular mission style in shades of ochre.

To say that I was occasionally made the butt of cruel practical jokes would be a gem of understatement. But once, at least, I was able to turn the tables and toss the joke squarely back into the face of its perpetrator.

Shortly after establishing myself in the White House, I received a strange, handwritten letter announcing the imminent arrival of "Mfusdi, Queen of Bechuanaland." New at the job of being the Nation's Hostess, I looked up Bechuanaland in one of Alice's old geography textbooks. It said little except that it was located in South Africa. Without giving the matter further thought, I marked the evening of the royal reception on my calendar, sent out invitations, and went about my business. Imagine my horror when, on the very afternoon of the Queen's arrival, I received a note reading:

Dear Madam Idiot,
Don't wait up for the Queen of Bechuanaland.

Lady Gladys Goldfoil

Burrowing through my personal files for the original letter announcing the "Queen's" arrival, I compared it with the rude note from Miss Goldfoil. The writing paper (stamped with the crest of a low Washington hotel), the handwriting, and the scent were identical. The envelope had also been postmarked "Washington, D.C." How could I have been so stupid?

I rang for my Press Secretary in a frenzy just as Mammy entered my room—feet bare, pipe in mouth, teeth in pocket, efficient as always—to present the menu for the royal reception. Suddenly, I was seized with an inspiration—Mammy would have to fill in as Queen Mfusdi! I dragged Mammy to my dressing room and snatched down a voluminous opera cloak of white paillettes. If Mammy held her breath all evening long, it might just go around her. Six seamstresses worked feverishly, fashioning the garment into a suitable evening dress, and while I coached Mammy as best I could on royal etiquette, my Press Secretary called the State Department to learn a little something more. He found that Bechuanaland was a protectorate of England, and had no queen other than Alexandra in Buckingham Palace. However, that would not make any difference to the people I had invited, my Press Secretary said. As the language was very limited—not more than five hundred words, I believe—a simple "Yambo" would do for "Hello," "Goodbye," "Pleased to meet you," and anything else that "Her Highness" would be required to say. Mammy practiced it a few times, sent down to the pantry for a case of Lohocla, and pronounced herself ready. Looking far more stately than some of our *genuine* visiting royalty, Mammy was standing in the East Room, a poised bronze monolith, as the first guest arrived. "Yambo," she said regally, and, in an aside to a waiter, "Get me a couple bottles of Lohocla, white boy."

All evening long, they kept coming—the cream of Washington society —bowing and curtsying to dear old Mammy. Once in a while, she took secret revenge on a guest who had displeased her in the past by stepping on a train or squeezing a hand too tightly, and by some diabolical legerdemain she managed to remove an heirloom bracelet from the wife of the Rumanian Ambassador, but most of the evening went amazingly well, and a number of people remarked on how daring I had been to bring Integration to the East Room.[3]

Everything was going beautifully, with no one the wiser as to "Her Royal Highness's" true identity. The Marine Band was playing its liveliest airs, and the reception was, up until then, one of the most brilliant and unusual affairs I had staged. Suddenly, the name "Miss Gladys Goldfoil" was announced. There was an audible gasp, and even the Marine Band struck a painful false note. Miss Goldfoil entered in her full theatre "war paint" and in a dress of the most immodest cut. Being nearest the entrance, I advanced and said, "Have you an invitation?"

"You bet I do, kiddo," she said. "Here." She thrust one of the engraved invitations to meet the Queen of Bechuanaland into my hand. How she could have come by it I shall never know. "Now, where's this here African queen?" she asked.

"Her Majesty is receiving right there," I said, indicating Mammy with my fan.

---

[3] Not entirely correct. Theodore Roosevelt had previously entertained Booker T. Washington at the family dinner table in the White House, but, as Mrs. Butterfield points out, the function in honor of Mammy was in the *East Room*. P.D.

"Well, well, well! I sure would like to meet this famous coon!" Miss Goldfoil shouted, and advanced upon Mammy. "Hey there, Queenie," she said, "haven't we met someplace before?"

Mammy emptied her glass of Lohocla, drew herself to her full height, and, with nodding plumes, said loftily, "We sure have, white trash. At Madam Thelma's sporting house in Valdosta, Georgia." Miss Goldfoil's face was a sight to behold.

Having had her say, Mammy gave me a sharp nudge and said, "Don't think it ain't been a lovely evening, gal. Now, send for my autymobile." Regal to the end, she swept out of the room, wearing thousands of dollars' worth of my jewelry and the glorious new mantle of leopard with which I had planned to achieve new heights in the world of fashion, and drove off toward Georgetown in the White House limousine. She did not return for several days—the leopard never. Mammy had saved the evening and had been an unqualified success in Washington society, but after that she gave herself such airs in the kitchen that it was almost impossible to live with her.

Ever since the first hideous twenty-four hours as President and First Lady, when my husband was either totally missing or else misbehaving so flagrantly with Miss Goldfoil that I would almost have preferred to have him absent, we had seen very little of each other, except in public. George had his suite of rooms; I had mine. While he was busy with affairs of state, I was occupied with luncheons and afternoon receptions, with opening bazaars, accepting bouquets, receiving delegations of prominent women, and so on. At certain important functions and at all White House evenings, we were seen together, but aside from these public appearances we lived almost entirely apart. After all, I tried to tell myself, he had his life and I had mine. Yet I knew that I was fooling only poor me. However, I had the gay and stimulating company of my young brother, Bubber, almost all of the time.

Slated for membership in the Cosmos Club, where Bubber planned to live, his election kept being postponed and postponed, because of the animosity of a man whom Bubber described as being in love with his mother. (Actually, I do not believe that this oversight was caused by anything more than carelessness. What exclusive men's club wouldn't welcome a gentleman like Bubber with open arms?) Therefore, Bubber moved into the old Lincoln Room of the White House as soon as my own quarters were redecorated and ready for me. I must say that Bubber's presence made me feel young again. He was so gay, so dapper, so dashing. It was wonderful to have a brother to protect me from the hurts and snubs of the politico-social swim—especially a brother who was not only Secretary of State but one who was also irresistible to the ladies.

Even to this day, I know too little about the ins and outs of political intrigue to be able to judge my brother fairly as a Secretary of State. Will he be recorded in history as one of the great ones? Only time itself will tell. But he certainly made the White House a place of wild excitement. True, I worried somewhat about what seemed to me to be his excessive drinking, and, Secretary of State or not, many were the nights when Mammy—to whom Bubber would always be her "baby"—was forced to undress him and put him to bed. But Bubber was able to cope with his many uncomfortable "mornings after" by installing a Turkish bath in the White House basement and doing much of his official work from there, thus killing two birds with one stone.

And then there was darling Clytie, the Countess Przyzplätcki, whose visit during March I anticipated with such excitement and pleasure. While I was more the stay-at-home, my sister Clytie was accustomed to travelling in court circles, the intimate of crowned heads, and the heart and soul of the International Set as it was in the days when it was composed of ruling monarchs. Clytie would be of such help to me in establishing a tone for the White House and in the festivities attendant upon Alice's engagement to Lord Lissom and the subsequent wedding.

Knowing that it would please Clytie, I had my Press Secretary arrange for an unusual amount of publicity to celebrate her landing. But, as had happened once before, a mysterious "tip" from an unnamed "extremely high source" marred Clytie's triumphal reentry to her native land and involved a certain amount of unpleasantness with immigration authorities and another prolonged and humiliating stay on Ellis Island—on grounds of *moral turpitude!*—until Bubber himself, in the dual role of Secretary of State and the Countess's brother, went to New York to release our poor sister.

Thus the dignified interviews I had planned with such journals as the New York *Times,* the *Herald,* the *Tribune,* the *World,* and the *Sun,* in which the distinguished genealogies of the Przyzplätcki and the Dinwiddie families would have been an important feature, were abandoned in favor of a Roman holiday on behalf of the gutter press. Once again, insulting headlines referring to Clytie as the "No-a-Countess" appeared all over the nation. However, the Presidential yacht collected my sister at

Ellis Island, and she was transported to Washington in the style that was only suitable to so distinguished a visitor.

Clytie was utterly delighted with Lord Lissom, whom she described in her fluent French as *"un peu de yum-yum."* Although the ancient Lissom family was not in Clytie's set, she knew of them and vouched for their authenticity. They were, she added, as poor as church mice, and she described Lord Lissom's widowed mother, Belgravia, Lady Lissom, as "a vulture on the wing." Still I was not worried. Discounting something for Clytie's picturesque turn of phrase, I was interested only in my little girl's happiness with the man she loved.

Clytie's visit, naturally, brought about a perfect rash of entertainment—luncheons, receptions, and teas—as I wanted all of Washington to know and love my charming sister as I did. The climax of Clytie's visit, however, was a period ball in the style of Louis XVI. George, whose figure was admirably suited for the role, dressed as Louis XVI. I wore the simple costume of a shepherdess, as Marie Antoinette (Queen of France) in pursuit of her rustic pleasures at the Petit Trianon. Clytie, resplendent in powder, patches, panniers, and jewels, appeared as Madame du Barry. Alice looked sweet as Princesse de Lamballe; Lord Lissom dressed as Count Axel Ferson; and Bubber was most distinguished in the robes of Cardinal de Rohan.

Dressing up can be such fun! It makes children again out of even the most staid and reserved of statesmen, and my ball was no exception. Truly it seemed to me that I *was* recreating Versailles on the banks of the Potomac. The gaiety was at its height when, on the stroke of midnight, a great sedan chair was carried in by two Negroes dressed as blackamoors. (As this was a *bal masqué,* guests were not announced by name but simply presented their cards of invitation at the door.) From the sedan chair emerged a sight that made my heart stop beating. It was none other than Gladys Goldfoil, who had not bothered to wear a mask—nor, indeed, anything else save a monumental hat, a tall staff, high laced boots, and skin-tight fleshings! I had put the keenest minds of the Secret Service to work trying to ferret out where and how Miss Goldfoil received authentic invitations to White House functions. After some investigation, their only verdict was "an inside job"—but *who?*

The silence was deafening as Miss Goldfoil crossed the East Room to where Clytie and I had been chatting with several of the Butterfield brothers.

"So this is the famous No-a-Countess," Miss Goldfoil said, quoting the yellow press.

A disastrous period ball

"*Je suis enchanté*," Clytie said, graciously extending her hand, then added, "Madam," giving it the English and not the French pronunciation.

"Talk with your mouth like you was born, cracker!" Miss Goldfoil snapped.

Never at a loss for the pert rejoinder, let me tell you, Clytie smiled and said, "So this is the President's concubine. Well, bedfellows do make strange politics."

"It takes one to tell one," Miss Goldfoil said. "What's this I hear about you and the King of—"

Clytie spat out a word in French with which I am not familiar and then, so that the point would not be lost on this unlettered nobody, employed a term in English that I would rather not repeat. At that, Miss Goldfoil grasped her tall, bejewelled staff as though it were a baseball bat and swung. Clytie ducked just in time, although Miss Goldfoil's staff removed the towering powdered wig that Clytie wore. From her crouching position, Clytie charged at Miss Goldfoil, butting her in the pit of the stomach. The two went down to the floor screaming and spitting, and I don't know what would have become of my lovely period ball had not the bandmaster had the wit to strike up the National Anthem. I cried myself to sleep again that night.

As though I had not enough problems as Hostess of the White House without the constant undermining interference of this vulgar home wrecker! I vowed that very night that something must be done.

XVII

Gathering Storm Clouds

1909

*Rumors of corruption. . . . Plagued by the press. . . . A rift in
the Bullfinch Party. . . . Trouble in the Dinwiddie-Butterfield
Enterprises. . . . The Secretary of the Treasury is censured. . . .
Pappa-daddy breaks with George. . . . La Goldfoil strikes again.
. . . Open scandal! . . . Lady Lissom. . . . A painful interview
with Gladys Goldfoil. . . . Overheard! . . . Alice's betrothal. . . .
Keeping a brave face.*

So occupied was I with keeping up my own end and establishing
the White House as the cultural and social center of the United
States—indeed, of the world—that for the first fortnight or so I
took little notice of what was happening on the political front. Indeed,
like all well-born Southern girls, I had been sheltered to such an extent
from rough, masculine pursuits like politics and business that I would
have had little grasp of the troubles confronting my dear husband, the
President, anyhow. But naïve as I was, I could hardly avoid noticing the
cruel cartoons and scurrilous headlines on the front pages of the dozens
of newspapers that arrived daily at the White House. Each periodical tried
to outdo its competitors in telling shocking tales of corruption, nepotism,
favoritism, and downright "thievery"—as they chose to term it—within
the Bullfinch Party. And day by day it grew worse. Even the very few
newspapers that had been "with" us during the campaign now mysteriously turned against us. Some gave the excuse that they had backed the
late General Lushmore in the Presidential campaign but had *not* ever expected my George to occupy the highest office in the land. How unfair!

We were constant fodder for such ferocious cartoonists as Gibson, Davenport and Sneed.

Others simply foresook the entire party, claiming that George had not lived up to the Bullfinch platform and had broken every promise ever made.

In addition to their constant sniping at the administration, the periodicals of the day even turned their guns on *me*—a poor, defenseless housewife—and, even more cruelly, on innocent little Alice. I had "ruined" the White House with my "unauthorized" and "barbarous" redecoration, they said. My parties were described as "outlandish" or "ostentatious" or "drunken" or just plain "dull." Alice, they said, was "plain," was a "social climber" because of her love for Lord Lissom; she was "dowdy" and "sang like a crow." Even Mammy's cooking was criticized. "Sticks and stones may break my bones," I told myself, "but names can never hurt me." And yet they did. Nothing I could say or do seemed to be right, seemed to please them, except when I supplied further ammunition for their brutal attacks on me and my little brood.

Further trouble cropped up almost immediately in the Dinwiddie-Butterfield Enterprises. True, the Bullfinch Party had been founded as a bulwark against Theodore Roosevelt's highhanded and Communistic invasion of the civil liberties of large corporations, trusts, and interlocking directorates such as ours, but George could hardly be expected to undo the work of seven years of the grossest interference overnight. Yet on March 5, 1909, the day after George's inauguration, Lohocla and all the related firms and corporations held by our family began to behave as though they, and not the President of the United States, were the law. Working hours were increased, salaries cut, monopolies reëstablished, and existing laws flagrantly ignored and broken. The entire Dinwiddie-Butterfield Enterprises seemed to feel that with George as Chief Executive no legislation that had ever been passed applied to them.

Nor was Pappa-daddy, who was getting on and, with the advancing years, failing somewhat, exactly suited to the office of Secretary of the Treasury. The poor darling, one of his first bold coups was an attempt to devalue the dollar from one hundred cents down to fifty cents. In his overpowering love for the humble workingman, Pappa-daddy felt that such a stroke would give the average citizen double his money's worth.[1] Feeling that the Secretary of the Treasury could simply carry out such an act without bothering to consult a lot of congressmen and senators, Pappa-

---

[1] It would also have done the same for Mr. Dinwiddie's own personal fortune, which at that time was estimated at very nearly one billion dollars. P.D.

Paying calls with Alice in our Franklin Runabout (pour le sport)

daddy simply halved the dollar and ordered a lot more currency struck off, with his own face appearing on the thousand-dollar bills. What a furor! Congress was up in arms, and several fist fights broke out in the Senate. Pappa-daddy was forced to peg the dollar back at one hundred cents (Franklin Roosevelt, some years later, blithely reduced it down to fifty-nine cents, just as my father had wanted to do), and all, or most, of the lovely new currency had to be burned.

This cruel pillorying all but broke my father's spirit. On that day, Pappa-daddy closed all his checking accounts and refused thenceforth to carry currency. Whenever he needed pocket money, he instructed his chauffeur to drive to the Mint, where he marched in and, as Secretary of the Treasury, helped himself. For large purchases, he simply signed the bills and had them sent to the Treasury. Not even Bubber could reason with him. Therefore, he—and we—had to undergo the pain and indignation of a public action of censure. In a fit of temper, Pappa-daddy resigned his post, ordered a fleet of vans and, on the way home, literally emptied the United States Mint. The reaction of the national press was devastating. At that point, my husband and my father had an open and complete break. George resigned from his every position in the Dinwiddie-Butterfield Enterprises, selling his various posts and titles back to Pappa-daddy for cold cash, which was naturally plentifully abundant, but again we suffered indescribable embarrassment when the moving vans filled with the contents of the Mint drove from Pappa-daddy's estate, outside Chevy Chase, to the White House to unload their contents. It made a perfectly honest and aboveboard business transaction seem somehow unwholesome and corrupt.

Naturally, it broke my heart to have my beloved husband and my adored father at swords' points—a rupture that was never healed during the little time left to each of them in this vale of tears—but an even more bitter blow was still to follow: a hopeless rift between George's adorable little twin brothers, "J.P." and "J.Q.," and a misunderstanding that cost many, many thousands of lives.

As Secretaries of the Army and the Navy, respectively, "J.P." and "J.Q." felt that it would be a wise move to demonstrate to the populace our nation's true power, both on land and on sea. Therefore, military and naval maneuvers were scheduled for late March, and the scene of this great sham battle was Atlantic City, then a flourishing and fashionable resort filled the year round with trippers and holidaymakers. This week-long military and naval exercise was widely heralded. The international press was invited, and even a few of the first newsreel cameramen attended.

With their typical youthful ardor and their desire to make wartime situations as realistic as possible, "J.P." and "J.Q." perhaps went a step or two too far by using real shells. The carnage was dreadful.

Once the rubble had been cleared away, the Boardwalk was a total shambles; both the Chalfonte and the Marlborough-Blenheim hotels were levelled to the ground; and our Navy had lost six ships. In addition to the loss of military and naval personnel, who, after all, had some reason to expect that their lives might occasionally be in danger during service to their nation, more than five hundred civilians were killed and over two thousand wounded—some quite seriously. It was a dreadful catastrophe, and the enemies of the Bullfinch Party made the most of it. Happily, the twins were unharmed.

Tragic and embarrassing as Operation Atlantic City had been, it did serve to show the rest of the world what a tremendous power the United States had become, and from the ruins of the Boardwalk rose yet another most embarrassing occurrence, which gave our enemies still more ammunition against the Butterfield administration.

Bubber, as I have said before, lived in the White House, and as he had always evinced a great interest in graphology, I was not unduly surprised one morning to find him in the Oval Room studying my George's signature. But imagine my horror when, on the very next afternoon, I was cut dead by the wife of the Nicaraguan Ambassador and when the evening newspapers announced that Nicaragua had severed diplomatic relations with the United States. It was a matter of some days before the ridiculous misunderstanding could be cleared up, and the ugly story that ensued was as damning as it was incredible. Rumor had it that my George was declaring war on smaller, less powerful countries, so that Bubber, in his role of Secretary of State, could go around and *sell* American friendship and amnesty to these less fortunate nations. Can you imagine anything so preposterous?

Dear George was beside himself with anguish when the ugly story reached him. Pounding his head again and again on his desk, all he could say was, "Why didn't *I* think of it? Why didn't *I* think of it?" He strode out of the White House and was gone for several days. I was beside myself with worry. Then Gladys Goldfoil struck again!

Whenever this common harlot had not been occupied in entertaining my husband (and, from what the reading public and I could gather, the entire Cabinet), whenever she had not been appearing all but naked at Dodge's Theatre in her low musical comedy, "The Chicken Inspector," and whenever she had not been bursting unexpected, uninvited, unannounced, and unwanted into White House festivities, she had busied herself with writing a vile and libellous series of memoirs entitled "The President's Mistress," for which a national newspaper syndicate had paid an alleged quarter of a million dollars!

My heart nearly stopped beating when the first installment of these ap-

palling revelations stared up at me from the front page of the local morning newspaper, as well as five out-of-town journals. Nothing or no one was spared. Names were named, dates were given. Letters were reproduced in full. This brazen strumpet even described George as "potbellied," but what could one expect from a woman of Miss Goldfoil's background? She included detailed accounts of her liaison with Bubber, and not satisfied to stop there, Miss Goldfoil even published passages concerning the amatory prowess of that saintly man *my father!* I trembled to think how a pillar of the community such as Pappa-daddy would react, but Mammy said that he was quite pleased and even sent Miss Goldfoil a case of pre-Roosevelt Lohocla. True, to forgive *is* divine!

To make matters worse, these shocking and outrageous disclosures had to appear on the very morning of the reception announcing Alice's engagement to Lord Lissom. Even as I read the first installment, aghast and stricken, His Lordship was aboard the train from New York, bringing his mother—Belgravia, Lady Lissom—and his six lovely sisters to Washington for the official announcement. "If only," I moaned to my faithful Press Secretary, "they were Greek or Chinese or Russian, and couldn't read English."

"Perhaps they can't read at all, like so many of the peerage," he said, trying to bolster my fading hopes, but, alas, I discovered that they could—just.

With eyes still red from weeping, I accompanied Alice to the station with a cortège of limousines and seven bouquets to greet my baby's future family. It was raining lightly, and I could not help noticing that each of the Lissom ladies held a newspaper over her hat and from each newspaper screamed the details of my shame.

Riding with me in the first limousine, the Dowager Lady Lissom did *not* seem overly friendly or easy to get to know. Lady Lissom—I cannot to this day think of her by any name as intimate as Belgravia, although I urged her to call me (which she did not do) Martha or sugar cake—was filled with complaints. The crossing had been rough and the ship uncomfortable, although it had been a *British* ship. She complained of the long, arduous trip by train from New York (four hours), and then complained because it had been so short. "I quite expect to be scalped by a red Indian whilst I'm here," she said, and then complained because she had seen no Indians between Union Station and Blair House. She complained also about difficult street names, such as Massachusetts and Pennsylvania Avenues, and then complained about the lack of imagination shown in naming the streets of Washington by letters and numbers. All told, she was not an easy guest.

As the arrival of the Lissoms had been well-publicized in advance by my Press Secretary, there was a throng of reporters at the doorway of Blair House. Unfortunately, the drizzle had stopped, so that Lord Lissom obligingly posed for the photographers with his mother, with his sisters, and with Alice, giving the reporters ample time to question the Dowager Lady Lissom. Needless to say, the name Gladys Goldfoil came up, and although Lady Lissom was ignorant of the woman's existence, a seed was planted.

I knew then that I must act. If a newspaper syndicate had paid Miss Goldfoil a quarter of a million for her story, I could offer her more. No sacrifice—even throwing myself on this hussy's mercy—was too great for the happiness of my precious Alice.

Having installed Lady Lissom and her daughters in Blair House, I returned to my own rooms and requested my Press Secretary to call Miss Goldfoil for an appointment that very afternoon. It was granted, and immediately after luncheon, heavily veiled, I took a public hack (I could not risk the notoriety of using a White House car) to the common theatrical hotel where Miss Goldfoil lived. "Miss Goldfoil is expecting me," I said, slipping a folded five-dollar bill into the hand of the insolent clerk. "You her mother or something?" he asked.

A shiftless bellboy led me to Miss Goldfoil's rooms, a dingy suite decorated in just the sort of taste one would have expected from such a woman. The slatternly maid who admitted me rudely indicated a chair and disappeared behind some plush portieres. I waited for just over an hour before Miss Goldfoil condescended to appear.

"Well?" she said, standing before me with her arms crossed over her tremendous bosom.

"Miss Goldfoil," I said, "I will come right to the point."

"That's good, because I've got a lot of things to do this afternoon," she said, blowing cigar smoke into my face.

"Miss Goldfoil, I have read the first installment of your memoirs. . . ."

"Pretty hot stuff, eh, Marty? Boy, you shoulda seen what they cut out. There was a part about this here big Supreme Court judge that likes to—"

"I am not interested in the Supreme Court, Miss Goldfoil—only in my own family and its sanctity and stability."

"Jeest! Listen to them ten-dollar words! No wonder Georgie-Porgie can't never figure out what you're sayin'."

"Just how many installments does your—uh, autobiography, your life story, run to, Miss Goldfoil?"

"Nine, so far. I'm kinda stuck for Chapter Ten unless I wanta go back to the time when—"

"And it is to run serially for how long?"

"Once a week till I've told all."

"I believe you are being paid two hundred and fifty thousand dollars for the complete series?"

"That's right, sister. Who says sin don't pay?"

"Miss Goldfoil, I am the mother of a débutante daughter—"

"What a dog!"

"I am not speaking of Fluffy, Miss Goldfoil, but of my daughter Alice. Tonight I am announcing her engagement to a British lord."

"No kiddin'? Jeest, if she can get a lord with a face like that, I oughta be able to get the Kaiser."

I tried to go on. "Lord Lissom comes from a very ancient and conservative family. My daughter's happiness means everything to me. I don't care so much what you and my husband have done—"

"I don't blame you, Marty. Between you and I, he ain't much. Now, your brother—"

"Miss Goldfoil," I said, plunging on, "if I give you my certified check for *half* a million dollars, will you print a retraction of this morning's story and give me the rest of your manuscript?"

"You know, that's the third offer I've had today. Some soft job being an orther. You can make more *not* writing than—"

"*Will* you?" I said, grasping her hand.

"No!"

Throwing my pride to the winds, I was soon on my knees to her, begging, pleading. My bribe rose rapidly to a million dollars, to one and a half, to two.

"Is that your final offer?" Miss Goldfoil snarled.

"That is my final offer."

Suddenly, she swept back the portieres. There was a flash of light.

"Caught in the act, eh, Marty? With pictures to prove it and every doggone word taken down by this here stenographer." A photographer and a young woman with a pad and pencil were indeed revealed behind the heavy plush curtains. "Well, thanks a million, Marty—*two* million. That takes care of Chapter Ten. See you at the White House tonight."

My humiliation

"You're *not* coming to Alice's engagement party?"

"Sure as shootin' I am. I got my invitation right here. In the President's own handwriting. He ain't much of a speller, either, is he?"

Rising from the floor, I confronted her. "Mark my words, you whore of Babylon, you will not set foot in the White House tonight!" With my head held high, I marched out of the suite, slamming the door behind me. If the heavens fell, I would see to it that that woman would not ruin my daughter's party!

Back at home, still trembling with fury, I summoned my ever-resourceful Press Secretary to do whatever possible to keep Miss Goldfoil from entering the White House that night: call out the National Guard and place a cordon around the entire building, if necessary—anything to prevent that harlot from ruining my baby's evening! Alas, he was out, busily trying to quash the ruinous stories springing from Miss Goldfoil's memoirs. In desperation, I turned to faithful Mammy.

Going down to the White House kitchen, where she was busily supervising the delicacies to be served at dinner as well as at the gala reception to follow, I took Mammy aside and presented my problem. Puffing away at her pipe, Mammy pondered the situation and then spoke. "Thing to do is cotch her *before* she git here."

"But how?" I asked. "Can you do it?"

Mammy thought again, excused herself, and returned. "I can do it. But it won't be easy. I'll need a autymobile, a clothesline, and fifty dollars."

"Take it!" I cried joyously. "Take anything you need, just so long as that woman does not set foot in the White House tonight."

The evening went—not well, not badly, but at least it went. At dinner, held for the immediate families and the British Ambassador and his wife, the two of Lord Lissom's sisters who sat on either side of Bubber—the Hon. Drucilla and the Hon. Lavinia—complained simultaneously of being pinched, a figment of their imaginations, I feel sure. Lady Lissom examined the Monroe *surtout de la table* and said that she had a far nicer one in silver at Cretins, their family seat. When a toast was drunk to the engaged couple, the Hon. Griselda burst into tears and had to be led from the State Dining Room. Yet so preoccupied was I, worrying that Mammy's plans—whatever they might be—would fail, that these things seemed minor annoyances.

The guests began arriving immediately after dinner, so that there was no time for the ladies to withdraw, thank heavens, and talk. For the rest

In the Red Room
Who could know my suffering?

of the night, I stood in the receiving line, wearing a brave, false smile, chatting and laughing artificially, and trying to keep George from collapsing. Yet behind my gay façade my heart was hammering against my ribs. As eleven o'clock approached—the time when the curtain fell on Miss Goldfoil's play—I grew absolutely feverish. What if she should appear? Yet she did not. Fifteen minutes passed, a half hour, another quarter of an hour. I was aware of a rustling behind some potted palms and looked up to see Mammy gazing at me through the fronds. She nodded in a conspiratorial way, and I knew that finally all was safe.

The evening, I suppose, was satisfactory. Lady Lissom said that she had been most agreeably surprised to find two or three Americans present who seemed civilized. The Hon. Solange met (and later married!) the courtly young Count von-und-zu Schmaltz-Geschlumpfert, then naval attaché of the German Embassy. All the lovely Lissom sisters were swept off their feet and danced unceasingly, save the exquisite Griselda, who wore deepest black, refused all invitations to dance, and spoke to no one but her brother. I thought that the party would never end, but finally—at nearly four o'clock—it did. Once again in my lonely room, after brushing Fluffy's hair and mine, I sank wearily onto my bed. But sleep would not come. Day was beginning to break when, from sheer exhaustion, I closed my eyes at last. As I did so, I heard newsboys on the street shouting, "Extra! Extra! Actress kidnapped!"

Everyone was curious to see us

April 4th,
A Day to Remember

1909

The impeachment papers. . . . Dyeing eggs for the Easter festivities. . . . George's strange visit to the White House kitchen. . . . The magenta dye is missing! . . . Bubber's unexpected call on Mammy. . . . Found—the New York City votes in the Lohocla warehouse. . . . A mass demonstration on the White House lawn. . . . A dinner that will live in infamy. . . . Had I ordered creamed hogs' lungs? . . . The Presidential Box. . . . A shot in the dark. . . . "Sic semper schlemielis"—Miss Goldfoil's final revenge. . . . The ordeal of finding a taxi in a town like Washington. . . . Revolutionary mobs. . . . A modern Dolley Madison —I flee the rabble, taking only a few mementos.

April 4th, a day to remember! From start to finish, it was a living hell.

To begin with, the ubiquitous Miss Goldfoil was once again on the front page of every newspaper, thus crowding Alice's engagement back to the obituary pages. ACTRESS KIDNAPPED! the banner headlines screamed. Stories three and four columns wide told a weird tale of Miss Goldfoil, dressed in a ball gown, jewels, and chinchilla coat (so she *had* been planning to come to the White House!), found bound and gagged on the Baltimore County line. Her picture, sporting a large black eye, was everywhere. In her own words, she had been leaving Dodge's Theatre by the stage door when set upon and forced into an electric car with a pillowcase over her head. She had been driven at breakneck speed, she said, out into the country, bound, gagged, and abandoned. Yes, she added, she had a *very* good idea of who had plotted the deed, but she was saving it for her memoirs.

No sooner had I finished reading this than I was summoned to the telephone to speak to Belgravia, Lady Lissom. Her Ladyship inquired as to my plans for the evening. Indeed, I had none. Thinking quickly, I suggested a quiet evening—dinner in the Family Dining Room and a bit of chamber music by the Marine Band.

"No outside guests or anything like that?" Lady Lissom asked.

"No. Just a quiet family evening. Get to know one another."

"Splendid. In that case, you'll have nothing to cancel. The girls and I are frightfully keen on seeing 'The Chicken Inspector.' It's an operetta, I believe, with that amazing Goldfoil creature, who was carried off last night. And it's to be my treat. I insist."

My heart sank. "It's terribly popular," I said. "I don't believe you could get tickets this late."

"The *President* of the United *States* not get tickets? Nonsense, my dear! If I can't get them for the President, I can at least get them for the *British Ambassador*. And *please* don't bother with dinner. We've been asked to the Embassy. I'll simply leave your tickets, and we'll meet in the interval." With that she rang off.

Knees trembling, I sank to a chair just as George stormed into my sitting room in a state of undress. "God damn it, Martha," he bellowed, "what kinda practical joke is this?"

"Wh-what, dearest?" I asked.

"This here," he said, brandishing a formal-looking document in front of my face. "It's an order of impeachment."

"I haven't the faintest idea what you're talking about," I said.

"Well, I have. They're trying to kick me out—dirty, lousy bunch of radicals! I'll fight, I tell you. I'll fight it."

"Can you?" I asked.

"Well, I don't know. Where's your brother?"

"Probably at the State Department. Did you look in the Turkish bath?"

"I been at it all morning. He ain't down there. He can fix this—just like he fixed the election."

"George, dear?"

The Secretary of State at work

"Now, what?"

"Lady Lissom has asked us to the theatre tonight."

"Oh? Well, that's better'n trying to talk to the old battle-axe. What show?"

" 'The Chicken Inspector.' " I said loudly and clearly, waiting for his reaction. There was none.

"I've already seen it—twice." Had the man no heart? "Well, it's funnier than that gimpy French actress you had yammering around here. It's got a little pep. Maybe take my mind off my troubles." With that he was gone. Could this, my husband—the man I had worshipped and cherished these many years—be so cruel, so selfish, so unfeeling as far as I was concerned? Ill with despair, I was about to fling myself onto the sofa for a good cry when my Press Secretary tapped at the door.

"What am I to do?" I wailed. "This Goldfoil woman and her ghastly revelations? Impeachment proceedings? Alice's engagement? And now being dragged—naked before mine enemy—to 'The Chicken Inspector' with Lady Lissom, of all people!"

"We're trying to make the public forget all that with a little good publicity," he said soothingly. "Now, if you'll just dress and come down to the kitchen, we'll do a human-interest shot of you dyeing eggs for the White House Easter Egg Rolling."

Down in the White House kitchen, Mammy and her staff had boiled hundreds of dozens of eggs, and on a table three of the Jefferson tea services were set out, containing Easter-egg dyes in every color of the spectrum. How gay it all looked and yet how black and leaden my despondency. Mr. Alexander's camera was all set up, and, forcing a smile, I posed as graciously as I could for the publicity pictures. But even as I did so, preparing a gay outing for the kiddies of the nation, I could almost see the headlines, the cruel editorials accusing the Butterfield family of wasting eggs on the White House lawn when children were starving. Was *nothing* we ever did *right*?

As the pictures were being taken, George himself entered—the first time he had ever set foot in the kitchen—looking most perturbed.

"Ah," Mr. Alexander said, "the Chief Executive himself! And just in time to pose for a picture with the Easter eggs."

"I haven't got time to mess around with—"

Preparing for the Easter egg rolling

"Mr. Butterfield," my Press Secretary said suavely, "if what I hear about an impeachment is correct, I think you'll have *plenty* of time in the future. We're *trying* to make you palatable to the public."

"Oh, all right, but make it quick," George snapped. Just then, his eyes lit on the open bottle of Lohocla that Mammy always had near at hand. "Ah, an eyeopener. Just what I—"

"Get that bottle out of the picture," Mr. Dennis said. "If there's one thing the public *doesn't* need to see, it's—" He removed the bottle with a flourish.

"Hey!" George called.

"They's some in that cup there," Mammy said.

George lifted the cup, drank it down in a single gulp, gagged, and made a wry face. "What are they putting into the stuff *now,* rat poison?" He managed a half smile as we posed together with our hard-boiled eggs at the table covered with cups of dye. "There," George said. "Now I've gotta look into every saloon in town to find your no-good brother." With that he was gone.

"Just one more picture, please, Mrs. Butterfield," the official photographer said. "In this one, please, dip an egg and then be admiring it."

"Very well," I said listlessly. "What color?"

"The orange or the magenta would make a nice tonal contrast against your dress," Mr. Alexander said. He had such an eye!

Placing an egg on a spoon, I dipped it into a cup filled with red-violet liquid, removed it, and smiled.

"Would you please try just once more, Mrs. Butterfield? The egg isn't colored at all."

Again I repeated the motions, and once again the egg came out still untinted. "How odd," I said. "The dye doesn't seem to be working at all, and yet on all the other eggs—"

"Fer Gawd!" Mammy cried, snatching up the cup and sniffing. "This ain't no aig dye. This here's Lohocla! The President done drunk the dye!"

My hands flew to my heart. "Drank the *dye*? But mightn't that be harmful?"

"If all that Lohocla ain't hurt him, I don't see how no old Easter-aig dye could make much difference," Mammy said philosophically.

"I must stop him!" I said, racing from the kitchen. I reached the front door just as George's limousine was leaving the gates. It was too late.

When I returned to the kitchen, the camera was gone and with it the Official Photographer and the Press Secretary. Instead I found Bubber, deep in consultation with Mammy.

"Bubber!" I cried. "Where have you been? George has been looking high and low for you. They—they want to impeach him!"

"Impeach him? That's a hot one! How can they impeach him when he ain't even President?"

"Not President? What do you mean?"

"Just what I said. You know the New York City vote that was missing? Well, they found it! We had it hidden in the Lohocla warehouse in Brooklyn. But it seems the Democratic Party ordered a couple of thousand cases for their Easter outing, and, instead of Lohocla, they got the Greater New York vote."

"But what does that mean?"

"It means that now they've found the votes, they'll have a recount. In other words, George ain't in. He never was in. He's out by millions of actual votes and I forget how many Electoral votes. It changes the whole of New York State."

"But didn't *anybody* in New York vote for the Bullfinch Party?" I asked.

"Fourteen people, as far as we can figure, including three repeaters."

"But, Bubber, what are we to do?"

"I don't know about you, but while I've still got this diplomatic passport, I'm going to use it. Someplace like Greece or Brazil, where there's no extradition. Want to come along?"

"Desert my husband in his hour of need?" I cried. *"Never!"*

"Suit yourself, stupid. Where's the Presidential yacht?"

"In drydock. Cecil's doing it over."

Bubber muttered a dreadful oath. "Don't forget what I told you, Mammy," he said, giving her a squeeze.

"I'll start cookin' it right away, baby," Mammy chuckled. "Bon appetite, eh?" She burst out laughing.

"Sure you wouldn't like to take a little trip, Sister?" Bubber asked.

"Not if my *life* depended on it."

"It may, at that. Well, au reservoir, as they say. Don't take any wooden nickels." That was the last I ever saw of him.

The events of the morning—disaster piled upon disaster—so stunned me that I moved like a zombie through my crowded day: luncheon for some Japanese students attending Wellesley; receiving a bouquet and a bone with Fluffy from the A.S.P.C.A.; presenting the Martha Dinwiddie Butterfield Medal of Merit to Jane Addams; tea with the W.C.T.U. Would it *never* end?

Opening a bridge

Winning over club wom[en]

Christening a ship

Youth wants to know

Decorating a grave

Laying a cornerstone

"Poems are made by fools like me"

With the poor orphans

Spreading cheer

Hot soup for lost souls

A cheese factory

As I was dressing for the dreaded evening ahead of me, once again I heard the chorus of newsboys out on Pennsylvania Avenue—this time screaming of "Fraud!" "Fraud!" "Fraud!"

When I emerged from my bath, there was a frightful commotion going on on the very lawn of the White House—those hallowed grounds—and a mass of rabble holding aloft torches and crudely lettered placards were protesting our very presence in this, our home! The telephone bell summoned me, and again it was Lady Lissom, this time complaining about the noise that had ruined her tea and her afternoon nap. "It—it's a demonstration of devotion to my husband," I said, through my tears.

Our enemies were relentless

"Well, please ask them to stop," Lady Lissom said. "I've a frightful migraine. Until the theatre tonight. I can't wait to see it. I've got quite a thing about poultry."

Dinner with George that night was a nightmare. He was flushed crimson and could barely move. I had no need to ask if he had been drinking. The two of us dined alone, save for the Official Photographer, who, in a valiant last-ditch stand to save the public image we had tried to create, wanted photographs of just the two of us at dinner together.

"George," I murmured when the photographs had been taken. "About the New York vote?"

He seemed not to hear me nor, indeed, to have heard as yet of the missing New York vote. "Try to impeach *me*, will they?" he muttered into his okra gumbo. "As for that woman-chasing brother of yours, he's finished. Out, d'ya hear me? Out! I'll get Hay or Bacon or Root—somebody knows something."

The footman removed the soup plates and laid down the next course. "Why, look, Georgie!" I said, desperately trying to be bright and gay. "Creamed hog's lungs—your favorite dish. I thought we were having . . ." My vivacious monologue broke off in midair. I had quite forgotten *what* had been ordered for dinner that night. "Don't they look yummy?" I said, lifting my fork. Just then, Mammy hustled out from behind the screen and snatched the plate away from my place. I embedded my fork in the rich tablecloth.

"Wrong dish," she said. "Yours is the one without the parsley." Quickly exchanging my plate with George's, she chuckled and said, "G'night folks." How thoughtful! Even on this day fraught with drama, Mammy had remembered my marked aversion to parsley. George finished his dinner—he could always eat, no matter how black things seemed—and washed it down with a great deal of wine and iced Lohocla. When one of the White House ushers appeared to announce that the car was waiting to take us to Lady Lissom's dreaded evening at Dodge's Theatre, George was in such a stupor that I could barely move him.

The theatre—a dingy, down-at-the-heel place—was thronged with curiosity seekers, willing to risk who knows what sort of vermin in order to see the notorious Gladys Goldfoil in her disgusting spectacle. Some bunting had been hastily tacked up on one of the stage boxes to create a "Presidential Box" in a theatre so disreputable that no President had ever entered it before George. In the boxes opposite I saw Lady Lissom, Alice, the young Lord Lissom, his six beautiful sisters, and Sir Mortimer Durand.

Did I order creamed hog's lungs?

As we entered the box, there could be heard the beginnings of a hostile demonstration. My heart sank. Fortunately, the orchestra struck up the National Anthem and the audience was silent. George was just able to stand on his feet during the music and then slumped to his chair like a man drugged. The lights went out, the overture was played, and the noxious performance began.

"The Chicken Inspector" was a far cry from the artistic, wholesome operettas (such as the unforgettable "Floradora" or "Mlle. Modiste") that had been my theatrical fare heretofore. It was a sleazy, hastily run-up production, with gross chorines in soiled, scanty costumes; flaking, badly painted scenery; and vulgar, low comedians. Almost every speech, every line of every song seemed to contain a *double-entendre* concerning the star's alleged relationships with my husband and with other important government officials. The audience—mostly the rag, tag, and bobtail of the Capital City—was in gales of laughter. Through my opera glasses I glanced nervously to the box opposite. Lady Lissom, thank heaven, had fallen asleep. Her daughters, unfamiliar with the American political scene and not easily able to comprehend the common accents of the cast, appeared not to understand much of what was going on. Lord Lissom himself seemed to have become acquainted with a bassoonist in the orchestra

and often smiled and gesticulated in his direction. Darling Alice—such a good sport!—giggled continuously, although I felt that it indicated a certain disloyalty to her father. As for George, he sat motionless in the seat beside me, apparently sound asleep. How I envied his nerves of steel.

Miss Gladys Goldfoil, the star, made her appearance, to a tremendous ovation of applause, whistles, and catcalls, wearing a gown that made me wonder that the Washington police could allow such flagrant indecency to be flaunted on the stage. After singing an extremely risqué and suggestive song (she had *no* voice!), she left the stage to change into a still more outrageous costume, while two ribald "Dutch" comedians in big shoes came out onto the stage to take the Chief Executive's name in vain. George, however, never batted an eyelid. Such poise!

After what seemed an eternity, the first-act curtain fell on an especially tasteless bedroom scene. "George," I said, "I have promised to meet Lady Lissom during the intermission." There was no reply. "George!" I said, nudging him.

Just then, I heard a loud explosion, saw a blue and yellow flash, smelled the acrid scent of gunpowder. A vulgar, familiar voice cried, *"Sic semper schlemielis!"* and then Gladys Goldfoil, brandishing a smoking pistol, leaped from the Presidential Box to the stage and disappeared. The audi-

Gladys Goldfoil—obviously demented!

ence was in an uproar. "George!" I cried, shaking him. "George! Speak to me!" It was no use. The President was dead!

The next few seconds—or were they minutes or even hours?—are a blur in my memory. I remember clutching my cloak about me and running, running I knew not where. Next I found myself on a dark, lonely side street in the depressed neighborhood of Dodge's Theatre, waving, shouting, and whistling hopelessly and helplessly for a taxicab. (It has always been next to impossible to find a taxi in Washington!) Where I was going or why, I could not exactly say at the moment, but I knew that with the President dead the ship of state must be saved and that *I* would be the one to do it.

Finally—and fortunately—I made my way to the Executive Mansion on foot, the soles of my French slippers worn through on the rough cobbles and pavements. As I reached Pennsylvania Avenue, I heard an ominous commotion. The gates to the White House had been torn down, and on the lawn was a revolutionary mob shouting, "Lynch him! Lynch him!" Had I made the White House *too* much like Versailles? It was ironical to think that, only a week earlier, I had even appeared as Marie Antoinette at the period ball to wind up Clytie's visit.

Stealing around the side, I let myself into the building by a little-known side entrance. The vast rooms and corridors were empty. Those servants and ushers who had not fled were loyally trying to prevent the doors from being battered down. I knew that escape was essential.

Hurrying to my room, I snatched the first thing I could find to wear and grabbed up my jewels, my memory book, and all the currency I could find. On the lawn below, the crowd had become larger and more unruly. Were the police doing nothing?

I knew then that the end was in view, that bloody revolution would replace the regime of democratic law and order we had fought so hard to establish. Torches appeared out on the lawn, and voices cried, "Let's burn 'em out!" Something of the grandeur that had been the White House *must* be saved! Thinking quickly, I emptied two pillowcases and made for the State Dining Room where the Monroe gold *surtout de la table* stood in stately display. As I was placing the last golden ornament into one of the pillowcases, I was knocked to the floor and felt something warm and wet on my face. It was faithful Fluffy! Dogs never forget those who love them. Fluffy would protect me if no one else cared for the life of the First Lady.

Together, we raced to the carriage house, as yet undetected by the lynch mob through the blessed darkness. Thank heaven the Newport Electric, my favorite automobile of the entire White House fleet, had been recently charged and was standing ready for action. I helped Fluffy in, took the tiller in my trembling hands, started the silent mechanism, and we were off. We reached one of the crumpled gates before any of the mob realized what was going on. "There he goes!" someone cried. "Get him!" But it was too late. Forcing the Newport to its maximum speed, we careened out into the deserted street and disappeared for parts unknown—a modern Dolley Madison and her faithful pet, valiantly trying to preserve some vestige of the splendor that had been the United States of America.

"First Lady" Loots White House

FROM AN ARTIST'S imaginary engraving, the daring escape of Martha Dinwiddie Butterfield, so-called first lady of the Bullfinch Party which ruled fraudulently from March 4 until yesterday. Mrs. Butterfield is reported missing, as are the priceless table ornaments in gold bequeathed to *[illegible]* matic by President James Madison, wh*[illegible]*

A modern Dolley Madison

XIX

The Sordid Aftermath

1909–10

The life of a fugitive. . . . A fool's paradise. . . . The Bullfinch
Party had never won the election! . . . Lord Lissom breaks an
engagement—and my baby's heart. . . . A mother's Gethsemane.
. . . Pappa-daddy and Bubber are apprehended. . . . Trials. . . .
Miss Goldfoil goes scot-free. . . . The mystery of George's death.
. . . The collapse of the Dinwiddie-Butterfield Enterprises. . . .
Holding the bag. . . . Heartbreak.

he bloody revolution died a-borning. The President was dead; his
wife had, to all intents and purposes, disappeared off the face of
the earth, as had the President's daughter[1] and the Secretary of
State. Even Mammy had completely faded away, never to be seen or heard
of again.[2]

As for me, I abandoned the electric car when it had gone as far as it
could go (to the outskirts of Baltimore) on its batteries, and put up in a
humble hotel under the name of "Martha Jones, widow." What a pang as
I signed the register! To think that only a few hours before, my darling
George had been at my side, strong, vital and alive. Now all was gone.

On the following morning, the whole sordid story was in every newspaper across the nation, including wild conjectures as to my whereabouts.
Sensing the folly of trying to continue my journey to I knew not where

---

[1] Miss Alice Butterfield, having been granted political asylum in the British Embassy, later
sought refuge under an assumed name in the Young Women's Christian Association. P.D.
[2] Actually, Mammy later married a Mr. Blubwell at the Liberian Legation and became the
uncontested social leader of Monrovia until her death, in 1921. P.D.

A tactless thrust—Scripps Howard

without some sort of disguise, I sent downstairs for several bottles of Lohocla, burned the corks, and made myself up as best I could as a "darky." Fluffy, however, remained a problem, as this immense white dog was already known and loved by newspaper readers the world around. In order to disguise my faithful companion, I had room service send up thirty pots of coffee, which I poured into the bathtub and proceeded to dip Fluffy until he became *café au lait*. Blacking his tongue with the remains of my burnt cork, I hoped that he would pass as a chow. Then, under the cover of darkness, we went to the colored waiting room of the railway station. Having no idea as to where I was going (being, in fact, barely lucid), I could not even answer when the ticket clerk said gruffly, "Where to, auntie?" My eye caught a poster advertising Asbury Park, New Jersey, and in desperation I mumbled, "Asbury Park."

As none of the grand beach hotels would accept what they took to be an old Negress with a large dog—even off-season—I was lucky to find a small furnished apartment for rent in the Negro section a few blocks behind the ocean front, where once again I registered as "Martha Jones, widow." It was from there that I was able to follow—if only vicariously through the newspapers, although they were filled with nothing else—the tumbled fortunes of my family.

I had been living in a fool's paradise all during the past month, when I had believed that my permanent address was "The White House, Washington, D. C." Nay, even longer—ever since the preceding November, when the astonishing news reached us that the Bullfinch Party had miraculously won over the others. But what Bubber had told me in the White House kitchen was all too true. The New York City vote had been lost or mislaid, and had mysteriously turned up months later in my family's warehouse. Those many, many ballots (cast by a polyglot urban society who had no feeling for the true needs of the *real* America) tipped the scales. We were out—never had been in—and the Presidency belonged to another.

But the worst was yet to come. Poor little Alice was betrayed, thrown over, jilted, and abandoned by that cad Lord Lissom! News of the broken engagement was everywhere. His Lordship maintained a stiff upper lip and said nothing other than that his betrothal with Alice had been terminated. His mother, Lady Lissom, however, had a good deal to say, pronouncing us "vulgar, corrupt, money-grubbing nobodies." The last that America ever saw of Lord Lissom was a newspaper photograph taken as he was boarding a steamer with his overbearing mother to return forever to England. Gone were my dreams of a noble marriage for my baby. And he seemed such a nice, simple lad, too! I wept aloud.

THE FUTURE LADY LISSOM

SUPPLEMENT TO THE BOSTON SUNDAY GLOBE

NOBILITY DEPARTS

LS
G EXILE

(fragmentary newspaper column, left)
rk Times
1—On the
h Burgen-
sternmost
...nced to-
...retary Gen-
...'s party had
...Habsburg to
...tively his right
ustria.
...and vote has been
a kind of refer-
...Habsburg issue.
...nn Withalm, the
...e of the party, was
...ve called on Dr.
...descendant of the
...perial family, at his
...ile, Poecking, Ba-
...make the plea. His
...tly was fruitless.
...of the conserva-
...party with the
...lists on continu-
...8-year-old coali-
...t broke down
...nsistence upon a
...n against Dr.
...n.
...hat the Burgen-
...wever it goes,
...e party or the
...coalition and
...ory in the
...he national
...ny propert...
...sition with-
...uld ...
...the
...uld

(fragmentary newspaper column, right)
sional
stitution...
districts
Nov. 3 g...
The de...
the state...
campaign
ground, th...
wide elec...
prove ch...
Maryla...
resentati...
Seven'
candidat...
19 M...
hopes.
wide co...
The c...
ish pres
Maryla...
for...
...ous...
with
T...
...at...
The...
draw t...
...nd cho...
in the F...
...ions.
They...
...ay's
...pealed
...admin...
Cong...
Lea...
mittee...
in Was...
...st in
R...
...f...
how...
of his
slim...
...ce...

THE EARL OF LISSOM, erstwhile fiancé of Miss Alice Butterfield, daughter of the former tenant of the Executive Mansion,
is seen boarding the S. S. *Histrionic* in the company of his mother,
Britannia, Dowager Lady Lissom. His engagement to Miss Butterfield ...ured for less... ...twe...y-four hou... ...ady Li...om

But that was not all. The blow quite shook my darling daughter's san-
ity, and, like Ophelia, she was found wandering at dawn over the grounds
of the White House, dressed only in trailing garments and a cascade of
flowers. (I had always wondered whether or not that course in Greek
dancing had been a wise choice for my little girl.) The newspapers went
on to say that she had been arrested for disturbing the peace and taken off
to a public asylum. I knew then that I could not remain in hiding a moment longer. That very day I sent Alice a telegram announcing my arrival, removed my disguise, bathed Fluffy, and returned to Washington.

"MOTHER IS COMING," the three-word message of my telegram to
Alice, was the headline of the day. I was besieged by reporters at the station, and had to fight to get into a taxicab and to the side of my baby. She
was in a pathetic condition, babbling senselessly. Through the aid of a

Miss Alice Butterfield, daughter of the late George Washington Butterfield representative of the Bull-Finch Party, was arraigned a the portico of the White House early this morning upon the death of her father and the termination of her engagement to Lord Lisson

Who can blame Ophelia?

kindly physician, I was able to locate a small and discreet rest home in Virginia, where I felt sure my little girl would receive the best of care. It was expensive, but money, or so I thought, was no object. Yet when I went to the bank where I had always kept a very large balance, I was appalled to learn that the account had been "attached!" Not one penny of the many hundreds of thousands of dollars on deposit could be touched! I demanded an interview with the bank president, and after storming into his office I was told that the entire Dinwiddie-Butterfield Empire had been placed under federal jurisdiction! Save for the currency any of us had on our persons, our money would be tied up for years and years and years of litigation.

Happily, I still had my jewels. By pawning my diamond parure and a rope of pearls, I was at least able to see that Alice would be cared for.

The next terrible blow fell on the following day, when the news broke that Bubber and Pappa-daddy had been apprehended at the Mexican border, my father in possession of several millions in currency and all the papers relating to the structure of the Lohocla Company, as well as the other family holdings; my brother, in the haste of his departure, had inadvertently packed a number of official documents inside the lining of his valise. Things looked extremely bad indeed.

What more can I tell you of the rest of that tragic year?

Sweet Alice grew gradually better, regaining much of her mental balance. She developed a marked interest in athletics at the rest home, where she remained until the end of 1910, and was fortunate to receive an offer as games mistress in a refined boarding school for girls.

The rest of 1910 was taken up with trials, trials, trials—not of the sort I had suffered up until that time but actual trials by judge and jury, held in various federal, state, and local courtrooms.

The trials of Bubber and Pappa-daddy were lost before the courts were even called to order. What chance had these elegant Southern aristocrats against a hostile new government hell-bent on selling them down the river? Pappa-daddy was charged with and found guilty of attempting to abscond with many millions of dollars from the United States Treasury. How ridiculous! No consideration was taken of that venerable gentleman's advanced age or of the many great things he had done for the country. The court was unwilling to give my father the slightest benefit of any doubt; his plea of having absent-mindedly filled a large suitcase with thousand-dollar bills was laughed out of court, and he was sentenced to a long term in a federal penitentiary.

Bubber, poor darling, fared even worse. Owing to the fact that his luggage contained a number of government code books, several documents, and correspondence from a foreign power offering to buy information, the court put two and two together and chose to arrive at an answer of *five!* In addition to this charge of treason—of all things!—there were a number of lesser charges that had to be answered and poor Bubber's various trials went on and on and on, my well-intentioned young brother being found guilty at the end of each. Finally, his accumulated prison sentences totalled 895 years! No quality of mercy whatsoever.

One bright note: Pappa-daddy and Bubber were led off to prison at Leavenworth, Kansas, *together*—father and son—separated only by the federal employee to whom each was handcuffed. Neither man lasted long behind bars. Their love of freedom was just too strong. Pappa-daddy breathed his last in 1914, and Bubber passed away, from unspecified causes, a scant three years later. They were but two martyrs from the gallant old Southland, trying to do their patriotic duty in the dog-eat-dog world of the Twentieth Century.

The most sensational of the trials, however, was the one at which I appeared as a witness against that brazen murderess Gladys Goldfoil. The District Court was jammed every single moment, and each word of testimony was telegraphed all over the world.

Let me state here and now that, like the trials of my father and my brother, this one was a mockery of democracy and a fiasco from the very outset. Not satisfied to have the short-lived Bullfinch Party completely routed and a thing of ridicule and unhappy memory, the new federal pow-

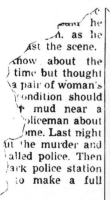

Locked Up!

FORMER "Secretary of State" (r.) and "Secretary of the Treasury" (l.) between a loyal American serv-
ant of the law as phot~~~~~hed by a Hearst cam~

ers did everything possible to make the humiliation a little more unendurable, to grind my tear-stained face into the mud and mire they had created with their endless investigations and scandal mongering. At the Goldfoil trial, they even went so far as to employ a claque to cheer Miss Goldfoil! Each time she entered the courtroom in her garish costumes, there was a standing ovation, with applause, huzzas, and whistles. She was called by the press "a modern Charlotte Corday." However, when *I* appeared gallantly trying—despite my manifold sorrows—to do my duty as a citizen of the United States and a resident of the District of Columbia, jeers and catcalls greeted me!

I was called to the witness stand several times by both the prosecution and the oily, unsavory "ambulance chaser" who served as Miss Goldfoil's legal counsel. Each time I told my story of the day of April 4th—and of the horrible, horrible night—I was hissed and booed until the court was called to order.

Honestly and without any prejudice of any sort, I told how Gladys Goldfoil had wormed her way into my family circle in spite of George's many attempts to avoid her company; how she had forced entrance into White House receptions; and how I had begged her to leave our little family alone, even calling on her at her hotel and begging her to desist. Not wanting to implicate poor, ignorant Mammy, I naturally glossed over the part having to do with Miss Goldfoil's kidnapping on the night of Alice's engagement party, but otherwise I told nothing but the actual unbiased truth right up through the moment when Miss Goldfoil had appeared in the Presidential Box.

I felt certain that in any court of justice, even with the mob cheering her perjured testimony on, things would go badly for such a cold-blooded killer. But once again I was wrong. I had not counted on the trumped-up medical testimony. What a shock it was! George, the medical witnesses said—and with many so-called sworn affidavits to back them up—had died of "natural causes" (a heart attack), helped along by arsenic poisoning (could it have been the Easter-egg dye?), ground glass (but how? where?), and (hideous lie!) acute alcoholism. The bullet fired by Gladys Goldfoil had missed its mark and lodged in the opposite theatre box—the one occupied by Lady Lissom!

Gladys Goldfoil was free!

CHARLOTTE CORDAY: Gladys Goldfoil, accused slayer of so-called President George Washington Butterfield, as she left the judge's chambers following her trial for the mur... Butterfield in Dodge's Th...

Although a wealthy woman in my own right, there were so many government liens on the Dinwiddie-Butterfield holdings, so many government investigations, that everything we possessed, from the Lohocla mother plant down to the tiniest railway spur, was seized, the records impounded, and all future income halted for years to come, pending the outcome of more than two hundred separate pieces of litigation! I alone was left holding the bag. Pappa-daddy and Bubber were behind bars; George was dead; Clytie had recently sold out her share of the empire for cash, and was, anyway, a citizen of a foreign land residing outside the country. The Butterfield brothers had scattered to the four winds. There was no one but Martha Dinwiddie Butterfield to bear the brunt of the whole, dreadful persecution.

With nothing but my jewels and faithful Fluffy, I was cast adrift, the relict of America's most misunderstood statesman, to fend for myself in an alien world.

XX

Decline and Fall

1910–64

A homeless fugitive. . . . Insults and injuries. . . . Poor little Alice. . . . The suffrage movement. . . . Clytie and Stanislaus— the end of an idyll. . . . War clouds. . . . Rebuked by both Mrs. Wilsons! . . . My war work. . . . Lohocla and the Volstead Act. . . . At home abroad. . . . Fabulous façades and false friends. . . . The wolf at the door. . . . My vaudeville tour. . . . Fluffy—the passing of a faithful friend. . . . Down and out in Monte Carlo. . . . War again. . . . A terrible crossing. . . . Routed by the (F.) Roosevelts. . . . Total war. . . . Lohocla wins World War II. . . . Winning the Nobel Prize. . . . Alice takes me on a little trip. . . . Bosky Dell—a home for children of all ages. . . . My correspondence with Truman, Eisenhower, Kennedy and Johnson. . . . Onward and upward. . . . My philosophy of life.

I was alone in the world, my husband dead and buried, my little girl still suffering from a complete nervous breakdown, and those two martyrs, my father and my brother, being held unjustly behind bars in a federal penitentiary. There was no one but darling Clytie, and she, for some reason, could not be reached either at her apartment in Paris or her house in London. Letter after letter was returned marked "Unknown" or "Not at this address" or "Moved away." I never heard from my beloved sister again, but then she was not a good correspondent.

"He travels fastest who travels alone," they say, but where was I to go? It was made all too abundantly evident that, having once been at the pinnacle of Washington society, I was no longer welcome in that city. In fact, all that I received from the White House was a van containing clothing and personal effects and, of all things, a *bill* for restoring the Executive Mansion and for replacement of the Monroe *surtout de la table,* which I had rescued at the risk of life and limb! So much for the gratitude of the United States government.

I could, perhaps, have returned to Pellagra and resumed my role of social leader there, but while mulling that possibility over in my mind I received an anonymous letter informing me that with all the Dinwiddie-Butterfield Enterprises closed down and with thousands unemployed, restive and resentful, it would not be wise to go back home just as yet. In the following mail, I also received a letter from Mrs. Wade Eubanks, her scorn and triumph faintly veiled, offering to purchase stately Dinwiddiewood for a sum so trifling[1] that it in itself was an insult.

As heiress to the Dinwiddie-Butterfield Empire I should have been, by rights, one of the richest women in the world. Instead, owing to the endless litigation brought against us by a vengeful and dishonest government, I was penniless, with nothing to fall back on save the sale of my jewels.

Poor little Alice gradually grew stronger in the isolated rest home to which I had sent her, taking an interest in weaving, basketry, carpentry, and hooked rugs. Her skill at things athletic was, as I have said, prodigious, and after a time she gave up calling the name of that bounder Lord Lissom and replaced it with the names of Susan B. Anthony, Elizabeth Cady Stanton, Carrie Chapman Catt, and Mrs. Emmeline Pankhurst. As I had been before her, my daughter became a staunch advocate of woman suffrage, and by 1912 she was occupying her own little apartment in New York and marching proudly up Fifth Avenue in the greatest of all suffragette parades, with such leaders of society and progressive thought as Mrs. O. H. P. Belmont.

However, the year 1912 was marked by horrible tragedy. My dear sister Clytie and her devoted husband Count Przyzplätcki were aboard the White Star Line's ill-fated *S.S. Titanic* on its disastrous maiden voyage from Southampton to New York. Although Clytie had not bothered to inform me of her impending arrival in the United States, I know in my heart of hearts that she was coming to surprise me with an offer of protection and support with the many, many millions she had received from the sale of her share of the business. Alas, it was not to be. Clytie's body

---

1 $10,000 unfurnished; $5,000 furnished.   P.D.

Alice for women

was never recovered, and it was small satisfaction to know that Archie Butt also perished in the same disaster.

Count Stanislaus, however, was rescued, wearing, of all things, Clytie's broadtail cloak, one of her tea gowns, and all of her jewelry. What strange things we will do in moments of panic! He was Clytie's sole heir, and although I tried desperately time and time again to reach him with comforting letters, it was a fruitless search. His trail led from London to Paris to Rome to Budapest to Belgrade and thence to the Middle East, where he developed a marked interest in Arabs and their customs. He died at Tangier of unknown causes during World War I, his enormous fortune left to a youthful acquaintance known only as Ali Mustafa. Thus passed from existence the proud, ancient line of Przyzplätcki.

I settled down in a small furnished apartment in Brooklyn, occasionally accepting an offer to lecture on politics, international affairs, and the Washington social scene, at various branches of the Eastern Star or Sorosis, although the honoraria they were able to pay were indeed pitiable.

Always a keen student of world affairs, I sensed the gathering war clouds long before they were apparent to the rest of this fun-loving nation, but they all called me Cassandra and laughed at my nervous apprehension. And then it happened! Sarajevo—that mysterious city, both Eastern and Western, that had brought such a turning point in my life—again produced an incident that was to plunge the whole of the world into turmoil. On June 28, 1914, Archduke Franz Ferdinand and his lovely wife, the Duchess of Hohenberg, were assassinated! I immediately dashed off a letter of condolence to my dear old friend, the Emperor Franz Josef, and then sat back to observe the inevitable. How right I had been. All of Europe went up like matchwood!

In an effort to speak to President Wilson, I took the first train to Washington and sped forthwith to the White House to call on his wife. Again, I—who had once been the First Lady and the ruler of that august mansion—was rebuked! As I had only a twenty-four-hour excursion ticket, I could not tarry in the Capital. Instead, I wrote to Mrs. Wilson at some length from the writing room of the Willard Hotel. The first Mrs. Wilson either did not receive or did not deign to answer my letter, in which I outlined in some detail the Martha Dinwiddie Butterfield Plan for International Peace. On August 1 Luxembourg was occupied; on August 4 Mrs. Wilson passed away.

But when the United States finally entered the Great War, in April of 1917, I was in the vanguard of eager war workers, even establishing the Martha Dinwiddie Butterfield Every-Stitch-a-Stitch-of-Love Knitting Unit, which was to meet fortnightly during the cooler months in the yarn section of Frederick Loeser's department store, in downtown Brooklyn.

Eventually and inevitably, however, the victory and the peace were

Rebuffed at the White House gates again

won, thanks to the singlehanded efforts of a few valiant patriots such as I. But it is an ill wind that blows no one good, and after endless waits and delays, suits and countersuits, a few of the Dinwiddie-Butterfield holdings had been released by the government during the war, beginning with a small gunpowder factory in Roanoke, Virginia, which Pappa-daddy had won in a poker game many years earlier. Following that—and largely because the government discovered that, at last, *it* needed *me*—three of our minor railways were placed back in operation. Although most of our holdings were confiscated during Star Chamber sessions so evil and corrupt that I will not even soil this paper by attempting to describe the proceedings, a few pieces of property were released to my custody, and by selling them I was able to enjoy some kind of security, although my income was not one-one-hundredth of what it should have been.

Finally, mighty Lohocla itself was freed in a Pyrrhic victory that brought but little after the staggering fines, suits against the company, and legal fees were paid. But Lohocla was never to rise again to the institution it had once been. Adverse publicity had wrought untold damage, and the product itself, off the market for nearly a decade, had faded from the memories of the happy users who had once sought nirvana from Mumsie-love's magical formula. Yet, with the aid of my devoted Press Secretary, who was back from gruelling war experiences, having done heroic canteen work at the Dayton, Ohio, officers' club, I was able to get the mother plant in Pellagra operating again, as well as four other factories in the North.

Having no experience in the manufacture of pharmaceuticals, but knowing deep in my heart that Mumsie-love and Pappa-daddy would have wanted their big girl to carry on their life mission, I set to work trying to reëstablish Lohocla in the sickrooms of our nation, little wotting the sinister use our product would be put to.

On January 17, 1920, the Volstead Act—or the Eighteenth Amendment —went into effect. "A blessing," I said as I watched the closing of the saloons and grogshops that had brought so much misery to the families of workingmen. "Thank heavens, Mr. Dennis," I remarked to my faithful ex-Press Secretary, "that sordid chapter in American history is over." So choked was he with emotion that he excused himself, telling me that he could be reached at a place called Tony's, and did not appear for the rest of the day.

Simultaneously with the enactment of the Eighteenth Amendment, the sales of Lohocla began to soar to such an extent that I was at last able to leave Brooklyn and establish faithful old Fluffy and myself in a large apartment on Park Avenue decorated by Joseph Urban. Always a fancier of fine motorcars, I found business so good that I managed to purchase a stylish Pierce-Arrow limousine, an Auburn roadster, and an Isotta-Fraschini phaeton. Whenever I inquired of Mr. Dennis as to the source of all this good fortune, he simply winked, said "Lohocla," and suggested that we split a bottle, although we were both in robust good health.

It even became possible to increase the price of a bottle of Lohocla from one dollar to five to ten to twenty! And our public itself even thought up Lohocla's *new* slogan, "The safest thing available."

The Twenties were a time of happiness and prosperity for all, and especially for me. Heeding the advice of my Mr. Stern, a cultivated young stockbroker whom I had met at a dinner party, I turned my income over to him as fast as I received it to be put into sure things. It was amazing! For an infinitesimal outlay of cash, Mr. Stern could often double my money in as little as a day through his clever manipulations on the stock market. If only his life had been spared,[2] who knows to what heights the two of us might not have risen on Wall Street? Once again, I was happy and content, sensing that I was doing good for the sick and unhappy, fulfilling the mission for which I had been put upon this earth.

But once again the bubble burst. The terrible blow fell in 1925, when, in the Isotta-Fraschini, I was touring Canada with Alice and Fluffy. Federal agents seized all the Lohocla plants, and our firm's fine old name was publicly villified and disgraced as that of a common moonshiner! Those who had been paying up to twenty dollars a bottle for my beloved mother's formula were doing so *not* because they were run down or ill but because of the medicine's *alcoholic content!* So shocked and stunned with disbelief was I that I shut myself into my bedroom at the Château Frontenac and refused all nourishment for forty-eight hours. When I emerged, a rather detailed letter was waiting for me from Mr. Dennis, who suggested that I leave directly from Canada for an *extended* European holiday.

It had been so long since I had visited Europe—not since my débutante year—that I hardly knew the place. Where, in my day, ladies in sweeping skirts and stately trains had moved with grace and elegance, being handed down from smart victorias and carriages by uniformed footmen—the example of deportment and style laid down for all the world to follow—they were, in the middle Twenties, slavishly aping the worst that American culture had to offer. Women from débutantes to dowagers were hav-

---

[2] He died of defenestration in November, 1929. P.D.

ing their hair shingled, were exposing their knees in flesh-colored silk stockings, were smoking and drinking in public, and were forsaking all dignity and femininity, with their frantic performances of such vulgar and ungainly American dances as the Charleston and the Black Bottom. I felt a total stranger in such beloved and familiar settings as Piccadilly, Belgrave Square, Mayfair, and St. James's.

Paris was much the same, and I discovered that all the marquises and comtesses and baronnes who had been the most devoted friends of my dear, dead sister seemed to have forgotten that Clytie had ever existed when I left cards at their apartments and town houses. The Europe I had known and loved so much had changed.

It was, however, the Crash that brought me back to my native land. Learning from faithful friends that "the heat was off," I arrived in New York on the very day of the Crash. Although Lohocla was now but a tender memory, I had been, until the autumn of 1929, still a well-to-do woman (on paper, at least). But when I finally telephoned my broker to request funds, I learned that he had just that day passed away and that I was not only destitute but actually in debt! There was nothing to do but go to work.

Through the offices of an enterprising theatrical entrepreneur, I accepted a role in vaudeville, then on its last legs. As the relict of a President, I considered it *infra dig* in the extreme, but I had little choice. As I could neither sing nor dance, just what my performance was to consist of was a mystery. However, there was always faithful Fluffy. Although a *very* old dog by then,[3] he had received only the best of care, and could still, when

---

[3] Thirty-one. P.D.

Alice finds her niche

prodded, lie down, roll over, and bark. My manager decided that if I was to bob my hair, learn to "talk" a little song, and have Fluffy do some tricks, it might be enough to "pack 'em in," along with a double feature, bank night, and free chinaware. How diligently we dieted and practiced, Fluffy and I, preparing for our joint theatrical début! At great expense, I had a dress especially made by the House of Tappé, and even paid for an impressive backdrop depicting the face of Martha Washington. After two months of feverish preparation, we were ready.

Fluffy and I opened at the State-Lake Theatre, in Chicago, and to try out our "potential" as a "box-office draw" it was decided that the entire stage presentation be built around a Presidential motif. Climaxing the usual jugglers, tap dancers, and so on, the State-Lake Adorables, as the ladies of the ensemble were called, were to parade down a red, white and blue staircase in lavish costumes, as famous First Ladies of history, while a tenor sang "Lady, Be Good," and then, as the grand finale, Fluffy and I were to appear, also dressed in patriotic colors, for our big act. Waiting in the wings, I felt tense and nervous in the extreme, and as had happened so many times before in my life, I sensed that *something* was about to happen—I knew not what. Just before our cue, I fed Fluffy a milk-bone biscuit, although he had but three teeth left, poor beast, and tried to rouse him from his lethargy. So old and tired was my faithful dog that he could

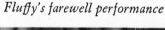

Fluffy's farewell performance

scarcely get to his feet, but when one of the stagehands gave him a playful nudge with the toe of his shoe, Fluffy rose painfully and trotted out onto the stage. The theatre was less than half filled, but the audience accepted my little patter song politely, one or two of them even applauding. Then it was time to do the little act that had been written for Fluffy and me. Herbert Hoover was, at that time, in the White House, and I was to ask questions of Fluffy—such as "Is prosperity really just around the corner?"—which Fluffy would answer with a series of moans and growls. Although old, crotchety, and forgetful, Fluffy managed his responses quite nicely and elicited a bit of laughter from the audience.

As a climax to our act, Fluffy was to jump through a hoop I held—a stunt he had always delighted in performing—but out there on the great stage he was strangely reticent. Even when I held up a milkbone biscuit my dog seemed totally disinterested. The audience became restive and there was even a faint hissing from the upper balcony. Embarrassed and humiliated at the amateurish performance we were presenting I spoke sharply to my beloved companion. "Fluffy!" I snapped, "jump!" For the first time in all of our years together the poor old dog refused. *"Jump!"* I said, even more harshly. Instead, he turned his back to the audience, yawned, stretched and proceeded to sit down right in the footlight trough. With that there was a crackling flash of light, a yelp and the whole theatre was plunged into darkness. I was conscious only of a ball of fur flying past my face in the cavernous gloom. The theatre was in an uproar.

When order had been re-established and the lights had come on once again there was no sign of faithful Fluffy. He had leapt his last leap, going all the way through the Martha Washington backdrop, behind which he lay dead! Although Chicago's finest veterinarians were called, there was no reviving poor Fluffy. "Old age, shock and overexertion"—that was the verdict. Today he lies beside George in the Dinwiddie-Butterfield family vault at Pellagra, a valiant comrade. I shall always regret that my final words to him were spoken in anger rather than with the love I always felt for that devoted animal.

I had just enough money left to eke out a meager existence—*if* I did it in Europe, where prices were still far lower than in my native land. Therefore, once again, I bade adieu to Alice and my few faithful friends and set sail for France.

France seemed the likeliest of all countries for me to live in on my extremely low income. In those days, it was possible to buy an entire dinner—and a delicious one—in Paris for as little as eighteen cents! Also I contemplated approaching M. Cesar Ritz, as a likely purchaser of the

Hotel Dinwiddie, the Lohocla House, and the George I. If I had to sell these beloved old family hostelries, I preferred to have them under the capable management of the man who had made the Ritz Hotels, in Paris, London, Madrid, Budapest, New York, Boston, and other brilliant cities, the synonym for luxurious living. Alas, there was little interest. The Ritz hotels themselves were all but empty, and M. Ritz did not feel that the tourist and transient trade in Pellagra would be sufficient to warrant taking three additional hotels under his wing.

Finding the damp, penetrating Paris winters too severe for one of my delicate constitution, I migrated to the South of France, and there established myself in a humble pension in Monte Carlo, where I soon became fascinated with the casino and the caprices of Dame Fortune at the wheel of chance. Too poor and too cautious to plunge with my minuscule income, I paid my admission to the casino every day, bought a few francs' worth of counters, and sat down with pad and pencil to figure out a system that would beat the roulette wheel. This was a project of many years' duration, during which time I kept careful notes as to black, red, odd, and even, sometimes risking a chip or two myself. The results were inconclusive, to say the least, varying daily from a few francs' profit or—on especially bad days—a loss, which I could ill afford.

By 1939, however, after tabulating my years of research, I felt that I was ready to edit and to have published the "Martha Dinwiddie Butterfield Sure System for Beating the Roulette Wheel," private publication of which I had negotiated with a printer in nearby Villefranche. What a gala summer that was—the last, did I but know, for many a year. Monte Carlo was at the zenith of its Elsa Maxwell period. Times were better, and free-spending tourists from all over were flocking to the little principality of Monaco. To my distress, however, I noticed arrogant Nazis and Fascists flinging money away as though it were contaminated. When I approached them with the information that I could tell them of a sure system for winning at the wheel, they laughed at me and, all too often, flung a few counters to me as a "tip"—*me,* the widow of a President of the United States!

My book appeared in the stalls of Monte Carlo and the Côte d'Azur on August 31, 1939, a day I had worked out as numerologically perfect. What its sales would have been, I cannot fathom. On September 1, 1939, Germany declared war on poor little Poland. On September 3rd, England and France retaliated with declarations of their own. Suddenly the casino was deserted. No one remained in that gay watering place except a few very old residents, and most of them had roulette systems of their own. I am

A ghastly crossing

told that the entire first edition of my book went to Les Amis de la France Libre, during their scrap-paper drive in 1943, so that the "Martha Dinwiddie Butterfield Sure System for Beating the Roulette Wheel" did fill a certain function, after all.

Having no place better to go, I stayed on in Monaco, confident that the neutrality of the tiny principality would be respected by the Hun and that, anyhow, the brave poilu would crush the Nazi horde in a matter of weeks. We all had such confidence in the Maginot Line! However, with the occupation of France and with the virtual starvation imposed on the helpless residents of Monte Carlo, I felt that I must flee. Converting almost everything I owned into cash, I fled to neutral Spain and thence to Portugal. The *S.S. Bilbao,* a tiny, disreputable freighter and the only ship on which I could book passage from Lisbon, was a far cry from the fine liners on which I had sailed during my palmier days. It was a winter crossing, and I was deathly ill from the moment we weighed anchor until the majestic skyline of Newport News hove into view.

Stopping in New York barely long enough to see my beloved Alice, I realized that my duty as a patriot was to proceed immediately to Washington and give President Roosevelt (Franklin, of course) my confidential report of actual conditions in wartime Monaco.

Although I had wired stating the date and time of my arrival in Washington, no White House car, no Secret Service men, not even a G-Man was waiting for me at Union Station. How careless, I thought, Mr. Roosevelt can be of security measures! Dependent upon public conveyances, I made my way to the White House and noted extra guards at the front gates. (F.D.R. could, at least, look out for his *own* protection!) Not wanting to let my presence be known in case of Fifth Columnists and other dangerous enemy agents lurking about the nation's capital, I availed myself of the secret entrance to the grounds that I had discovered during my own tenancy of the Executive Mansion, entered, and crossed the lawn—darting from tree to tree until I reached the great portico. I announced myself and told the flunky who opened the door to me that I had informed President and Mrs. Roosevelt of my pending arrival. Mrs. Roosevelt, I was told, was out of town, while the President was conferring with Cordell Hull and Henry L. Stimson, *was not expecting me,* and "could not be disturbed!" Another Roosevelt, another political party, but still the same slipshod, inefficient way of running the country. The door was slammed in my face! I had been rebuffed again! There was nought for me to do but to return to New York.

My money was extremely limited and prices were soaring during the early years of World War II. I had thought that it might be possible to move into Alice's little flat in Greenwich Village, however, the manual-training teacher with whom she shared the apartment—a most brusque and extremely ungracious young lady with Leftist tendencies and absolutely no respect for her elders—would have none of it. And I was Alice's own mother! Alice herself suggested the Peabody Home for Indigent Gentlewomen, but there was a lengthy waiting list. Instead, I found lodgings at a residential hotel for older women, where I threw myself, heart and soul, into war work—knitting, rolling bandages, Civil Defense, and all the rest of it.

However, it was not long before I received a visitation from representatives of the United States government. A delegation of distinguished scientists and War Department officials called on me. Their all-consuming interest seemed to be Lohocla, to which I was the sole remaining heir. I was most mystified. Heretofore, every time the government had shown any interest in Lohocla, the results had been disastrous, bringing hardship and disgrace to the proud name of Dinwiddie. I was most guarded in my responses, fearing that this visit was perhaps some delayed inquisition concerning the federal agents' raid on the few Lohocla plants operant during the Twenties. However, the gentlemen (and this time I use the

Another Roosevelt rejects me

term advisedly) who called upon me on behalf of the government were charm, dignity, and generosity personified. They were, their spokesman explained, interested in Lohocla on behalf of the armed forces.

"For the canteens?" I asked brightly. "It was ever so popular during the Spanish-American *contretemps.*"

"Good God, no!" one of the scientists said. "Our losses in battle alone are enough to—"

Interrupting him, one of his colleagues explained to me that the government was interested in Lohocla not for the consumption of the troops but as *the* integral part of a secret experiment that was being carried out. "Not any of the newer formulas," he added, "but the *original* Lohocla formula. All records of it have disappeared from the Patent Office."

"Aha!" I said. "And who have you to thank for tampering with the original scientific formula but that man Roosevelt!"

"Franklin Delano Roosevelt?" one of the men asked.

"Theodore Roosevelt!" I shouted.

"Ah, yes." (You see, I was not alone in my feeling about the Rough-rider.) "But we were wondering if you had any idea as to the components of the original Lohocla."

"Gentlemen," I said, "I have the original formula in Mumsie-love's very own handwriting, right in my mother-of-pearl box. However, I will not move without legal advice."

They understood. Immediately, I telephoned my faithful Press Secretary, who was at that time residing in a home for elderly gentlemen. He was at my side as fast as his wheelchair could carry him. A favorable contract was drawn between the government and myself.

From that day on, my financial troubles were at an end. The United States government, having refused me the pension, the postal franking rights—every privilege accorded to even the widows of the most undistinguished Presidents—behaved quite ethically in paying me the regular royalties for the use of the original Lohocla formula. And it was used in such quantities!

With the money coming in each month, I found that I was able to lease a very smartly furnished apartment in Sutton Place, and also—just for the company—to invite Mr. Alexander and Mr. Dennis to share the place with me. What fun we had talking over old times!

Just what the government had wanted with the Lohocla formula I had never asked, but immediately after that fateful day in August, 1945, when the first atomic bomb was dropped, it was made abundantly clear to everyone. The basis of the terrible bomb that had brought an end to World War II was Lohocla! And the very government that had condemned it had, at last, found a vital function for it! How ironical is life!

From being scorned and despised, an outcast among my countrymen, I was suddenly the toast of the nation, receiving honorary degrees from many distinguished universities, and much in demand as a guest speaker. It all culminated in my being summoned to Stockholm, where I was awarded the Nobel Prize in the hallowed name of Mumsie-love. What a thrill!

With the prize money, I immediately set about commissioning Carl Milles, the famed Swedish sculptor of heroic monuments, to do a statue of my late, lamented pal, Fluffy—the finished work to be somewhat larger than the Statue of Liberty. It was my intention to purchase Ellis Island, where I had first met my beloved pet, and turn it into a private park honoring the memory of that noble beast.

It was then that Alice suggested that I get out of New York for a while, and took me on a little trip up the Hudson River, accompanied by my two dear old friends and three attendants, to the glorious estate that is now my permanent residence—Bosky Dell Home for Senile and Disturbed. It is a

Stockholm—1946

TIME

THE WEEKLY NEWSMAGAZINE

MARTHA DINWIDDIE BUTTERFIELD
"Mother knew best"
(National Affairs)

home, as the medical director says, "for children of all ages," and oh, the fun we have here!

Formerly the vast country estate of an ex-president of the New York Central Railroad, Bosky Dell is comprised of an enormous manor house of Jacobean persuasion, with numerous annexes and outbuildings of Tudor, Georgian, Mediterranean, "moderne," and assorted other styles. While not inexpensive, the manifold activities and merry times we all have make the monthly "tuition" worth every penny. In addition to occupational therapy, physical education, and hydrotherapy, we are in a perpetual social whirl, with card parties, movies, concerts, dances, picnics, athletic contests, and outings planned for every week. "Iron bars," as I said to Mr. Alexander only yesterday, "do not a prison make."

Here, at last, among ladies and gentlemen of the most delicate sensibilities, I am treated with the respect due a former First Lady. Having taken an avid interest in matters political, I now lecture—at no charge—on international affairs, foreign policy, and related subjects to all who wish to attend, and a surprisingly large number of my fellow-guests[4] do.

Ever since the Truman administration, I have kept up a weekly correspondence with the successive Presidents, and *now* each letter is answered and signed not by the President's full name but intimately "Harry," "Ike," "L.B.J." and so on. What is more, they are of such top-secret importance that they come to me on White House letter paper

---

[4] The word "patients" is frowned upon at Bosky Dell.   P.D.

without being stamped, franked, or even postmarked. By *special courier*, as the envelopes all read!

Mr. Dennis—printer's ink is *really* in that one's veins—is quite active in the printshop at Occupational Therapy, and is forever running off letterheads for me, for the other guests, for the hospital, and sometimes quite fanciful ones reading, "Buckingham Palace," "The Vatican," "10 Downing Street," and so on. He has such a lark playing jokes and writing crank letters with them!

As for Mr. Alexander, he has advanced from being Official Photographer of the White House to Official Photographer of Bosky Dell, and he is ever so happy snapping pictures of all of us at work and play here in this wonderful place of enchantment.

Alice, now retired from the public-school system, visits once or twice a year, as often as her busy schedule will permit, and always takes away mountains of my handiwork (hemstitched corset covers, petit-point evening bags, crocheted "hug-me-tights") to sell, the proceeds going to Girls' Town, Alice's favorite charity.

There are times, it is true, when I think back to the grandeur that was mine as First Lady of the Land, but, rather than dwell on the glories of the past, I must look onward and upward to greater victories in the future.

My life has been a turbulent one—a thing of sunshine and shadow, heartbreak and happiness, triumph and despair. I have my memories, as who has not, but, rather than look backward, *I* believe in looking to the future.

Tonight, for example, I am giving a little party for the other guests at Bosky Dell, and even now my nurse is laying out my gayest ensemble and mixing my tranquillizer for the gala affair. True, it will be a party with music and dancing and refreshments for all, but it will also be a party with a *purpose*. In discussing politics with my faithful Press Secretary and dear friend, Mr. Dennis, it seems to me that so many minorities are aiming for the highest office in the land—and, in some cases, getting there—that in this big election year why not a *woman* for President? Yes, my dear readers, at tonight's big affair I am going to fire the first gun with my fellow-guests—Martha Dinwiddie Butterfield for President. With all *my* experience, how could anything go wrong?

Bosky Dell
April 1, 1964

CAST OF CHARACTERS

Martha Dinwiddie Butterfield .... *Peggy Cass*
Mary Margaret McGillicuddy, R.N. .... *Rhoda Fleming*
Patrick Dennis .... *Patrick Dennis*
Cris Alexander .... *Cris Alexander*
Nurse .... *Kaye Ballard*
Nurse .... *Annie Russell*
Mumsie-love .... *Mary Ross*
Pappa-daddy .... *Wally Mohr*
Clytie .... *Dody Goodman*
Bubber .... *Harold Lang*
Mammy .... *Corry Salley*
Mrs. Prouty .... *Allyn-Ann McLerie*
Office Boy .... *Caesar-Augustus Delano*
Margaret Peavey .... *Sondra Lee*
A Waiter at Sherry's .... *Roland Vazquez*
Mrs. Ada Civet .... *Vicki Cummings*
Count Stanislaus Przyzplätcki .... *Shaun O'Brien*
Peasant Girl .... *Thelma Pelish*
George Washington Butterfield .... *William Martel*
Poultice Grout Butterfield .... *Carl A. Reynolds*
Grandma Butterfield .... *Carl A. Reynolds*
The Butterfield Brothers .... *Lorenzo Bianco, Dell Hanley, Johnny Kuhl, Robert Locklin, Harry Percer, Steve Shapiro, Steve Shapiro, Merrill Sindler, Eugene Tanner, Stuyvesant Wilmerding, Baby LeRoy Zuckmeyer*
Tattooing Artiste .... *Kathleen Ryan*
Alice Butterfield .... *Alice Pearce*
Chairman of the Board of Lohocla .... *Allen T. Smith*
Fluffy .... *Ch. Bela a Bator de Eszterhazy*
A Working Man .... *Bruce Laffey*
The Eubanks Brothers .... *Whitney B. Leffingwell, Jean-Claud d'Harnoncourt*
General Lushmore .... *Byron Russell*

Mrs. Lushmore .... *Mary S. Riddle*
Gladys Goldfoil .... *Dagmar*
A Seamstress .... *Phoebe McKay*
An Urchin .... *Michael Tanner*
Cecil Lambrequin .... *Leslie Blanchard*
Maestro .... *Robert Irving*
H.R.H. Ruth of Ruthenia .... *Mary E. Hoban*
Sarah Bernhardt (as Hamlet) .... *Shaun O'Brien*
Anna Pavlova .... *Melissa Hayden*
Boris Nijinski .... *Jacques d'Amboise*
Belgravia, Lady Lissom .... *Mrs. John D. Crimmins*
Lord Lissom .... *Philip Van Rensselaer*
The Hon. Misses Lissom .... *Nan Badian, Fanny Brennan,*
    Mary Sykes Cahan, Jennifer Plain, Bita Dobo, Denise McGregor
Dame Moonyeen Mulligan .... *Elsie Foley O'Brien*
H.R.H. Maharanee of Ghozapore .... *Elaine Adam*
H.R.H. Rorschach of Ocarina .... *Elizabeth Tanner*
The Regent .... *Edgar Daniels*
Graf von-und-zu Schmaltz-Geschlumpfert ..... *Carl Fisher*
The Eunuch of Angora .... *Lester Judson*
H.R.H. Ranavalona .... *Rowena Dewlap*
Her Consort .... *Carl A. Reynolds*
Generalissimo Junta y Flotilla .... *Guy Kent*
Max, Pretender to the Throne of San Marino .. *Alvin Colt*
Zizi, his Consort .... *Marina Stern*
Grand Duchess Sirene .... *Sirene Adjemova*
Piua, Infanta of Brazil .... *Louise Tanner*
An Interpretive Danseuse .... *Astrid des Loges*
Secretary to the Secretary of State .... *Jan Sterling*
Masseur .... *Fred Kagan*
A Schoolboy .... *Matthew Gaynes*
An Orphan Girl .... *Iya Gaynes*
A Government Man .... *Robert Riley*
Citizens of Pelagra, Innocent Taxpayers,
White House Guests, Servants, and Distin-
guished Persons .... *Francis X. Ahearne, Elmo*
    Avet, George Borton, Florence Fleming, Marie Grand, Dick Hinds,
    Julia Johnston, Guy Kent, Karl Lindborg, Francisco Moncion, Kevin

Noonan, Harry Percer, Walter Pistole, Modessa Lee Priddy, Mrs. Sidney Ratchit, Vincent Secundo, Francis X. Toohey, John Valjean, Katherine M. Walch.

Guests and Staff of Boskey Dell ....*John Battles, Peggy Brooks, Leslie Copeland, Robert Craner, Florence Fleming, Rhoda Fleming, Elsie Foley, Nanette Frumkin, John Fuller, Warren Galjour, Carolyn George, Murray Grand, Karen Katzel, Guy Kent, Deni Lamont, Joan Luria, Kip MacArdle, Donald MacLerie, Kenneth MacMillan, Jane Anderson Moses, Sybil Musgrove, Portia Nelson, Elsie O'Brien, Shaun O'Brien, Modessa Lee Priddy, A. T. Smith, junior, Ilona Royce Smithkin, John Stern, Patrick Tanner, Lorraine Titweiler, Wanda Warner, Daniel Yankelovich, Hasse Yankelovich.*

The Butterfield Cabinet ....*Francis X. Ahearne, Abraham Badian, Marvin Barouch, Geoffrey Barr, Ralph Boelsen, Frederick Brisson, John Benson Brooks, D. A. R. Bumpass, Harry Chapin, Maurice Crain, John Dixon, Joseph Doherty, James C. Finkenstaedt, Otis L. Guernsey, junior, Norman Hall, Bill Helmuth, Lawrence Hughes, Harold Lang, John T. Lawrence, Duncan McGregor, Bill McLeod, James G. Milne, Wally Mohr, Thomas J. Morrissey, Julian P. Muller, Michael O'Brien, Ralph Ong, Walter Pistole, Martin Schneider, Vincent Secundo, Steve Shapiro, Steve Shapiro, William Shelburne, John Shinn, Merrill Sindler, Allen T. Smith, Edward E. Tanner, H. D. Vursell, John C. Willey, Lyonel Zunz.*

and
Lois Dwight Cole as Miss Kunkel,
Postmistress General

Costumes by GUY KENT

Special thanks for authentic period fashions are also due to *Robert Riley* and the *Design Laboratory of the Brooklyn Museum*; to *Andrew Geoly, Cousin Andrew Geoly, Guy Geoly, Thomas Geoly, Evelynne Greene, William Kimble* and *William Loger* of *Eaves Costume Company*; and to *Jack Hynd* of the *National Broadcasting Company*.

Miss Cass's hair styles by *Leslie Blanchard*
Period pieces from *Rosella Baskind* and *Brandon's Memorabilia*
Jewelry from *Marvella Pearls*

Book Design by MARSHALL LEE

Hon. Mr. Butterfield
Secy. of the Navy

Hon. Mr. Pistole
Secy. of Deportation

Hon. Mr. Ong
Secy. of Wild Life

Hon. Mr. McGregor
Secy. of Vital Statistics

Hon. Mr. Bumpass
Secy. of War

Hon. Judge Boelsen
Secy. of Pest Control

Hon. Mr. Helmuth
Secy. of Weights and Measures

Hon. Mr. Brisson
Secy. of Public Exhibitions

Hon. Mr. Dixon
Secy. of Excesses

Hon. Mr. McLeod
Secy. of International Ad—

Hon. Mr. Crain
Secy. of Eskimo Affairs

Hon. Mr. Zunz
Attorney General

Hon. Miss Kunkel
Postmistress General

Hon. Mr. Barouch
Secy. of Hospitals and Nursing

Hon. Mr. Tanner
Secy. of Oaths and Ora—

Hon. Mr. Morrissey
Secy. of Secret Affairs

Hon. Mr. Milne
Secy. of Fine Arts

Hon. Prof. Hall
Secy. of Education

Hon. Mr. Chapin
Secy. of Natural Gas

Hon. Mr. Schneider
Secy. of Interior Decor—

Hon. Mr. Dinwiddie
Secy. of State

Hon. Mr. Barr
Secy. of Adjustments and Controls

Hon. Mr. Shelburne
Secy. of Border Activities

Hon. Mr. Willey
Secy. of Bottling and Spirits

Hon. Mr. Badian
Secy. of Emergencies